Generis
PUBLISHING

D1328220

See Jimmy Run

Memoir of a 3rd Grade Flunk Out Who Became a
Fulbright Scholar

James S. Payne

Title: See Jimmy Run

Memoir of a 3rd Grade Flunk Out Who Became a Fulbright Scholar

ISBN: 979-8-88676-138-2

Author: James S. Payne

Cover image: www.pixabay.com

Publisher: Generis Publishing
Online orders: www.generis-publishing.com
Contact email: info@generis-publishing.com

Table of Contents

Acknowledgement

It's Christmas, my daughter-in-law, Nicole, "You need to tell your story."

"What story?"

"About your struggles with reading. Most of my ESL (English As Second Language) kids have trouble reading. Their parents would be encouraged by your story. It would give them hope."

Two years, ten number two pencils, a case of paper, reveal 84 years of living with dyslexia.

Michelle, my typist, confidant and copy editor of many years, after typing the chapter about Mrs. Goodrum, my mother-in-law, said, "I laughed and cried. I identified with your mother-in-law. It touched me. The Redskin story intrigued me and your brother – WOW, what a character."

Mary Ann Bowen agreed to story edit my work. She commented, "What you did with Allen in the restaurant got me. It is fascinating and the chapter about your brother needs to be placed at the end. It is climactic.

My wife, Esim, after reading the chapter about how I met and fell in love with her replied, "It is exactly as I remember it. Let's go get a drink on the Square."

Bob, my son-in-law, called. "I don't think Kim is going to be able to complete reading your memoir. She reads a few pages and goes to the bedroom to cry. She has been doing this for the past couple of days."

"Crying? The book is funny. It isn't supposed to be sad."

"You may want to look at it again."

Kim called a week later, "Dad, I don't know what to say. I didn't know you had so many problems. I was the first and only white in your Head Start program and I loved it. I fondly remember helping you in your Rehab class and selling Girl Scout cookies at the back of the auditorium. The two marriage licenses scene I remember, but I really didn't think you and mom were stupid. The flashbacks on Nanny grabbed me. I cried all the way through. As your daughter I thought I knew you. Now I really know you. Thanks for sharing your Memoir with me."

Dr. Walter J. Cegelka, my advisor and mentor at The University of Kansas simply said, "I visited Head Start many times, and as you know, I was so impressed with what the kids were learning and the many creative things you did. I had no idea the pressure you were under. Simply amazing."

Tom Kergel, longtime friend and spiritual advisor, after helping me correct the chapter on religion commented, "This is the best piece of writing you have ever done. This is going to help a lot of people."

Bill Herbert, former student of the Rehab class and continuous reviewer of much of my work said, "You've got to tell how you survived. People want to know how you did it. They want to know the secret."

"I don't know. I've thought about it a lot but I honestly don't know. There is no secret."

"There is."

"What is it?"

"You simply stayed in the game of life despite setbacks. You had the will to hang on as a result of the love and support of your family. You were open to the possibilities that life threw your way. Maybe an inspirational leader, a job opportunity, a trick that hid your weaknesses or magnified your strengths. You paid attention to how the game was played. You waited for those pitches you could hit and in the meantime you learned to get out of the way of pitches that might hurt you. You were dealt a bad hand, dyslexia. Despite every known methodology on how to teach reading, you were never able to compete, but you kept finding other ways to play the game and you kept swinging."

Pencil

2018

Taught 2nd grade
(I learn from second graders)

I am not the sharpest pencil in the box but throughout life I've stayed sharp enough to weather the storms and experience the good times.

I've been issued a small storage room that doubles as the teachers workroom in Batesville Intermediate School in Batesville, Mississippi, to teach second graders how to work a Rubik's Cube:

J.C. enters. Drops his book bag on the floor next to his chair. Round face, Mohawk haircut dyed orange, tee shirt sporting Sheldon Cooper's face, wellworn black Nike tennis shoes. As he sits, he slaps a 5" x 7", eight-page booklet on the upper right corner of his desk. It's really a table that functions as a desk. Grabs the cube and starts working.

My desk/table, just like his, joins on the right. J.C. on left, me on right. I glance at the booklet. "What's that?"

"My reading assignment." (hesitation) "They are teaching me how to make a cake."

J.C. turns right side of cube one click clockwise, bottom of the cube counterclockwise two clicks. Stops. Head rotates clockwise, looks me straight in the face, "As if I'll ever make one."

Returns to cube.

At the end of the year J.C. recorded a 1.5 year gain in Reading and 1.7 gain in Math.

Frank, repeater of second grade, tallest in the class, slides into the room and tags the leg on my chair as if second base. Jumps up, hugs me and without a sound sits and starts turning the sides of the cube faster than I can see. He completes Step 1, the cross. Proudly displays it so I can see. I nod with approval. He immediately mixes up the cube and solves Step 1 again, and again, and again. I brag, smile, slap him on the back and brag some more. I get as excited as he.

He abruptly stops, turns to me, "I'm working on Step 2. You want to see?"

"You can't do Step 2."

"Watch."

He completes Step 1 with a whiz and as he starts Step 2, stops, analyzes the cube, finds the desired die, rotates it to the front, right, bottom position. In a flash, Right minus, Bottom minus, Right plus, the desired die ends up in the correct position on top – placed and oriented.

Frank leans back, holds the cube up for both of us to admire. A pat on the back and the search for a second desired die is afoot.

He definitely has mastered Step 1 and well on his way to 2. The hyperactive, rambunctious second grader is glued to me, the cube, and the lesson. I know he will master Step 2 within a week or at most two. But most importantly, I know he knows he will master Step 2.

He gets up, hugs me and takes two steps toward the door, turns, comes back and sits.

"Dr. Payne, how are you always so nice?"

His choice of the word 'how' not 'why' puzzles me. Before I can respond…

"You always brag on us. Even when we make mistakes. You call us smarty pants. At home we always fight, yell, argue, get loud. And you smell good. Do you use cologne?"

"Aramis."

He repeats thoughtfully as he gets up to leave, "Aramis. Never heard of it."

Frank gained 2.8 years in Reading and 2.2 in Math.

Christmas is approaching. Clyde comes in, pays no attention to the cube. Turns his chair toward mine, "Dr. Payne, you won't believe what I saw Saturday."

"What?'

"I saw Santa Claus, in Walmart, buying toys."

"Clyde, give me a break, that wasn't Santa Claus."

"Was too. Red suit, hat, black boots, white beard and hair. Real white."

I sense this is deep and not up for discussion.

He cocks his head to the side and with a questioning wrinkled brow, "That's what the Elves are supposed to be doing."

He turns, attacks the cube, Step 1, 2 and beginning 3.

As I watch I realize Clyde thinks those Elves are slackers. Just what are they supposed to be doing, anyway?

Clyde, end of year, 2.4 year gain in Reading and 2.2 in Math.

This is the fourth time I've seen Leigh one-on-one. Thin, but not skinny, hair uncombed, same blouse for the week, run down flip flops, dirty toes. Uncared, unkept, smart as a whip.

We work on the cube. Really she works, I watch. She is ahead of most of her classmates. I love working with her because… I don't know why. I just do.

She holds up the cube. Smiles. She completed Step 3.

"Leigh, you are one smart cookie."

"Dr. Payne, every time I come in here you tell me how smart I am. When you see me in class you hug me and call me a smarty pants. My dad thinks I'm dumb. He calls me stupid."

Stunned, "Leigh, you are not stupid. You are very smart. Maybe next time your dad calls you dumb or stupid tell him 'Dr. Payne thinks I'm smart. He would be glad to show you what I've learned.' Then maybe your dad will call or ask me to come over. I'd welcome a chance to show your dad how smart you are."

Leigh, expressionless, looks at me. Returns to the cube and works Steps 1, 2 & 3 over-and-over without comment. She finishes, gets up, heads to the door. Turns before leaving, "Dr. Payne, you don't have to talk with my dad. I know I'm smart."

Her dad needs to know she gained 1.5 years in Reading and 2.3 in Math.

At the end of the year, of the 24 second graders in Batesville, Mississippi, all mastered Step 2 and are working on 3 including the two special needs students. Ten mastered the cube, all five steps. Test scores show the class gained significantly more than a year in reading, topping the scores of the other 13 second grade classes in the same building. Unheard of. Why did the kids continue to work the cube for a full year and not give up even though they experienced failure and made lots of mistakes? Why did they gain in reading when the reading program remained unchanged and the methods and technology stayed the same?

Why do unsharpened pencils succeed? But most importantly how do you sharpen unsharpened pencils?

I know why and I know how. It isn't luck or in the DNA.

It has taken me a life-time to figure out how unsharpened pencils keep writing and in some cases learn to re-sharpen themselves to write better.

I flunked out of third grade because I couldn't read. After the second try, I still couldn't read any better than I could the first go around. I graduated from high school illiterate, received a B.A. in Psychology and couldn't read a newspaper. Presently, as a Professor Emeritus, I read no better than 6th grade.

I received a doctorate with honors, wrote three of the best-selling textbooks in my field, became a Fulbright scholar to teach a theory I developed on how to help people achieve. The theory was presented at the American University in Cairo Research Conference and selected as the feature article in the conference proceedings.

I also actually worked for a living: paperboy, dishwasher, fry cook, iron foundry worker, farm hand, paint store clerk, oil field worker, semi-pro baseball player, used car salesman, school teacher and rehabilitation counselor.

Administratively, I have been a restaurant manager of one of the largest restaurant chains in the Midwest, furniture stripping and repair proprietor buying a company out of bankruptcy and developing it into one of the best in the state, General Manager of one of the most prestigious automobile dealerships in the South, first Director of one of the largest Head-Start programs in the nation, and Dean of Education at a Research I, flagship university.

As an unsharpened pencil and at times downright dull, I have managed to re-sharpen myself from time to time. I have learned how to help others get sharp and stay sharp.

There is no silver bullet. I present to you no guiding principles, no secret recipe, no universal truths.

I present to you my life as it sharpens, un-sharpens, re-sharpens, becomes almost illegible and occasionally point perfect.

Walk with me as my pencil takes shape. Let me show you how you can sharpen your own pencil. But, more importantly, how you can help others sharpen their pencil.

Batesville Second Grade Cubists

End of Year Celebration

–Chapter 1–

Double Dip

1937

Born, Topeka

1945

Repeated 3rd grade

(I learn I can't read)

We enter the school -- Mother on my right, Father on my left -- and report to the office. We are told that my teacher is waiting for us in her room. My room.

Miss Campbell - third grade teacher, Gage Park Elementary - greets us at the door, motions for us to be seated, positions herself in her rightful chair behind her desk. It is indeed her room not mine. I sit in a desk chair designed for third graders. My mom and dad squeeze into two adjoining, brown oak desk chairs. A three inch diameter hole in the upper right hand corner designed for an ink well never to be used by me, my classmates, or anyone we knew.

I snap to attention while my parents adjust into their seats. Miss Campbell sits erect behind her desk. The desk is marred in places and shows wear from years of abuse much like Miss Campbell's face. Behind her is the chalk smudged blackboard that spans three quarters of the wall. In the right corner, an American flag stands upright, at attention, like we students must sit and stand, in-line for recess and lunch. Between the flag and next to the blackboard is a four foot by four foot cork bulletin board that cries out three class rules: No Chewing Gum, No Hitting, No Talking.

I believe Miss Campbell thinks herself proud but I see her as arrogant. Her speech is tight, her sentences sculpted by her incisors. Her words are clipped and ominous. I wonder, "Does she bite?"

No small talk now, no thank you for coming. "Jimmy is failing. He can't read. He will have to repeat third grade."

Mother and Father listen, expressionless, dutiful, unsurprised. They know I am failing, struggle with reading and most likely will repeat third grade.

For a brief moment, I question why this information needs to be shared via a parent conference. Why not a simple letter or phone call? What follows reveals the need for a face to face conference. Miss Campbell explains why I am failing in detail. Simply, blatantly put, I cannot read. Much to my surprise, I learn the reason I cannot read is that my parents are not helping me. As Miss Campbell continues her lecture, for the first time I realize I am not dumb. It is my parents' fault. They are the slackers. They are not holding up their end of the learning process. They allow me to goof off.

Miss Campbell does not plead, she does not ask, she instructs. For me to pass, to learn to read, my parents must …goodness gracious they must do a lot of stuff. This explanation goes on for some time. I begin to wonder if my parents are able to do it all; Miss Campbell wonders if they are willing.

Just when I think the meeting is over, but before Miss Campbell can get up and escort us to the door, my dad says, nicely but purposefully, "I don't think you understand. If the student hasn't learned, the teacher hasn't taught. You are the teacher. We are the parents. Your job is to help Jimmy learn; our job is to parent. Parents take their kids to the movies and picnics. They play catch with them, take them fishing. They eat ice cream together. This coming year, why don't we continue to be good parents and you try to be a good teacher and teach Jimmy. Otherwise, we might be back here next year, and I can't believe you want him in your class a third time."

My dad gets up and simultaneously my mom gets up. I look at Miss Campbell still seated. I'd describe her as stunned. Her wide open eyes stare into space and her mouth forms a perfect "O," big enough to stuff a ping pong ball through. She has no bite. She has no sting. She is paralyzed by my dad's elegance. I get up and the three of us exit the building in silence.

As we walk down the sidewalk away from the school hand in hand, I feel good. Two supportive parents make me proud. I look up at my dad, "What are we going to do now?"

He looks down, "We're going to get some ice cream."

This day is special, a double dip day. Cake cone, strawberry on top, chocolate on the bottom. I savor every lick.

Dad in his milk route uniform

Mom and I walking downtown
Topeka, Kansas.

Me, eight years old, in my
Cub Scout uniform.

Miss Campbell's third grade class. I'm in the middle row, second seat from the front.

-Chapter 2-

Jo Ann

—

1946
Knee catches my eye
(I learn not everyone sharpens their
pencil the same way)

Repeating third grade is supposed to be a bummer but, you know, maybe it will help me catch up. It is no fun not to be able to raise your hand to answer questions you don't know the answers to. I can't figure out how all the other kids know the answers. Even Ellis, God. Ellis is dumb as a stump, but even he got to go to fourth.

Sometimes I know the answer but am too slow. My mind works funny. The teacher asks "Who was the first President of the United States?" To begin, I think 'who.' That means a person. Next I think 'first.' That means started in the beginning. Then I think 'President.' That is the person that runs things. Finally, I think 'United States.' Oh yes, the United States. I get it, what person started and ran the United States of America. Of course, George Washington. I raise my hand and everyone has gone to recess.

I don't think Miss Campbell knows how my brain works because I don't know how my brain works.

I don't know why I'm so slow and I don't like being last. Mom and Dad don't care if I'm slow or last, but they hope I'm going to do better this year. They hope, but they really don't care how I do. Mom, dad and my dog Cactus love me. They think I'm great. They even think I'm smart.

This year is going to be different. I'm going to get a fresh start. At least, I won't be last. I'm going to have new friends and on the playground and after school I'll have my old friends. My old friends like me because I can run fast, catch and hit a ball. They always pick me first to be on their team. We have so much fun.

I already know half of my new third grade friends. They can't wait to get me on their team.

I bet I'm going to know how to read this year. I wonder if I'll be in the Bluebird group. I'm not smart enough to be a Cardinal. Those Cardinals know everything. I don't want to be a

Cardinal. My dad warns me not to get too smart for my britches. Those Cardinals are too smart for their britches, except for Kevin. I like Kevin. He is almost as fast as me and we usually end up on the same team. We are buddies.

Yeah, this year will be different. It will be fun. It will be exciting. Since I was in third last year, this year will be easy as pie. I bet I'm going to know everything and I'll be able to raise my hand first. Washington was our first President. Topeka is the capital of Kansas. Eight times nine is … I'm only up to my six's, but I'll get to those crazy eights later this year.

I'm going to keep my mouth shut, keep my hands to myself and sit up straight. When Miss Campbell talks, I'm going to look directly at her. I bet she won't yell at me even once this year. I will know where everything is and how to act. This year will be a snap.

I feel so good I can't wait to get to class. It is the first day of school. The air is so fresh. I have to skip. "Skip to ma loo, skip to ma loo, skip to ma loo my darlin."

Once, two, three, Up the steps. Through the door. Down the hall. Three doors to the right. Yep. Miss Campbell's name is proudly displayed above the door, 'Miss Campbell, 3rd Grade.' I'm the first to enter the room.

"Jimmy, this year you sit here." She points to a center, front row desk immediately joining her desk. Last year I was center, two rows back. I sense a tone in her voice, she doesn't trust me.

As I put my stuff under my seat in the storage area, Miss Campbell greets each kid with a smile and directs them to their rightful place. I notice the flag is in the same place, the same rules displayed in the same place. Da je vu. Everything, I mean everything, is the same. Miss Campbell must own only one pair of shoes. This may not be as good as I had hoped.

The days crawl by and everyday the same boring stuff, presented the same boring way. I wasn't able to get it the first time. Do they think by repeating the same stuff in the same way

I'm going to get it the second time around? I've got news for them. I couldn't read the stuff then and I can't read the stuff now and neither can anyone in my group, the Crows. I guess once a Crow, always a Crow. My Crowean friends this year are just like last years. We can't read a lick.

I hate this, I can't stand it. I'm a prisoner trapped in third grade for a second time. Just as I am about ready to have a mental breakdown I notice, out of the corner of my left eye, a knee. I don't dare move my head. I just roll both eyes left to get a more focused view.

Jo Ann just crossed her legs telegraphing her knee. I've been suspicious of Jo Ann from the start. She is a Cardinal but rather than look down her nose at me like the other Cardinals do, she always smiles before turning her head away.

Jo Ann is not a kid. She is a creature.

Jo Ann is a good foot shorter than me. Like me, she is fit and physically attractive. Her hair is short and curled with a black sheen that makes me want to stare, but I haven't and won't. Brows are thick and eye lashes flipped up. Those unusual eye lashes accent two brown eyes that resemble deep glossy M&M's. A nose slightly up turned, lips that are the thinnest of all the girls and perfect teeth. She always wears a white blouse with wide lapels. My favorite is the one where the points of the lapels span to her shoulders. I've never seen anything so white and I can't imagine any piece of fabric so wrinkleless. Her blouses are so clean, white, and perfectly ironed I want to run my fingers along the lapels but dare not to even think about it. Her skirts are thigh high revealing indescribable knees. White socks with lace or fancy embroidery dancing around the top edges. My favorite is the pair that has a string of tiny clowns holding hands circling slightly above the ankles. If the socks weren't classy enough, they are neatly tucked into a pair of black patent leather shoes, each with a small strap across the instep to secure a snug fit.

Suddenly, without warning, the legs uncross and she rises. She walks toward the door, not too fast, not too slow, but with purpose. As she grabs the knob she turns her shoulders, and ever so briefly glances my way. Cardinals never look at Crows but I swear she looked directly at me.

I honestly don't know what happened to me but my mind snapped a mental photo of her glancing over her shoulder as she departed.

I think I must have had one of those 'out of body' things you hear about. Without thought or reason I snatched a piece of paper from my notebook and with my number two pencil, drew a picture of her glancing over her shoulder leaving the room. Those eyes, that hair. I imagined a perfectly formed back with a spine that reached to the crack between her buns. Those buns never to be seen by me or anyone in the class, must be as perfect as her knees. As I draw those buns my pencil moved...I swear to you, the pencil moved as if guided by God.

When I finished, I reveled in my masterpiece. A naked drawing of a model stepping out the door, glancing over her shoulder with a back so straight it would make any ballet teacher proud.

I looked around and much to my surprise and delight no one had noticed me or Jo Ann. I carefully placed my work in a beat-up, used folder I had from last year and tucked it under my seat.

A week following her exit from the room, she rose to sharpen her pencil. Third graders sharpen pencils by turning the handle clockwise in a nondescript way. Everybody does it the same way except for Jo Ann. When Jo Ann sharpens her pencil she uses her whole body. As she shimmered and shook, instinctively, I pulled out a piece of paper and put my number two to work. But this time, unlike last, I got a profile shot: An unclothed, stark naked picture of a creature sharpening a pencil. I drew her looking down at the pencil being held in her left hand while her right turned the crank. I don't know what made me do it but I imagined her sharpening her pencil standing on her tip toes.

Again I looked around, no one noticed me or Jo Ann. I slipped my work in the folder and stashed it under my seat.

My parents were right. Repeating third grade was a good thing. As the days rolled on, my beat-up folder becomes a treasure trove of magnificence.

Unknown to me, Mrs. Campbell uncovered my work. I thought what I kept under my seat was private. She thought what was under my seat was in her room, thus, what was under my seat was available for her preview. She didn't have the guts to tell me, she told my mom. I enter the house, naïve of a conspiracy. My mom pours me a glass of ice cold, cherry Koolaid, my favorite. She put in three scoops of sugar rather than the usual two. I should have suspected something but I didn't. I sit at the kitchen table where I usually sit while mom fixes her coffee, as she usually does.

"Jimmy, how was school today?"

"Fine."

"What did you learn today?"

"Nothin."

"How you doing in your studies?"

"Good."

Mom, with her coffee, sits at the head of the table, where she usually does, cattycornered from me. "How's the Koolaid?"

"Great."

"Your dad and I want us all to go to the movies Saturday."

"Oh mom, can we go to the Hopalong Cassidy one?"

"That's exactly what we were thinking."

"Afterward we want to go for ice cream."

"Do you think I can get a shake, chocolate?"

"I think so. Are you involved in any new projects in school?"

"No."

Mom looks up from her coffee and in a normal unassuming tone, "Jimmy, are you drawing pictures of naked girls?"

Quickly, I look up from my Koolaid, staring straight across the table, staring at the wall, not daring to look at my mom: wide-open eyes, in shock, "No, mom."

Mom looks down at her coffee, same unassuming tone, "I know you wouldn't do anything like that. You are such a good boy."

She slowly looks halfway up, "But someone in your room is." Her head turns toward me, "And when you find out who it is." She leans forward while the two of us look straight at each other, eyeball to eyeball, "YOU TELL HIM TO STOP IT." She picks up her cup and as she rises to return to the kitchen in a pointed voice, with her back turned, "Because it ain't nice" punctuating the 'ain't nice' part.

That ended my career in Fine Arts. But no matter how hard I tried, I couldn't keep from looking at Jo Ann out of the corner of my eye.

–Chapter 3–

WashburnUniversity

1954

Graduated, DeSoto High School

1954

Started Washburn University
(I learn the phonetic alphabet)

I arrived at Washburn University to find that classes do not meet every day. I don't have any money. So I get a job with Famous Brands Wholesale Liquor, a delivering boy. The job is only part time, but the hours are regular. As are the class hours at the university. At the university I am expected to be on time, every day. No problem, except on Tuesdays. My last delivery is at 9:45 a.m. and my history class begins at 10:00 a.m. The time it takes to park the truck, punch out, and get to class puts me arriving at 10:05 a.m. The history teacher is a stickler for being on time. Being to class on time is more important than delivering liquor. Since I am being paid to deliver liquor and since I put out money to take the course, I mistakenly think otherwise.

The history teacher explains, "The only excuse for being late or missing class is a death -- your own." For some reason he thinks that is funny. Every day I come in 5 minutes late. As I enter he stops talking until I am seated. He looks at me out of the corner of his eye in disgust. The fifth day of class, I arrive five minutes late to find the door to the class locked. The door having no window, I place my ear against the wooden panels. The teacher is droning on. I jiggle the handle. To no avail. I knock quietly. No response. I knock more firmly. Still no response. I don't know what comes over me -- anger, determination, stupidity. I drop my book bag to the floor, doubled up both fists and begin to pound on the door left, right, left, right, left right while simultaneously, yelling, "Let me in, let me in. I love history, I am a sponge of knowledge. Learning from history is the most important thing on earth. Let me in, let me in."

As I began to repeat my demands third time the door opens. I pick up my bag and walk to my seat. No one smiles or snickers. Everyone watches me then they watch the instructor return to the lectern. The professor continues where he left off and no one, absolutely no one, ever says anything to me afterwards. The door is never locked again.

I earn a D for the course -- not because I didn't learn history, but because I could not read the text or the tests.

For some reason, I take a speech course under a Mr. McCausland. The course centers on speaking proper diction. We learn the phonetic alphabet. The first day every student reports to the lectern, and, from a pre-prepared list, reads 25 words into a recorder. Throughout the semester, we learn how to project and to breathe through our diaphragms. Then, at the end of the semester, each student returns to the lectern, reads the same 25 words as a final exam. Mr. McCausland would play the before and after readings of each student so we can all realize what we had learned. Pretty clever. A before and after test. Everyone could pass and would actually realize our proficiency. No one was embarrassed. Each student anxiously waited for his time to demonstrate a skill that none had possessed at the beginning of the semester.

Although functionally illiterate at the time, able to read at about a third grade level, reading the 25 words for the first time seemed a piece of cake. I remember clearly, as if it were today. I was the sixth student. I confidently strode to the lectern and confidently read the 25 words into the recorder. Afterwards, Mr. McCausland jumped out of his seat, hustled to my side, put his arm around my shoulders and with the sincerity of a surrogate father said, "Mr. Payne, please read the words again. I've been teaching this course for over 15 years, and that is the worst performance I have ever heard. You will learn so much in this class. And we are going to learn so much from you." His arm never left my shoulders. Later he listened with amazement as I read the 25 words a second time. When I had completed the list he hugged me, and I noticed a small tear roll down his cheek.

From that point on, throughout the semester, in each class session, when it came time for me to present, every student along with Mr. McCausland watched and listened in anticipation. Each time I made a mistake, Mr. McCausland rushed forward, stood next to me, in front of God and before every student, and made me do it over and over until I got it right. One time, he actually kissed me on the forehead. That semester, I mastered the phonetic alphabet.

One night, I was home watching television with my father. Something came on the screen that my dad wanted to remember. He directed, "Jimmy, get me a pin." I dutifully retrieved a pin from the bedroom to be corrected by my dad, "Not that kind of pin, a pin you write with."

"Dad, you don't want a "pin," you want a "pen,"' I proudly explained.

"What?" queried my father, who did not know Mr. McCausland.

With the excitement of a young child, I held out a pen and articulated with a clarity that would have made Mr. McCausland weep, professionally projecting, "This is a pen that you write with," and then displaying the pin in my right hand, "This is a pin you stick with." I continued pompously, "Pen, pin."

My dad looked up from his beat up lounge chair with little pieces of cotton sticking out from the corners of the arms. "Where did you learn all that?"

Proudly, I announced, "Washburn."

Overhearing the conversation, my mother, asked, "Washburn? I thought it was Worshburn."

"No, Mom, it's Washburn not Worshburn. Also, you don't "worsh" your clothes you "wash" clothes. No 'r'. Wash not worsh."

"Who told you that?"

"Mr. McCausland," I proudly proclaimed.

"Well, the next time you see Mr. McCausland, ask him what type of soap I should use."

I got a B in Mr. McCausland's class. But more importantly I certainly got my money's worth.

My dad taught me how to
enjoy living.

Mr. McCausland taught me the
phonetic alphabet.

–Chapter 4–

English 101

—

1955
Failed, Washburn University
(I learn I have style)

It is the first day of my freshman English class. I am sitting with 23 other boys. No females. I sense this isn't the Cardinals or the Bluebirds. Miss Margaret Southworth enters. Solemn, horned rimmed glasses, scholarly and smileless.

- "I want you to hear it from me before you hear it from anyone else. You are enrolled in what is commonly referred to as 'Bonehead English.' The reason: you are boneheads. You scored so low on the English entrance exam people believe you will fail to graduate. So you are in this class. I have but one goal in life: to pound enough English in your heads so that as seniors you will pass the English proficiency test and graduate.

- The best grade you can get in this class is a C. If you were capable of getting a better grade you would not be here. Get it into your head right now -- you are shooting for a C. I don't like to give D's or F's but I can and will if necessary. A theme is due every week. If you have more than five misspelled words, you will receive an F.

- Get out paper and pencil. Put your name in the upper right hand corner. At the top of the page write, "Why I Came to College." Now, tell me in your best writing why you came to college."

We wrote as she looked on. At the end of class, we placed our papers face down on the desk in front of her. Two days later I get my paper back 'F'. I misspelled "college" 32 times. I spelled it "collage."

The class met twice a week. We sat in alphabetical order. Each session began with her calling roll. During week three she called out, "Norris."
"Here"
"Owen"
"Here"

"Payne"

"Here"

"Robinson"

No   response.

"ROBINSON"

Still no response

Miss Southworth leaned way over to her left so she could see the chair right behind me. It was empty. She asked in a dictatorial tone, "Where's Robinson?"

A student from the back of the room meekly explained, "Miss Southworth, Robinson is having trouble. He is dropping your class."

"He doesn't have my permission to drop this class. Ridiculous." She turned and walked out of the classroom. "This class session is over."

We all looked at one another. We were stunned. We didn't know what to do. More importantly, we didn't know what was going to happen to Robinson.

The next class session,

"Norris"

"Here"

"Owen"

"Here"

"Payne"

"Here"

"Robinson"

"Here"

"Stevenson"

"Here"

She continued calling out the names. All were present. At the end of class several of us cornered Robinson. He explained in detail, "She came to my house. I opened the door. She asked 'What's up?' I explained I was dropping her class, in fact, I told her I was quitting school. She explained in no uncertain terms I couldn't drop her class; I didn't have her permission.

Furthermore she said she wouldn't give me permission. She saw potential in me, and she had too much time invested in me to let me drop. At this point she jammed her foot against the door so I couldn't close it, and she moved her head about six inches from my face and said 'Get your butt back in my class and don't even think about quitting school. I'll see you Thursday.'"

I look back on that day and I realize we were either so dumb we didn't know we could drop her class without her permission, or we were so scared we didn't dare. Maybe, just maybe, she was on our side, in our corner. She would not let us fail. We were going to learn English.

By mid semester I had received an 'F' on every paper. I was having trouble in every course, but English was a disaster. I mustered up enough courage to go to Miss Southworth's office. I knocked on the door. "It's open."

I opened the door to find Ole Miss Southworth at her desk grading themes. Papers were stacked all over the place. She looked up at me. "What do you want?"

I explained. "I am Jim Payne and ...."

She cut me off, "I know who you are. You are Jim Payne in my third hour Bonehead English class. What do you want?"

"Miss Southworth. The first day of class you said you were going to pound enough English in our heads so we would pass the English proficiency test as seniors. I'm not going to get that far. I'm failing your class. I have an 'F' on every theme."

She laid down her indelible red pen, "You can't spell. Get a dictionary."

I explained, "I have a dictionary but how can I find the word if I can't spell it?"

She directed, "Turn around."

I turned around.

"Turn sideways so I can see your profile."

I turned sideways.

"Face me."

I faced her.

She advised, "Mr. Payne, you are a handsome young man. I'd suggest you go over to the Union. Walk up and down the cafeteria. Look for an attractive young coed sitting alone with books scattered all over her table. Ask if the vacant seat is taken. After she says 'no,' cautiously sit down. Put your book bag on the floor and take out one book. Open the book and act as if you are reading it. After a couple of minutes explain that you are going to get a Coke and ask if she would like one also. When she says, 'Yes', run, don't walk, to the fountain. Get two Cokes and take her one. As she begins to sip the Coke start a conversation. 'Are you from here? What's your major? Are you planning to join a sorority? What courses are you enrolled in?' Somewhere along the line she will start asking you questions. Now don't get excited. It's like fishing. She has to take the bait. At the right moment explain you are having trouble with English. Do not mention the word 'bonehead.' Just say English. Explain you have a lot of trouble with spelling. Now for the kicker -- say your teacher told you to get a dictionary. Then you say, 'I've got a dictionary but what good is it? How can I find the word if I can't spell it?' If she smiles she has taken the bait.

Now, start reeling her in. Ask if she might have time to check your themes for spelling errors. When you do it right, and if you have selected the right person, she will help. Each week, make arrangements to show her your theme. After she corrects it, rewrite it and you are on your way to a 'C.' By the way, if she's any good take her to dinner.'"

I leave Southworth's office, go to the Union, find a coed, get two Cokes and like magic I've got my own personal spell checker.

The very next class session, before having the benefits of a personal spell checker, Miss Southworth hands out a paper for us to look over. It is my paper, my name removed. She had made copies for each of us to study. After giving us enough time to look the paper over she asks the class, "What did you see in the paper?"

Albertson, on the front row says, "I see more than five misspelled words."

I could have throttled him but Miss Southworth calmly responded, "Yes, but I'm thinking of something positive."

"Something positive" -- what could that be? I frantically looked over the paper again as does the rest of the class. No one can find anything positive with this paper. Nor can I.

Then Miss Southworth says, "It's got style."

I quickly glanced at the paper again. Of course, it's got style. I've got style. I walk with style. I dress with style. I talk with style. If there is one thing I've got, it's style.

Miss Southworth points out, "Notice how the words jump off the page. Notice how you kept reading because you want to know what's coming next."

She went on and on. I begin to realize I've written a masterpiece. After exhausting the accolades of my paper she begins to return each student's paper. I receive my stylish paper, the one with my name on it, graded "F".

Miss Southworth was relentless but I loved her – no, I adored her, and so did everyone in the class.

With the help of my spell checker, after a case or two of Cokes and an occasional dinner, I ended up with the grade of C. I left that class believing I had style, value. I had something worth writing about. How could I write and not be able to read? Short sentences and low vocabulary. That was the key to good writing. You don't have to be able to read to write.

At the end of the first year of college I had a below C average, not good enough to go on. Not having enough sense to quit, I transferred to Dodge City Junior College.

Me as a freshman at
Washburn University

I adored Miss Southworth.
She made me believe I had style.

–Chapter 5–

Dodge City Junior College

—

1958

Graduated, Associates Degree, Dodge City Jr. College
(I learn a little French)

I arrive at Dodge City Junior College with a baseball scholarship. The scholarship pays tuition, books, and room. A 10 hour a week job at the Lariat Café gives me enough money to live on plus one free meal per day.

My room at the fire station is offered as a community service to the college. Located on the second floor, a window overlooks Boot Hill. In fact, if I wanted, I could drop a pebble straight down from my window onto Boot Hill. The firemen show me how to slide down the fire pole. On occasion they share a meal with me. They even let me ride on the back of the truck during test runs. Every fireman is a professional. They take their jobs seriously, are courageous when necessary, and daring. Yet, with all the professionalism they are kids at heart.

Dodge City loves parades. Their parades always end up at Front Street, now turned tourist attraction. Dodge City, Kansas, The Cowboy Capital of the World. During my second month there was a big celebration with, of course, a parade. But this time the parade's marshal is Hugh O'Brien, the Hugh O'Brien who played Wyatt Earp on television, and he is coming to lead the parade and host the ceremonies. Unknown to Hugh O'Brien, the firemen, or the city fathers, a group at Garden City was plotting to raid the parade and capture Hugh O'Brien. All make-believe of course. People who have never visited the western part of Kansas won't understand. In the western part of Kansas, adults still play cowboys and Indians; they ride on real horses. It's hard to believe but it's true. It's great.

So the parade begins. The streets are lined with cheering fans. Hugh O'Brien on his white stallion leads the parade, followed by the fire truck -- my fire truck. Occasionally, the sirenblasts away. The high school band plays and the twirlers twirl.

Just as the parade nears Front Street, the Garden City gang come riding out to capture a surprised Hugh O'Brien. Six Garden Citians, bandanas covering their faces to resemble movie bandits, surround him. The white steed spooks, rises up on its hind legs and throws its rider to the ground. The horse rears up, jumps around, one hoof unfortunately landing on Hugh O'Brien'sboot. The boot is cut and O'Brien's leg bleeds. The firemen -- I am so proud of them -- spring into action. They shoo the Garden City rascals away, swoop up O'Brien, put him in the fire engine's spare seat and speed him to the fire house three blocks away.

At the firehouse they place O'Brien on a folding chair, slice open his boot with one of their special knives, easily removing the boot without harming his leg.

All the time O'Brien is cussing like a drunken sailor. The leg is just scratched. The firemen, experts in first aid, spray the wound with disinfectant, wrap it in gauze and seal the leg with a piece of tape. All this just in time for their patient's limousine to arrive. Hugh O'Brien continues his tirade, drops into the back seat and is whisked away.

I look around and the fire chief is marking off a three foot square where Hugh O'Brien sat.

Before I can process everything that has gone on, one of the firemen joins the chief with an artist's brush and a small jar of black paint. The chief in his best penmanship bends down and prints "Hugh O'Brien 1958" inside the marked square next to a small drop of blood.

I look at the chief and I look at the fireman and instantaneously, I give them an ovation. They bow with pride. I can't believe I am living rent free in the fire station at Dodge City, Kansas, and do not have to pay extra for the entertainment. Is this America or what?

Dodge City was an experience, but the junior college was a gift in disguise. The gift came with Monseigneur Ballou, a portly French teacher who loved French food and France. The class gave five hours credit. Its text was written in French, which no one could read. Most of the tests were oral. I thought I had died and gone to heaven. I struggled, but so did everyone else. I wasn't the best in the class, but I also wasn't the worst. Monseigneur Ballou liked me and I liked him. Truthfully, Monseigneur Ballou liked everyone and everyone like him. I learned to count in French, speak a few phrases, and actually read a little.

But what made me shine was that a good part of the grade was determined by a closing five minute presentation, in French, delivered at the class dinner at the end of the semester. I recited my version of Little Red Riding Hood. I studied, rehearsed, incorporated all of Mr. McCausland's best teachings and came before the students. When I finished, the class showed their respect with applause. Monseigneur Ballou came to the front of the class and embraces me in front of all my classmates.

A few days later I received a call at the firehouse asking me to report to Monseigneur Ballou's office. When we met, he asked me to present the Little Red Riding Hood sketch to the faculty at their next meeting. The faculty applauded. Most came up to shake my hand and compliment me. My picture along with an article about the class dinner appeared in the local paper.

The firemen cut the article out, framed it, and gave it to me as a going away gift. I received a B for the class. Add a one hour credit A for playing baseball, an A in art and a batch of B's and C's for biology, math and whatever, I ended the year with an Associates Degree. And a ticket to return to Washburn as a Junior.

I loved and
respected all the firemen.

Me in front of the lockers
at the Firehouse.

I really got into it.
Some were more enthused than
thers.

Dodge City College's French Classes
Enjoy Dinner, Entertainment Program

LITTLE RED RIDINGHOOD—Jim Payne, fresh- man at Dodge City College, gave his mono- logue version of Little Red Ridinghood in French Wednesday night at a dinner and pro- gram given by the college French class at

Scholle's Serva-Teria. At left, Payne is attire for the part of Little Red Ridinghood and, the right, he dressed for the part of Grandm
(Globe Photo

The article made me feel important.

45

–Chapter 6–
Psychology

—

1962
Graduated, Bachelor's Degree, Washburn
University (Psychology)
(I learn from a rat and Emily)

My previous education led me to Washburn as a junior. I received a small scholarship for playing baseball to help offset expenses. Over time, I had learned some survival techniques for passing classes. Sit up front, look alert, nod approvingly on occasion, and act like you are taking notes.

I still could not read a newspaper. I could write if someone helped me with spelling. So in classes that required a paper or a project I was fine -- not good, but okay. I attended all classes. Some instructors actually gave credit for attendance. Also, sometimes credit is given for participation. I learned to ask questions at appropriate times and join in discussions. I learned that credit for participation is assessed by volume (the number of times you talk) and not necessarily evaluated on the quality of your input. Also, no credit is given for listening.

Fill-in-the-blank questions on tests usually require rote memory, and I was ok on this type of test except for the spelling. Most teachers don't count off for spelling on fill-in-the-blank tests. Essay tests were fine. Giving credit to Miss Southworth, I could write a good paragraph. I excelled in see-and-tell projects, presentations, role playing and even oral quizzes. Because of Mr. McCausland I could pass anything oral. The multiple choice tests, however, killed me: I couldn't read fast enough. In many cases, I couldn't understand the question. My female freshman spell checker had given me good advice. If you don't understand the question or don't know the answer, mark the same response on each answer. So if I don't know, I always mark "A." Marking "A" every time automatically gives me a 25 percent success rate if my options are A B C D. On occasion option D is "all of the above." "All of the above" is seldom the correct answer so my success rate increases to 33 and 1/3 percent.

All of my psychology professors were excellent. Some, maybe most, didn't know how to teach but they all knew their subject matter. They amazed me. I was fascinated with what I was learning, but enjoyed the experimental labs the most.

I took a course in stimulus response theory in which we learned about reinforcement. In lab, each student was issued a Skinner Box and a rat. The Skinner Box resembled a large shoe box about a foot deep, a foot wide and a foot and a half long. A straw-like tube was diagonally fastened to one end of the box. I would drop in a pellet of food. It would go down into a small receptacle inside the box and land in a small dish about the size of a quarter. Six inches above the dish was a little handle or bar. When the bar was pushed down and released, a spring mechanism returned the bar to its original position.

The idea was to teach the rat to depress the bar. The experimenter-student would drop a pellet of food through the tube and into the dish every time the rat pushed the bar down. Simply put, the rat learned that when the bar was pushed, he got food. Common sense to us students. But to B.F. Skinner it was a revelation. It's not rocket science, its psychology and, believe me, volumes have been written about this phenomenon.

During lab each of us would get our box, grab a handful of pellets and fetch our rat. We would deposit the rat in the box, quickly put a pellet between our thumb and forefinger, hold the pellet slightly above the opening in the tube outside the box and ready ourselves to drop the pellet when the rat pushed the bar.

At first, we would religiously go through our routine only to observe our rat lumber over to a corner of the box, curl up in a ball, and go to sleep. This routine went on for about a month. I was told that some of the students nudged the box and a couple even shook the box without result. One student actually poked the rat with a pencil. That was cheating. I just watched my rodent, hoping something would happen, and occasionally wondered how I would earn a grade.

After a month, just as we were about to give up, Emily's rat pushed the bar. We couldn't believe it. Not Emily, with her thick glasses, kinky red hair and ugly ankles! The whole class gathered around as Emily dropped her varmint in the box to see it immediately scamper to the bar and push it down. Emily continued to deposit pellets, her rat would push the bar, swallow the pellet, push the bar, swallow the pellet, over and over until our 30 minute class time was up. You would have to see it to believe it. Emily would proudly return her rat and her box to their rightful places and leave the lab without comment.

Emily was smug. I don't think anyone liked her. After three or four lab sessions, one of the students accused Emily of being given a gifted rat. Talk about a cat-fight (in this case a rat fight)! Emily jumped up and down, stomped her feet, insisted her success had nothing to do with the rat; it had to do with her own skills. She was a superior lab scientist.

I was offended by her arrogance. She might be able to read but she wasn't superior to her peers. Yet I began thinking - maybe our grade in the lab depended on successful experiments. We did keep a journal but we could hardly be graded on it. There was no presentation. There was no mid-term or final. My God, my grade didn't depend on me, it depended on how fast my rat learned. Ok, Emily will get an A. But what about me? I began to panic. Psychology was my major. I had to get a C, at least.

The next lab session Emily showed off like a movie star. She reported to the lab carrying her box under her left arm and a bag of pellets in her left hand. She proudly displayed her rat, holding it high above her head, in her right hand, just like a movie star would show off an Oscar. I looked closely and by gosh, she was wearing a little eye shadow. She placed the box down, moved her rat from side to side for all of us to see, as if saying "See -- no strings." She plunged the rat in the box and like magic the rat began pushing the bar and eating pellets. That day that rat pushed that bar so fast so many times, I got tired watching it. That rat pushed that bar at supersonic speed. I began to sweat. My hands began to tremble. Then all of a sudden I had an insight, an "ah ha" experience. I don't know where it came from but I thanked God for it.

As the lab session ended, Emily returned her rat and her box as before, with dramatic flair. As she left the lab, walked down the hall and out of the building I followed her, not so close she could see me, and not so far behind that I would lose her. She walked around Henderson building, turned right past Benton. I knew it, I knew it, she was going to the Union. I hung back a little. I wanted her to get settled. Sure enough, she went to the cafeteria, positioned herself at a table next to the big window and began to unpack her book bag. Before anyone else could get close to her table I nonchalantly passed by and asked if anyone was sitting in the vacant chair.

She motioned me to be seated. I put my book bag on the floor, took out a book and pretended to read. I turned to her and said I was going to get a Coke and asked if she would like one.

She said, "Yeah, that would be nice."

I got up, hastily went to the fountain, returned and positioned her Coke on the table. As anticipated, she began to sip the Coke. I asked if she was from Topeka? I asked if she was a psychology major? Are you connected with a sorority? And then I threw out the bait. I turned, looked her in the eye and accused "Your rat is gifted; it's not fair."

She came back, "It is not. It's me."

I said, "It's not you."

"Is so," she said.

"I can tell you this," I said, "I bet you can't make my rat push the bar."

She said, "Push the bar? Give me two minutes with your rat. I can make it hump that bar like a sexually deprived rabbit."

I said, "Wait a minute, let's don't get dirty here. All I say is, you can't get my rat to push the bar." She took the bait, I had her hooked. Now all I needed to do was reel her in, "Bet you can't, you ain't woman enough."

She jumped up from her chair and said "How much?"

"Ten dollars."

"Ten dollars, you couldn't get me to spit for ten dollars."

"Twenty," I said.

"Forty," she said.

"Thirty five."

"Pick up your bag and follow me," she said.

I not only had reeled her in; she was in the boat.

She gathered up her satchel and I followed her to the lab. As majors we both had lab keys, but when we entered, she began to look around carefully; she didn't want anyone to see us. Once she was sure the coast was clear, she instructed me to get my box while she got the food pellets. I got my rat. She motioned me to hand it to her. "Get a pellet ready to drop. We are going to do it," she confidently pronounced. This gal thinks she is Wonder Woman in sneakers!

Before I could get composed, she held my rat up in her left hand, slapped its head a couple of times with her right, jammed the rat into the box and pushed the bar down with the rat's nose. Then she dropped it face down into the dish. She snapped the rat out of the box and said, "Damn it, drop the pellet the minute the bar goes down."

51

Next she instructed me as if I were an idiot. "Get a pellet."

I got the pellet.

"Hold the pellet next to the opening in the tube."

I placed the pellet next to the opening as instructed.

Then she said, "When I push the bar down with the rat's nose, drop the pellet. Ready?" She slapped the poor thing around again, plunged it into the box, smashed its nose against the bar. I dropped the pellet. As the pellet dropped into the dish, she jammed the rat's face into the dish. The rat sucked up the pellet and she quickly pulled the rat back out of the box as the rat consumed the morsel.

She instructed me to get ready again. I nodded. Slap, slap. Rat enters box, nose jams on bar, pellet drops, head butts dish, pellet is consumed.

This we repeated four more times. Then with pride she said, "Watch this." She began to gently stroke the rat. I watched the rat relax and grow calm. "Ready?"

I nodded.

This time she slowly lowered the rat in the box with her left hand while gently holding its paw between the finger and thumb of her right. She gently placed the paw on the bar, pushed it down, I dropped the pellet, she moved the rat's mouth toward the dish and instantly the pellet was consumed. We repeated this four times. She lifted the rat from the box and said, "Watch this." She took a handful of pellets in her right hand, placing one pellet between her thumb and forefinger. She lowered my rat and placed it on the far side of the box opposite the bar. When she released the rat, it briskly went to the bar, pushed the bar with its right paw as Emily dropped a pellet. The rat consumed the pellet and instantly pushed the bar again while Emily dropped another pellet. The rat kept pushing and Emily kept releasing a pellet. It reminded me of dropping BBs down the slot of a Red Rider Daisy Riffle.

I learned a great lesson that day. Don't judge anybody by their fat ankles. It was the best 35 dollars I ever spent. I got an A for lab. Emily was better than Wonder Woman.

I graduated with a degree in Psychology, only to find I wasn't employable. Nobody hires a person just because he earns a BA degree in Psychology. My first job -- and I was glad to get it -- was washing dishes at Allen's Drive-In.

Blues' Bearded Baseballer

Washburn first baseman Jim Payne displays a beatnik-type beard as he awaits the season's opener with Kansas Wednesday at Lawrence.

I got a small baseball scholarship and was featured
in the local paper several times.

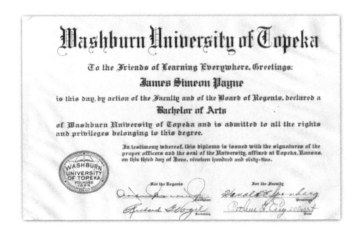

No one would hire a person with a B.A. degree in Psychology.

–Chapter 7–

Red Scooter

1962

Hired, dish washer, Allen's Drive In

(I learn how to manage)

My job search after graduation quickly taught me no one needed an educated person with a degree in psychology. My first job as a university graduate was washing dishes at Allen's Drive-In.

The 60's were a car culture. People, young and old, enjoyed going to a drive-in restaurant, ordering food from a teletray unit and waiting for a car hop "usually on roller skates" to deliver their food to the car. Allen's Drive-In was the biggest in Topeka supporting 60 teletray units. The main building was the size of a Shoney's or a Denny's. A canopy jutted out both sides of the building with teletray units lined side by side much like at a Sonic. Allen's had an additional canopy lined across the back of the lot serving 20 cars. The back canopy units were popular with teenagers. They would back their cars into the stalls, order a Coke and fries, then sit and watch other cars circle the building.

Inside the building a row of booths filled one wall while the grill, garnish and fountain, referred to as the "Line," filled the other. A wall separated the Line from the dishwasher in the kitchen but there was no door just an opening to the kitchen. A counter with stools divided the Line from the booths. Customers choosing to dine in could and would watch all the commotion involved in taking, preparing and serving the food. Many people came for the fun and excitement of it, leaving half their food uneaten. It doesn't make any sense now, it didn't make any sense then either.

Truthfully, I was thankful to get the job. I was still living with my parents and two brothers. My dad had been laid off for some time and was developing a drinking problem. My brothers were too young to work legally and my mother had been a housewife all her life. She did manage to snag a part time job as sales clerk at a small dress shop in downtown Topeka.

The dishwashing job was perfect for me. Not only was Allen's Drive-In just three blocks from our house, it was, by far, the best, fast food establishment in the city. It was famous. Although the job only paid 52 cents per hour, I could work 50 to 60 hours a week. The result was my mom and I made more than enough money to squeeze by.

I was in charge of the kitchen. A 30' by 30' cubical. A row of three sinks lined the east wall. A state-of-the-art, L-shaped, stainless steel Hobart dishwasher stood against the west wall.

This dishwasher was an engineering marvel. Dirty dishes were loaded on a 3' by 3' square tray; the big stuff was sprayed off with a nozzle attached to a hose that hung from the ceiling. Once sprayed, the operator pulled up the left door, pushed the tray in the machine, then closed the door and pushed the "On" button. And the machine did its magic. Once the machine cleaned and sanitized the dishes, the right door opened and out came a piping hot tray. The dishes dried themselves.

The summer after my junior year in high school I had washed dishes at the B and B Restaurant in Olathe, Kansas. The midnight shift from midnight to 8:00 a.m. My job was to bus tables, wash dishes, and peel potatoes. I hated peeling potatoes but washing the dishes was no picnic either. There were three big tubs: the first got the gunk off, the second scrub everything down with soap and water, and the third rinsed everything off in a dunk tank. I hated that dishwashing job, but I loved the dishwashing job at Allen's Drive In. Simply put, the job at Allen's was easy -- the Hobart did everything automatically. And I didn't have to peel any potatoes.

The dishwashing at Allen's was so easy and so fast that I had time to scrub and clean every square inch of the kitchen. By the second day my kitchen and everything in it was hospital clean. My second week the state health inspector came in and gave me the highest rating possible. It was rumored I was talked about at the state health department's office as if I were a wizard. And I'd only been working two weeks.

Think of it: no lectures, no projects, no tests and nothing to read.

Not only was the kitchen clean, the equipment was clean. So were the floors and dishes. I was fast as lightning. I kept up with every rush hour. I was so good I was promoted to the Fountain my fourth week. At least I wanted to believe that. The truth is the Fountain guy quit. I moved to Fountain and a new Dishwasher was hired. Although he was a nice guy, he was uneducated.

He hadn't even finished high school.

The Fountain was adjacent to the L shaped stainless steel Hobart dishwasher but separated from it by the kitchen wall. During my high school years, afterschool, I had worked as a fountain jerk at the Sunflower Drugstore. If you have seen one fountain you have seen them all. I already knew how to make shakes, sodas and sundaes and to draw soft drinks. The position was a letdown: I was over qualified.

I was good and I was fast. They couldn't cover me up no matter how busy we were. I wore the customary company-issued black pants, white shirt and paper hat, but as a fountain jerk I was issued a black, clip-on bow tie. That tie made me show off. Kids would come and sit at my counter and watch me perform. Most of the time at least one of the 10 counter stools was filled. When I made shakes, there was always a little left over in the bottom of the container, so I'd give it to one of the kids sitting there. If there was a lull in business, I'd make an extra shake and give each kid a little sample. I was so good, I had kids waiting in line to occupy a stool.

My success was short lived. By the end of the second week I was moved to Garnish. Like fruit basket turnover. I moved to Garnish, the uneducated dishwasher moved to Fountain and they hired a new dishwasher.

I moved from Garnish to Assembly, from Assembly to Fry Cook, from Fry Cook to Grill Man, from Grill Man to Day Manager, from Day Manager to Night Manager and from Night Manager to the real manager sometimes referred to as the Head Honcho. This all happened within nine months.

As the Head Honcho, one of my responsibilities was to hire and train the staff. I liked this assignment more than all of my duties. Not long afterwards, I was approached by a Placement Counselor from the Division of Vocational Rehabilitation with a request to hire a client who had spent his entire life in an institution. It was during the Kennedy Administration and the President had launched a national initiative to hire the mentally retarded, now referred to as intellectually handicapped. I had no clue what I was getting into but I agreed. The first Rehab client I hired was 50 years old; Allen had never worked a day in his life and had an IQ of 52. I had no idea what a 52 IQ meant and I didn't care. I wanted a dishwasher who would show up every day on time.

The first problem was, Allen came to work on a bicycle and would not leave it outside. He wanted to keep his eye on it. I was tolerant. I allowed him to chain his bicycle to my revered L shaped stainless steel Hobart dishwasher. I personally trained him how to run the Hobart. He could handle it except during a rush. When he got covered up I'd run back to help him out. After

58

a couple of months he didn't need me.

I decided to hire another client from Rehab. His name was Kyle, in his 50's and wasn't as sharp as Allen. Now we had two bicycles chained to my Hobart. In the beginning I assigned Allen to teach Kyle. Later, when there was a need, I'd move Allen up to the Fountain. This didn't work. The problem wasn't with Allen; Allen was a good teacher. The problem was that, Kyle just couldn't get it. He would forget to spray the dishes. He would forget to push the "On" button. When I began to work with Kyle, I realized, the problem: Kyle was retarded; very retarded. Allen and I both worked with Kyle, but he wasn't any better the third week than he was the first week. As we started the fourth week, Allen came to me and suggested Kyle only spray everything, push the tray in the machine, and punch the "On" button. Allen would do everything else.

Allen may have had a 52 IQ but he was one smart cookie. By the second day, under Allen's tutorship, Kyle could spray the dishes, shove the tray into the machine, push the "On" button, even during rushes. Without my saying anything, Allen also had Kyle pulling the cleaned and sanitized dishes out of the machine. Next, he had Kyle sorting china from glass, and by the sixth week he had Kyle running the Hobart all by himself.

I moved Allen to Fountain and began using his training techniques. In the beginning, I only had Allen draw soft drinks. Once he mastered drawing soft drinks, I taught him how to make shakes. After making a shake I'd let him go to the kitchen and drink what was left in the bottom of the can. The second a person ordered a shake. Allen could make it Olympian fast. Sodas and sundaes were added one at a time. Before we knew it, Allen was a certified, manager approved fountain jerk.

Not leaving well enough alone, I hired a third client from Voc Rehab: Sam. Now, we had three bicycles in the kitchen. Kyle trained Sam using Allen's training techniques and within two weeks Allen was training Kyle on the Fountain.

After Kyle mastered the Fountain I placed Allen at the Garnish table, but it was disastrous. Our routine was to place every sandwich on a bun board with garnish specifics written on a ticket placed under the sandwich. The garnish person took the ticket, read the specifications and garnished the sandwich accordingly. Allen couldn't read. Allen couldn't even recognize letters.

Garnish ingredients were identified on the ticket as letters: O for onion, P for pickle, T for tomato. Allen and I worked side by side but he just couldn't get it. I called his counselor and we sat down to discuss the situation. The counselor didn't know what to do, and told me I was the only employer that hadn't returned a client. In fact, I was the only employer who had hired more than one client.

I decided I'd teach Allen letter identification using flash cards. I bought some three inch by five inch index cards at an office supply store. On each card I put a letter in upper case on one side and on the reverse side I taped a picture of what the letter represented. During slow times I'd sit down with Allen at the back table and drill him. He got frustrated, fidgety, anxious and occasionally he got mad -- so upset he'd leave the table and go in the kitchen to sulk.

I needed something that would get him, to focus, to try harder. I decided to use a shake as an incentive. After getting 10 cards correctly identified I'd give him a shake. I tried that, but before he got the 10th card correct, he would be in the kitchen sulking. The next session, before presenting a card, I made a chocolate shake, put a straw in it, and let him take a little sip every time he got a letter correct. I presented three cards. He took a sip of shake after every correct response. Then he reached over and pulled the stack of cards from me. He would take a card, name the letter represented, turn the card over to see if he was correct, and then sip the chocolate shake. When he misidentified an item, he would place the card to the side. I sat there watching. Soon he moved the shake right under his chin, put the straw in his mouth, and as he went through the cards he took a sip when he got it right. Then he would move the card to the side when he got it wrong, without taking a sip. Right or wrong, the straw never left his lips. He did this for fifteen minutes, and never got mad or fidgety. When we started to get busy and had to go back to work, he put the cards in his pocket.

I got busy and he took the cards home with him. The next day, I made a shake and we sat at the back table as before. This time he went through the entire stack without making an error.

He wasn't fast, sometimes he would look at a card for five, maybe ten seconds before he named it, but he was always right and always took his reward. Within a day or two he could correctly identify each card as fast as I could.

The card game transferred to the garnish table, except he was slow. He was always correct when garnishing each sandwich but he was way too slow.

I remembered that after his shift he would come to the register and buy five, two cent mints to take home. I liked those after dinner mints myself and would consume one now and then on the job while no one was looking. I couldn't let him eat the mints at the garnish table but I came up with the idea of placing a cup next to the table as a receptacle for pennies. When he garnished a sandwich correctly in a reasonable amount of time, I'd drop a penny in the cup and say "Allen, I like how fast you garnish."

I placed myself at the assembly position next to the garnish table. The assembly person's job was to take the garnished sandwiches, put them on a tray along with the specified drinks, and either shove the tray out the window for a car hop to deliver or sit the tray on the corner of the counter for a waitress to deliver. I wore a smock and filled one of the pockets with pennies. As I worked the assembly, I could easily supervise Allen. Every time he completed a sandwich in a reasonable amount of time I'd drop a penny in the cup and say something like, "Allen, I like the way you garnish so fast." When things slowed down, Allen would empty the cup of pennies in his hand and buy some mints. Mints turned to candy bars, then bags of jellybeans, and ultimately to cigarettes. He would earn enough pennies to buy anything he wanted. One time he chose a cigar. He went outside around the corner of the building and lit up the stogie, much to the delight of the carhops. The carhops loved Allen and Allen loved the carhops. He could and did garnish sandwiches as fast as anyone.

Because of Allen, Kyle and Sam, I learned and mastered the techniques of breaking a task down into simple, easy to understand parts, and the value of reinforcing a task well done with shakes and pennies. Armed with an arsenal of sound teaching techniques, I called the placement counselor and asked for three more workers. Before making the call, I installed a bicycle rack outside the door leading into the kitchen. Within two weeks I had a fully functioning dishwasher, fountain jerk, and garnish person for the day shift and a dishwasher, fountain jerk, and garnish person for the night shift. Within a month I had a finely tuned machine of workers that never missed a day's work and were always on time. They loved their jobs and I loved them. Eventuallywe filled the assembly and fry cook slots with clients, too.

After about a year and a half Allen came to me and asked if I would help him buy a motor scooter. I explained that motor scooters cost money. He informed me he had money. No, I explained, motor scooters cost a lot of money. He asked how much. I told him, "two to three thousand dollars." He reached in his back pocket and showed me a First National Bank Savings book with over three thousand dollars in the account.

I immediately called his counselor, who came over to talk. I asked if he had told Allen he could buy a motor scooter. The counselor confessed he had, if he saved his money. Then he added, "How did I know he was going to stay on this job so long? How did I know he could possibly save that much money?"

I said, "I don't know, but he has the money and he wants a scooter. I can help him but he needs a driver's license and he can't read."

At that point the counselor got up and left, shaking his head.

I went to the Department of Motor Vehicles, picked up a driver's handbook, took it to work and had the day manager help me read it. I took notes, made flash cards and readied to tutor Allen.

Allen and another employee and I went to the cycle shop in the company station wagon. Allen bought a bright red scooter. I drove it back to the drive-in while they returned in the station wagon. I parked the scooter next to the bicycle rack. I made arrangements with the Recreation Department to use the ball field as a place to teach Allen how to drive his motor scooter. Since he could ride a bicycle, it didn't take him long to master the scooter. He zipped around that ball park so fast he was almost a blur. He could stop it on a dime. Actually, he could probably drive it better than I could. Every day after work, we would take him to the ball field and let him drive for 30 minutes.

To prepare him for the driver's test, we broke the handbook down into small learning chunks. The waitresses and carhops made flashcards with pictures of road signs on them: stop, slow, caution, yield. When Allen walked by a waitress or carhop, if they weren't too busy they would flash him a sign and he would have to react accordingly. He loved it and they loved it. On breaks everyone took turns quizzing him.

We all felt he was ready. I contacted the motor vehicle department and made arrangements for him to take the test orally. Before taking the test we drilled him and drilled him. He never got mad nor did he ever go sulk. The big day came. He took the test, passed it the first time, and that night we enjoyed the most jubilant celebration Allen's Drive-In had ever experienced.

He got his license and drove that motor scooter all over town. Everyone knew him and when they waved, he waved back. As exciting as it was and as much fun as it was, in the back of my head I wondered what would happen if he had an accident.

I get a call at the Drive-In. It's Allen. He is excited. He tells me he got hit but he wasn't hurt. He needed me to bring the station wagon to pick-up both him and the scooter. He tells me where he is. I run to the station wagon and drive frantically. Allen is skinned up a little but nothing serious. The scooter, however, is in bad shape. The policeman tells me a young driver ran a stop sign and hit Allen from the side. The driver went into shock. Allen called the police. When they came the driver was still incomprehensible. The policeman told me Allen explained everything to him, fully in charge of himself and the situation.

Everything settles down. I back the station wagon over to the mangled scooter. I open up the rear gate. Allen gets on one side of the scooter and I on the other. Together, we prepare to lift the scooter into the station wagon. Allen turns to me with tears in his eyes and says, "Mr. Payne, be careful. Don't scratch it."

Allen, in glasses, eating a
Thanksgiving dinner at our
home with a coworker.

Allen's Drive In, a good place to work and a good place to learn from.

–Chapter 8–

Corporate

1963
Married, Ruth Ann Goodrun
1964
Reassigned, Trouble shooter, Allen's Drive-In
(I learn the restaurant business)

I pick up the phone. It's Mr. Jones, President and CEO of all the Allen's Drive-Ins: 35 drive-ins scattered throughout Kansas, Missouri, Oklahoma, Colorado. Even one in Hawaii. He commands, "Come to corporate tomorrow, 10 a.m."

The corporate headquarters including the business offices, bakery, meat processing plant and commissary that ships out all the supplies to the individual drive-ins, is located in Kansas City, Missouri, a little over an hour and a half from Topeka.

I arrive early. Mr. Jones is already waiting in the conference room, a plush room with a large walnut conference table surrounded by 18 cushy executive chairs. Mr. Jones is seated at its head and Mr. Llewellyn, part owner of the Kansas Drive-Ins and my immediate boss is seated to his left. They greet me and instruct me to be seated on Mr. Jones' right.

Mr. Jones explains that Mr. Llewellyn has told him about what good things I had done in Topeka. He asks about my hiring practices and training program. I explained my relationship with Vocational Rehabilitation and what I have learned about training. Mr. Llewellyn chimes in with how the Topeka site has regained its market share and profitability under my direction. Mr. Llewellyn likes me and I like him. I want to emulate him in every way. He was handsome, well built, well groomed – shoes always shined, his pants always creased, his shirts fitting like a glove and all of them white, oxford cloth, heavily starched, and short sleeved. Snazzy.

The two men explain my transfer to Fairway, one of their first acquisitions, located in one of the suburbs of Kansas City, Kansas. My assignment is simple: manage Fairway, hire and train the staff, regain market share and profitability. Then I would move to another Drive-In to do the same. I would become the trouble-shooter for the organization, so to speak.

Allen's Drive-In at Fairway is situated in an upscale neighborhood. The drive-in was run down and dirty. Surprisingly, the staff were bright, reasonably educated, but poorly trained. They lacked motivation. I contacted my younger brother Dan to come help me. He commits to work with me for three months, and within two weeks we had the Fairway Drive-In as clean as the Topeka Drive-in. My brother and I retrained the staff. No new hires so that saved time. We established some basic rules. We initiated a fundamental system for food preparation and a procedure to turn our products out quickly and efficiently. We began by retraining the dishwashers,then the fountain jerks, then the garnish servers and so forth. Everyone learned to do his job correctly. Once the system was established, a team emerged and we became competitive by the endof the sixth week.

By that time we were as good as the Topeka operation, except our ice machine kept breaking down. When our ice machine broke down, we had to buy bagged ice from an outdoor ice machine located a block away. Ice was fifty cents a bag. In times of need, I'd take quarters out of the register, drive the station wagon to the outdoor ice machine, load the back of the station wagon with eight to ten bags, return to the drive-in and empty the bags of ice into our malfunctioning machine.

We were in the middle of a noon rush when the dishwasher reported we were running out of ice. Instinctively I opened the register, snatched a roll of quarters, gave the quarters to the dishwasher along with the keys to the station wagon and told him to get ice, quick. Before I knew it, the dishwasher was back -- the outdoor ice machine was out of ice. It would take our money, the conveyer belt would roll, but no ice would come out. I knew some incompetent fool had forgotten to load the bags on the conveyor belt. The dishwasher and I ran out the back door and drove to the machine. The dispenser that took the coins was located about five feet above the two' by two' square opening that delivered the bags of ice. The mechanism was far from being anengineering marvel.

During my teenage years and early twenties I had worked part time as a magician. I entertained at parties and other events. In those days, the theaters would show double features on Saturdays, and between the movies there would be live entertainment. Typical entertainment mightinclude a juggling act, yo yo contest, clown skit, or magic show. As a member of the Society of American Magicians, known to us professional performers as SAM, I possessed a repertoire of tricks. I was better than any juggler or clown and almost as amusing as a yo yo contest. I became captivated by the works of Houdini. I subsequently billed myself as the Great Paynedini. I learned how to escape from a straight jacket, get out of handcuffs, and pick a jail cell lock.

That square ice hole was no match for the Great Paynedini. I dropped down on my knees, shot my right arm through the opening, relaxed into a subconscious state and slithered into the machine easier than sliding out of a straight jacket. Inside the machine, I grabbed a bag of ice and pushed it through the hole for the dishwasher to load into the back of the station wagon. We only needed six bags but I was so mad I shoved out fifteen bags. After unloading fifteen bags I exited the hole with the skill of a seasoned performer -- except my left foot got caught. When I pulled my leg out, my shoe stayed safely inside the machine. The dishwasher, my assistant, looked on wide-eyed, as if he had seen something significant. I stood before the machine, one shoe short, thinking what the hell was I going to do now.

All of a sudden, without my saying a thing, my assistant stepped forward, deposited two quarters in the machine. Like magic my shoe came rolling out.

On stage it would have merited a standing ovation. I put a sign on the coin dispenser "out of order." Then I wrote a nasty note telling the owner what I had done and to come to the drive-in to get his money. If he dared to do so. I put the note in an envelope and taped it to the machine.

He did dare to do so and he came in mad as the dickens. Equally mad, I gave him his money. In quarters. I told him if he ever forgot to load that machine again I'd jam him through that hole.

He left spitting fire but we never found his machine unloaded again.

After five months I was moved to Stateline, located in Kansas City. The location was run down, the drive-in was run down and the employees were, let's say rough around the edges. They liked to hunt, fish, and drink. They drove beat up trucks. I don't think any of them owned a pair of socks or a comb.

My brother had returned to Topeka two months before and had picked up a full time job there so he couldn't help me. I subcontracted with a local custodial company and within three weeks we had that drive-in almost as clean as the ones in Topeka and Fairway. The employees had been there forever and they were not only dirty, they were poorly trained. For some reason every employee wanted to wear his own dirty clothes rather than the clean uniform supplied by the company.

I called a meeting. Every employee was required to attend and would be paid to attend. I held the meeting at the close of the midnight shift. The employees filled the place. We served coffee and donuts. The purpose of the meeting was to underscore the importance of wearing a clean uniform, every day, supplied by the company. I displayed a uniform. I explained it was free. Put on a clean uniform in the morning and discard it at the end of your shift.

I talked about customer's perceptions. I tried not to talk over their heads. They must have got tired of hearing me go on and on, because all of a sudden one of the older employees cut me off in the middle of a very important sentence and asked "Do you want us to wear a clean uniform every day?"

"Yes," I said.

He said, "Then, just tell us."

"O.K. everyone is to wear a clean uniform every day."

They nodded, looked around and before I heard a motion to dismiss, they were in their trucks and on their way.

The next morning everyone put on his clean uniform and deposited it at the end of his shift. From that day forward, uniforms were not an issue.

I now had another training technique to add to my arsenal of managerial tools. One, break the task down; two, reinforce performance, both in accuracy and speed; and now, three, tell 'em what to do. I had learned a lot as a psychology major; now, I could write a book.

By the end of the second month both the day crew and the night crew were functioning like a finely oiled machine. At Stateline, the sandwiches were always garnished correctly. Sometimes a part of a pickle would droop over the side of the sandwich and sometimes the shakes were served with a little bit of shake on the outside of the glass, but, boy, those workers were fast. Faster than either Topeka or Fairway.

I became fascinated with how much they enjoyed their work. Their language was basic, at time gutterized. They liked me and I liked them. They took me to my first wrestling match and introduced me to tractor pulls and mud races. I shopped with them at Goodwill and the

Salvation Army. I was exposed to a side of life that began to be fun, exciting, and even dangerous.

One night, passing by the drive-in at two in the morning, I noticed that someone had forgotten to turn the lights off in the dining room. I stopped, opened the kitchen door, and there before my innocent eyes, was the day manager screwing one of the car hops on top of the Hobart dishwasher. Naked as jaybirds, up on the Hobart.

They shocked me but I petrified them. The car hop jumped off the stainless steel table and ran into the dining room to secure her clothes. The day manager stood in front of me trembling, and mumbled, "What was I to do? She was going to quit."

I wasn't paying attention. I just stared at the virgin violated Hobart. The two put on their clothes and reported back to me.

I don't know why, said, "The next time you have sex, do not, do not do it on the Hobart."

I never went into an Allen's Drive-In at two in the morning again.

After five months I was off to Lawrence, Kansas home of the University of Kansas and the Kansas Jayhawks. Allen's Drive-In was situated at the bottom of the hill on Naismith Drive and University Avenue. Being a university town most of the employees were part time students working to make enough money to get by. This drive-in was clean. University students knew how to clean and they would and did. But they didn't care about the customer; they just went through the motions. I never had to fire anyone because the students would come and go with little or no notice. I contacted Voc. Rehab and told them to send me two clients. Within four weeks two more came. Within six weeks, two more. Within three months I had a day and night crew I'd put up against anybody. They were accurate, clean, fast and reliable. My training techniques had been honed: tell them exactly what to do, break each task down to understandable parts, reinforce accuracy and speed. With the clients I used pennies; with others I used praise and recognition.

The only difference between Topeka and Lawrence was that instead of depositing the pennies in a dispenser, I'd snap the pennies between my thumb and forefinger with enough force to make a clinging sound on the stainless steel counters.

I got that idea visiting casinos. I heard slot machines. The noise coins make when they drop into the metal tray stimulates the brain in such a way that the player wants to continue playing. I learned so much from Allen's Drive-In, I thought about writing a textbook, a psychology textbook. I was getting smart.

Allen's Drive-In at Lawrence was up and running at full speed within six months, but Mr. Llewelyn wanted me to remain. It had to do with image. He wanted me to get involved in the community, do civic things. This was all foreign to me. I had been a restaurant manager not a community servant.

The restaurant could pretty much run on its own. The day manager and night manager adopted my techniques. They could dispense praise and pennies. I was free to involve myself in community activities.

I decided I wanted to know more about mental retardation. I searched the university catalog, found a course with the word "retarded" in it and enrolled as a graduate non-degree-seeking student.

The course was entitled "Teaching Parents How to Teach the Retarded." It was taught by Dr. Norris Haring. I didn't know it at the time but Dr. Haring was nationally recognized in special education. The first day of class he asked each student to stand up, tell who he was, what he was doing and why he was taking the course. I was sitting in the back of the room, the last person to stand up. All of the students stood, gave their name and said the same thing: they were teaching at such and such school and needed certification.

My turn came. I stood up. "I'm Jim Payne. I manage Allen's Drive-In. I'm here to learn what mental retardation is."

Dr. Haring looked up from whatever he was concentrating on. "What was that?"

I repeated, "I'm Jim Payne, I manage Allen's Drive-In and I'm here to learn what mental retardation is."

At this point, all eyes were on me. Dr. Haring broke the temporary silence. "Mr. Payne, would you stay after class. I'd like to talk with you."

At the end of class, after everyone had exited, I went to the front of the room. I think Dr. Haring thought I was in the wrong class. He was used to teaching teachers and counselors. He'd never had a manager of a restaurant in his class before. But I attended each class and every time Dr. Haring would ask me to stay after class. At first I explained what Allen's Drive-In was. He had never been there. Later I brought him a menu. I talked with him about my Rehab clients and how many I had worked with and what I had learned from teaching them.

Halfway through the course, I invited him to visit the restaurant. He surprised me by saying, "I thought you would never ask."

The very next day he came in at midmorning. I took him on a tour, introduced him to each employee, offered him some coffee, and for a brief moment we chatted at a back table. I excused myself at eleven and told him, we were going to get busy.

The Lawrence operation had the reputation of having one of the biggest lunch hours in the business. Everything was stocked up; everyone was in his position. Customers filed into the dining room and the teletray unit lit up. That noon hour, as usual, the crew went through their routines. They worked at break neck speed with the gracefulness of gymnasts.

All of the Rehab clients had IQ's below 50. I didn't know it, but the Academics believed that to be very low. Persons with IQ's below 50 were supposed to be extremely limited. I admit the clients looked a little different but their work was stellar. During the hurry scurry rush, I dispensed a few pennies here and there. Immediately they were scooped up and placed into the pocket of the deserving recipient.

In the middle of this organized chaos, I noticed Dr. Haring had moved from the back table and was sitting at the end stool next to the kitchen wall. When things calmed down I joined Dr. Haring at the counter. He was so complimentary it was embarrassing. We talked and talked and he stayed to watch the dinner rush. Afterwards, he insisted I spend some time with him. He wanted to take me to the Children's Rehabilitation Unit at

The Kansas Medical Center in Kansas City and Parsons State Hospital Training School in Parsons, Kansas.

At the children's unit in Kansas City I met and observed Dr. Frederic Girardeau conduct research sessions using tokens to reinforce subjects having the condition of mental retardation. At Parsons, I met and observed Dr. Jim Lent using tokens to teach adolescent patients with the

72

condition of mental retardation to sort and assemble things.

Back in Lawrence, Dr. Haring complimented me by saying I was way ahead of my time. He wanted me to leave the restaurant business and come to work with him as a placement counselor on a federal grant he was being awarded. First, I would need to work in Topeka as a placement counselor for Vocational Rehabilitation for six months. After six months, his grant would be in place and he would hire me to work as a rehabilitation counselor in Kansas City, with the understanding I would became a part time Master's candidate in special education at The University of Kansas. He agreed to set up everything, the six-month job in Topeka, the placement job on his grant, and assuring my acceptance in the Master's program.

I got so excited. I forgot I couldn't read.

My brother Dan seated at the counter of
Allen's Drive-In. We were a great team.

The largest selling text in Special Education.
I didn't know Dr. Haring was famous.

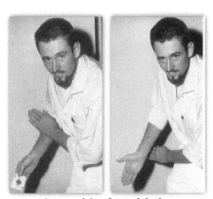

As a magician, I wasn't bad.

As a hypnotist, I was dazzling.

Dr. Lent was researching the use of
tokens at Parsons State Hospital.

–Chapter 9–

Voc Rehab

———

1965

*Hired, Counselor, Vocational Rehabilitation
Unit, Kansas Neurological Institute
(I learn how to read at a newspaper level)*

I got the vocational rehabilitation job in Topeka. I was a placement counselor assigned to the Vocational Rehabilitation Unit at the Kansas Neurological Institute, known as KNI. It was the first professional job I ever held. I was required to wear a suit and tie. I bought three suits, six white shirts and 10 ties. I loved wearing a tie and when I went to the cleaners I required all my shirts to be heavy starch. I actually thought I looked better than my old boss, Mr. Llewellyn.

My job was to place clients diagnosed with the condition of mental retardation on jobs, and to follow them until their case had been closed as "rehabilitated." At the Allen's Drive-in job I was on the receiving end and at KNI I was on the placement end.

During the first week I reviewed the client files, learned the rules and regulations, and got acclimated to the facilities. My first Saturday I experienced a wakeup call. I arrived at the Unit to find the parking lot vacant. The door was locked. I looked through a couple of windows: no one was there. It took me a while to realize I didn't work on Saturdays or even Sundays. I couldn't believe they were going to pay me not to work on weekends.

Jim Young, my assigned mentor, had worked as a counselor for over 20 years. Elderly, silver haired, distinguished, kind, he loved his job. The second week I was to follow him and observe. They called it "shadowing."

We took the company car and headed to a small town in Kansas to follow up on a client named Clifford. As we drove, Mr. Young explained Clifford's background. He was 53, with an IQ of 46. He had been admitted to Kansas Neurological Institute at the age of two; he had spent his life in an institution. This was his first job. For almost a year, he had worked in the laundry at a small cleaners. He was capable of loading the clothes in the big washing machine, running the extractor, folding flat stuff like sheets, pillow cases, socks, and he was beginning to master tee shirts.

Jim explained Clifford was not having trouble on the job or in the community. The town of less than six thousand had adopted him. He had a place to stay where the landlord looked after him. A church had taken him in and made arrangements to pick him up each Sunday. He was doing fine on the job. The problem was he was over-eating. He loved food. Jim explained if he continued to over-eat he was in danger of killing himself. Our primary job was to get Clifford to teach himself to regulate his food intake, to eat in moderation.

We entered the town and just as we turned the corner, Jim said, "There he is."

It was about 10 a.m. Clifford worked nights and he was heading home. At first, Clifford was just sauntering along but when he saw the Kansas state car his pace increased, not to a run or gallop but just a quick walk. We pulled up next to Clifford, and he stopped.

Jim had emphasized that the main issue was over-eating, but added "Clifford will not lie. I can tell you he won't lie. He doesn't know how to lie but he is clever. You have to watch him."

As we approached him, Clifford looked at us, like a deer in the headlights. Jim introduced me, and before I knew it Jim and Clifford were in a conversation I'll never forget.

Jim began "Clifford, what did you have for breakfast this morning?"

Clifford responded slowly, "Mr. Young, I h-ad j-u-s-t some e-g-g-s, t-o-a-s-t and b-a-c-o-n."

Young, "How many eggs?"

Clifford, "T-h-r-e-e."

Young, "How many pieces of toast?"

Clifford, "F-o-u-r."

Young, "How many pieces of bacon did you have?

Clifford, "E-i-g-h-t."

Young, "What did you have to drink?"

Clifford, this time quicker, almost at a normal speed, "One glass of milk is all I had. I promise only one glass."

Young, "How many times did you fill that one glass up?"

Clifford in a long draw, "F-o-u-r, w-i-t-h a l-i-t-t-l-e b-i-t of chok-o-lit. A l-i-tt-l-e t-e-eny b-i-t."

Jim shook his head, went to the trunk of the car, and whipped out a bathroom scale.

Clifford reluctantly stood on the scale. He had gained three pounds since last week. Jim went through a tirade. Clifford just stood there and took the verbal beating. From time to time, Jim took a handkerchief from his back pocket to wipe the drool from Clifford's mouth. Clifford had a terrible drooling problem and his nose dripped. But as I watched Mr. Young counsel Clifford on this day while wiping Clifford's face, I understood what was going on between Young and Clifford: it was not professional; it was paternal, fatherly. Young loved Clifford and Clifford, aslimited as he was, loved Young.

We got in the car and drove away as Clifford continued to walk home. Jim talked to me while looking straight ahead, "If I don't do something, he is going to kill himself. He will eat himself to death."

All I could think about was that Clifford was one clever dude. He might have been smarter than we were.

After visiting each of my clients I noticed that all of them were over 50 years of age and all of them looked the same, just like Mr. Young's clients. They were all pear shaped and over-weight. Jim explained to me years ago people thought mental retardation was inherited, so every male patient that entered an institution in the state of Kansas was automatically castrated. When a human male is castrated he puts on weight around the hips, just as a castrated hog does. With humans, as weight is put on around the hips, a problem with varicose veins occurs. As a rehabilitation counselor, I needed to be aware of the problem and treat it before the condition became severe.

During the six months I worked for Voc Rehab, something happened that changed my life forever. As a placement counselor, after visiting a client I had to document the clients' progress. I was issued a hand-held, portable dictaphone. While driving back to the Unit I would dictate my observations. The format went something like:

On this date the client was observed at such and such. The client continues to perform the duties of such and such. The client is satisfactorily blankety blank. Presently the area targeted for improvement is blankety blank. Etc, etc. etc.

When I returned, I would give the dictated tape to a secretary. By afternoon the tape had been transcribed, and the narrative was returned to me to proof, correct and place in the client's folder. It is difficult for me to explain what came over me. I would talk into a machine, which I enjoyed. Then, somehow, my talk would return to me in print form.

I loved to read what I had said.

The third week, I was called into the director's office to learn that the secretaries had concerns about the length of my reports. The other counselors' reports were two to three paragraphs in length; mine were eight to ten pages. The director read my reports and concluded they were accurate and appropriate. He told me to continue what I was doing - much to the chagrin

of the secretaries.

A miracle happened. By the sixth month my reading level had jumped from third grade to sixth grade level. Just exactly what did that mean? It meant that for the first time in my life I couldread a newspaper. Not fast but I could read it. Once an individual passes fourth grade reading levelhe has cracked the code. From then on, it is all vocabulary and context.

For the first time in my life I could compete academically. If I tried hard.

At the end of my sixth month as a rehabilitation counselor, I left KNI to become the first placement counselor for Dr. Haring's federal grant, The Kansas Vocational Rehabilitation and Special Education Cooperative Project. I was automatically admitted to The University of KansasMaster's Program in Special Education.

At this point in my life, I believed I not only looked better than Mr. Llewellyn, I was smarter.

–Chapter 10–

Dr. Haring's Grant

———

1965

Hired, Counselor, Kansas Vocational Rehabilitation

and

Special Education Cooperative Project
(I learn relationships are very important)

I move from Topeka to Kansas City. I am the placement counselor and my time is split between the Shawnee Mission School District and the Kansas City Kansas School District. I am assigned a fulltime personal secretary.

The grant was high profile. It was the first educational grant to combine the services of two major departments, Special Education and Vocational Rehabilitation. The official title of Dr. Haring's grant was "The Kansas Vocational Rehabilitation and Special Education Cooperative Program." The project required me to present at State and National Conferences. I loved talking about what I did, was doing and what I planned to do. No reading required, just talking about what I knew. I couldn't believe someone could get paid to talk.

As a part of my position I am required to provide narratives each day related to my work with students, much like I did for my rehab clients. The major difference is, rather than the narrative being dictated and later transcribed via a machine, Rhonda takes my dictation face to face using shorthand. Rhonda writes faster than I can talk. Believe me, talking with someone face to face is a lot different from talking to a machine. This was a marriage made in heaven. I wrote, well actually Rhonda wrote, volumes. I dictated letters, narratives, grants, proposals, I even drafted a book, which years later was published. As a requirement for the job, I had to continue as a graduate student at KU. Graduate students read a lot, but they also write a lot. With ole Miss Southworth's knowledge and Rhonda's skills I was academically competitive, and if a presentation were required, using Mr. McCausland's techniques I was exceptional. It is sometimes hard to believe I was consistently in the A-B range with only an occasional C.

The grant was a research and demonstration project designed to help special education students, diagnosed as having the condition of mild mental retardation, get jobs upon high school graduation. This was my first exposure of working with individuals having reported IQs between 55 to 70. At Allen's and The Topeka Voc. Rehab the individuals I worked with had reported IQs below 55.

As juniors the Special Ed. students would work in the school an hour, two to three times a week. Typical work settings were cafeteria, custodial, and physical plant. In the classroom the students were involved in remedial math, reading, science, etc. As seniors they were placed on parttime paying jobs outside the school. Job placements included restaurants, laundries, small manufacturing, custodial and car wash. As seniors, to graduate, the students were required to have two successful job placements. The classroom curriculum included life skill training -- like cooking, washing clothes, ironing, operating a vacuum cleaner, etc.

Money management was also included. The students were taught how to complete an application and the basics of interviewing. The program was commonly referred to as work-study: students were in school half of the time and working or in work training half of the time.

To motivate students and keep them interested, we initiated one of the first, full blown, token economy systems in a public school. Students earned tokens for correct responses, speed, and appropriate behavior. They could exchange the tokens for items thatmight be found in a 7-11 or Quick Mart. Items like candy, fruit, tobacco, comics, magazines, billfolds, purses, hats, scarves, sport equipment like balls, bats, gloves. The most expensive item was a bicycle.

The token system was identical to what I had devised for Allen, except with Allen, pennies were used. In the work-study program tokens were used and exchanged for far more elaborate rewards.

The research part of the grant was to determine the most effective ways to use tokens. Offering tokens for academic achievement proved to be the simplest and easiest to understand. Tokens earned for accuracy and speed within a 10 to 15 minute time period resulted in greater gains and maximized attention, focus and effort. The success of the token system made me proud. At the beginning of the program, none of the students could read at the fourth grade level. Using tokens, along with a well-designed reading program administered by master reading specialists, all of the students upon graduation were reading at the fourth grade level or higher. Fourth grade reading level is considered to be literate. All of the students graduated literate, could count money, and work competitively in the community.

But the research involving the effect of tokens on behavior was much more complex. To start off, the students had not liked school. They were fidgety, hyper, and anxious. They liked to fight, cuss, and talk back. They had trouble paying attention, behaving themselves and just acting civil.

Using tokens to reinforce good behavior did not work. We quickly learned that behaviors had to be broken down into understandable and observable parts. For instance, when standing in line a token could be earned for keeping one's hands to oneself. In the beginning of the study, as the students lined up for some type of activity, either the teacher or I would hand a token to a student while saying, "Henry, I like the way you are keeping your hands to yourself."

Keep in mind, the students wanted the tokens because they could be exchanged for items they could not get at home or in the community.

Students who wouldn't stay seated were issued tokens for "bottoms down" behavior. We never required them to sit for more than 25 minutes at a time, but issuing tokens for sitting three to five minutes worked, as long as the student knew exactly what he or she was getting the tokens for. Within a reasonable period of time the composure time could be eight to ten minutes. Another secret was never to have them sit without something to do or without something to interest them. In other words we integrated "bottoms down" behavior with interesting academic tasks. We avoided trying to pump up a dull curriculum with token reinforcement.

In the beginning, the store was placed in the back of the room, and students could exchange tokens any time they wanted. Later, most of the students would save their tokens and exchange them for a more expensive item.

A couple of the students just couldn't delay their gratification, even though they would tell us they were saving for a more expensive item. The tokens "burned a whole in

84

their pocket," so to speak. One student wanted a billfold but the student would have to work hard, behave himself for at least ten days and save.

The student could not do that. So we took a Polaroid picture of the billfold and cut it. into six parts. Every other day, the student would come to the store, buy one piece of candy and receive one piece of the Polaroid picture, which had to be paid for. The twelfth day he could buy the last piece of the picture and be issued the billfold in exchange for the six pieces of the picture. He was some happy kid. He would show that billfold to everyone.

During the second year he wanted a bicycle. It would take him approximately four months to earn enough tokens to buy a bicycle. We took the bicycle apart. Each week he would buy one part of the bicycle. He had his own storage place in the back of the room and within four months he not only owned all the parts but he had learned, with the help of the class, how to put the bike together. He was one happy fellow riding that bike.

The classroom was a regular high school classroom, but since we only had eight students we had the luxury to have plenty of room for activities. The back half of the room served as the store and a small gym, each taking up a fourth of the floor space. On the store side, shelves lined two walls from floor to ceiling. An old glass display case was positioned there. Inside the case were candy and cigarettes. The lower shelves were stocked with cheap items like magazines, marking pens, and comics, while the higher shelves held more expensive items like ball gloves, hand tools and clothing. A space next to the display case was reserved for bulky items like a bicycle, camping equipment and a beach chair. An old beat-up teacher's desk was placed in the store vicinity. Two cigar boxes on top served as cash drawers.

The mini gym area contained an exercise bike, a small set of dumb bells and a four' by six' mat used for stretching exercises and pushups. The mini gym and store took up the back half of the entire classroom space.

In front of the mini gym were three cubicles lined side by side made out of refrigerator boxes. These cardboard boxes had one side cut out. Inside each box was a small folding table and chair outside the box facing inward. The cardboard cubicles were used as individual study areas or offices for fun reading and personal writing.

A teacher's desk butting the front wall was primarily used for stacking stuff. On the wall above the teacher's desk was a traditional chalkboard and next to it a tall military-greenmetal, storage cabinet held supplies.

The rest of the room contained eight student desks with attached seats, used for formal instructional purposes.

The school, built in the late 30's, had never been renovated, but the kids grew to really like it. It became their second home. We had lots of space and no one bothered us.

Within a short period of time all the students were behaving and trying hard, but we also noticed social growth taking place. First, we saw the students save tokens and delay gratification. Next, we saw them buy birthday items for some family member, even grandmother or grandfather. Next, some bought birthday items for a nonfamily member, then gifts for family or friends without any special occasion. On a couple of occasions we saw two students pool their money to buy a board game. Another couple of students pooled their tokens to buy a basketball. Obviously, the token system also helped them learn how to make change with real money and how to understand banking.

My most unusual case was Mike, a tough kid but I really grew to like him. He behaved himself in class, but we were told he was a terror in the community. However, and was a hard worker.

All of our students went regularly to music class and gym. Mike would attend music class but he didn't like it. He behaved himself but didn't really participate. Gym class was way on the other side of the school building and he wouldn't ever get there on his own. We would have to drag him there. By the time he got dressed, the class was over.

I talked with the gym teacher. He told me Mike never participated like the other kids. The coach had had Mike's older brother but he had never come to class either. Even his dad had never come to gym class. The coach suggested it must be in the DNA.

86

The hallway from the special education classroom to the gym had six turns. So when the bell rang for gym I positioned myself just around the first corner. All the other kidswhizzed past me and eventually Mike rounded the corner. I jumped out at him, putting three tokens in his hand. I said, "It only took you four minutes to get here. Nice going."

I went back to my office, called the gym teacher, asked if Mike got there. Nope! The next day I waited around the first corner and this time he came to the first corner in less than aminute. I jumped out, gave him three tokens and reached in my packet for two more. "Wow I didn't know you could move so fast," I said.

I left, went to my office, called the gym teacher: no Mike.

The next day I positioned myself at the second corner. I don't know how fast he got tothe first corner but it took him five minutes to make it to the second corner. I held out three tokens in my right hand and took one of the tokens away and put it in my pocket. I gave him the two remaining tokens. "Five minutes, not bad but disappointing."

No Mike at the gym.

The next day at the second corner he beat all the other kids to that spot. He earned fivetokens and a pat on the back. Still, no Mike in gym.

Within a month I had sucked him down into the locker room using the token rewards,but I was exhausted. Now to get him dressed. The school furnished the socks and the shorts but not the tee shirt. Since Mike always wore tennis shoes it wasn't much of a trick for me toget him into the socks and shorts. The trick was the tee shirt. First of all, he didn't own a tee shirt. So we bought some tee shirts and put them in the store. The tee shirts didn't sell very well even when we put them on sale. Finally, we had a tee shirt give-a-way for anyone who spent more than 25 tokens on a single day. Mike loved to smoke and cigarettes were 25 tokens each. It was like taking candy from a baby -- he got his cigarette and a tee shirt and I got a chance to see him put it on.

Using tokens, I was able to get him to the locker room and suited up just like the others, but I couldn't figure out how to get him to make it on his own without tokens. I gave up. Not long afterwards, Mike got in a fight as he was coming into school. He had been doing so well for so long. I was beyond disappointed. In fact, I, was furious. His fight was with a girl; supposedly, she called him a name. Regardless of the reason, fighting was not permitted. The principal called me to his office to get Mike. The principal was disappointed but not surprised. He explained his disappointment in front of Mike. He told me to handle it.

I grabbed Mike by the arm and escorted him to the track that circled the football field. I told him we were going to run laps until he dropped. I don't know what made me do it. Well, the two of us started running side by side, as I continued to lash out at him verbally.

We continued to run and I continued to chew him out. I began to get tired. After the first lapI ran a little slower than a trot. Next I held to a fast walk, then a walk, then I stopped and dropped to my knees. Then I rolled over to my side in a fetal position.

Mike who never got more than five feet ahead of me, he stopped and looked back at me in my fetal position. Then he rushed to my side. He held my head in his hands and began to explain how sorry he was. Suddenly, he gently laid my head down and darted off. He ran and got the coach. The two of them came back, and with Mike on one side and the coach on the other, they took me to my office. Mike ran to bring me a cup of water from the fountain in the hall.

That very day I'm in my office, embarrassed by my collapse. The principal said the next time he told me to take care of it, let the kid run, not you. He thought that was very funny.

My phone rings. It is Coach. Get down to the gym, Mike is suited up and participating.

I ran down to the gym and there was Mike, leading the pack in calisthenics. As the class left to go to the locker room, I caught Mike and told him to come to my office after he dressed. He sheepishly entered my office. I motioned for him to follow me. I took him outside to the track. We walked the track to the far side of the field and down the hill adjacent to the end of the football field. Out of sight from the school I sat down and then Mike sat down. I reached in my pocket and took out a cigar. I clipped the end of my cigar, licked the end and lit up. Next I pulled out a second cigar, clipped it and gave it to Mike. Mike clumsily licked the end. He put it in his mouth and I lit it for him. The two of us sat at the bottom of the hill and savored every puff. We never said a word. We finished, discarded our cigar butts, and then he went to work. I returned to my office where Rhonda was waiting at the door with her steno pad in hand. She knew something major had just happened.

Mike continued to suit up for gym and vigorously participate until the day he graduated -- never to earn another token (or a cigar) for his behavior. What I learned that day, and I'll never forget it, relationships are more powerful than tokens.

Dr. Haring gave me the opportunity of a lifetime.

–Chapter 11–

Wyandotte County

—

1966

Born, 1st child, Kim

1966

*Transferred, Director, Wyandotte County
School and Sheltered Workshop*

(I learn I must be brilliant)

I was transferred from the Vocational Rehabilitation, Special Education Cooperative Project to become the Planning Director of the Wyandotte County School and Sheltered Workshop. I worked a one year federal grant to determine the number of special needs individuals with IQ's below 50 who resided in Wyandotte County Kansas, and to design a state-of-the-art facility to serve them.

As director, I was provided a personal secretary. The staff included two psychologists, a social worker, four special education teachers, an additional secretary and a maintenance person. We were housed in an old two story farm house on the property where the facility was to be built.

All of the equipment, furniture and supplies were brand new. The dining room served as a conference room. My office was in a large bedroom on the first floor and my secretary was stationed outside my office in the living room. All other staff members were positioned on the second floor.

As the director I was required to do a lot of traveling, attend a lot of meetings, and write reports, make observations, and prepare mini grants. I learned to take pictures with a high quality camera. I traveled all over the country visiting schools, residential facilities and workshops. I met with directors and superintendents. We hired as consultants some of the most respected special educators and psychologists in the world. We used a first class architectural firm to design the proposed school and sheltered workshop. I periodically presented our recommendations to congressmen in D.C.

One might think this job was a little out of my league, but dress me up, trim my hair, splash a little cologne on me, sit me in my executive chair behind my big executive desk and I could fool anyone. By this time I was reading on a seventh grade level and pushing eight. I knew words like "cultural-familial," and "epidemiological," and, could spell both of them correctly.

Within a year, with the expertise and talent of the staff, consultants and architectural firm we designed a world-class school and a sheltered workshop that were recognized in the highest of professional circles. Everyone, except my secretary and staff, thought I did it alone.

92

The creation of the facility was based on the foundation of a Prevalence Survey that identified the number of severely, profoundly handicapped individuals residing in Wyandotte County Kansas. The survey, conducted by the staff, was the only prevalence study ever conducted that actually visited every subject, validated their condition, and verified the service needed. Much of the data was used in my Master's thesis. At the conclusion of the grant, portions of the Prevalence Study were published in professional journals and cited as the most comprehensive and informative survey ever conducted in the United States.

Although this grant provided me the opportunity to be recognized as a viable professional in the field of education and supplied data for my thesis, what really changed my life was the graduate course I took just prior to writing my thesis.

The course was a seminar that included three students: Don Ball, who later became a nationally recognized statistician; Jim Kauffman, later to become an internationally known special educator, and me. Don Ball and Jim Kauffman could not only read, they could think. The professor was new. She was quite pretty and I enjoyed it when she turned to write on the chalk board, only to find available space at the very top of the board; she had to stretch up on her tip toes which made her skirt accentuate her gluteus maximus. I don't think Don and Jim noticed.

She had been conducting research at one of the high schools in the surrounding area. About three quarters through the semester, she entered our class in a state of disbelief. She explained she had discovered a group of graduating high school students who could not read. They were illiterate. Then she said something I'll never forget, something that changed my life forever. She queried, "Do you realize how intelligent they have to be?"

Don and Jim looked at one another. "What do you mean?"

"Think how you would navigate through school if we took away your ability to read."

There was dead silence in the room. Don and Jim looked at the professor in disbelief. I looked down at my shoes and thought, "I repeated third grade, graduated from high school illiterate, and earned a BA degree in psychology, unable to read a newspaper. If those students are intelligent I must be brilliant."

Dr. Ball and I coauthored many articles in professional journals.

Dr. Kauffman and I coauthored the bestselling introductory text in mental retardation.

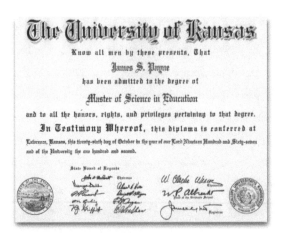

My master's diploma. Data from the Wyandotte County Project was used for my thesis.

–Chapter 12–

Head Start

—

1967

Graduated, Master's Degree, University of
Kansas (Special Education)

1967

Hired, Director, Head Start
(I learn from little kids)

From outside my office, "Dr. Plucker's secretary is on line one."

"Hello."

"Mr. Payne, Dr. Plucker would like to see you. Could you come around four today?"

"Sure. What's it about? Do I need to bring anything?"

"No. Just come. It's not about the Wyandotte grant."

Dr. O.L. Plucker is the superintendent of the Kansas City, Kansas school system. Persons at my level seldom get a chance to talk with someone that high up. In fact, I've never met him personally and I've never been in his office. This must be important or I've done something terribly wrong.

The central office building is a tall towering building just like all the other buildings in downtown Kansas City. Concrete, ugly but intimidating. Dr. Plucker's office is on the top floor, corner office of the executive suite.

His secretary has me wait. I sit on an expensive couch flanked by two side chairs and a coffee table with Dicken's, *Tale of Two Cities* on top.

I'm summoned. Dr. Plucker shakes my hand. I sit in one of the guest chairs in front of his beautiful mahogany desk. He sits in his black leather high-back executive chair. Book cases line three walls from floor to ceiling, each filled with books, side by side, placed in even lines on each shelf. I feel like I'm in a library, a very nice library. Behind his desk is a large picture window overlooking the city. Wall to wall carpet, beige with light sprinkles of cinnamon match two drapes on each side that frame the showcase window.

"Jim, you've got the Wyandotte project off and running. Good job. I'm going to turn it over to someone else now. I need you to take over this new program, Head Start. Our grant has been approved and we need to get on it. Dr. Caruthers will help with the transition. He will handle the details. By the way, congratulations on finishing your Master's. While director of Head Start you will continue taking courses at KU, just as you did with the Wyandotte project. We won't pay for the courses but we can give you some release time and pay for your travel backand forth to Lawrence. Do you have any questions?"

"What's Head Start?"

"It's part of President Johnson's War on Poverty. It's a preschool program to get kids from poor areas ready for kindergarten. You will be working in the northeastern part of the city and your office is at Rosedale. By the way, Dr. Haring is going to put you in a couple of classes that will help you."

Dr. Plucker stands up. I stand up. He walks me to the door. It's final. It's official. I'm the director of the first Head Start program in the state of Kansas.

I enter my office at Rosedale High School. Nothing more than a bare empty classroom stripped of student's desks and chairs. No bookcase. No file cabinet. Totally bare except for one used pine teacher's desk and an army surplus chair covered with army-green paint. On the desk is a rotary dial phone. On the Wyandotte County grant my phone had buttons.

The principal, Mr. Davies, greets me. "You must be Mr. Payne. I'm Walter Davies. Welcome. Let me show you around."

The building is of the early thirties. Two stories. Halls lined with gray metal lockers. Hall floors topped with warn out gray tiles, some removed showing patches of black dried up glue. Classrooms all the same, well-worn wooden floors, old high school type desks with attached seats. Bathrooms clean with the scent of Pinesol. We end up in Davies' office. He explains, "Your main office is here. Personnel will handle the hiring. You worked with Mr. Burns before. He's the same. Nothing new. Purchasing is the same as you did on the Wyandotte project. Dr. Caruthers will help you set things up. His office is down the hall from Dr. Pluckers."

He hands me a 1'x2'x1' cardboard box filled with notebooks, manuals, and papers, "Here's some stuff for you to look over. Dr. Haring has made arrangements for you to get ideas about teaching preschool kids from Drs. Wolff and Risley at Juniper Gardens. They will be invaluable to you. Here's their numbers. I'd suggest you get a hold of them soon. If you need me, see my secretary, Sharon."

I return to my office. Skim the materials. No staff, no equipment, no supplies, no noth'en. Just like when I started the Wyandotte grant, except lots more money. The project is to serve 750 children. In addition to education, transportation, breakfast, lunch, and snacks, medical and dental services are to be provided. The district's facilities are full so we will operate out of churches, yet to be selected.

The Juniper Gardens Project is nationally recognized, using direct instruction and reinforcement to teach preschool aged children and their parents. The program is located in the middle of the impoverished northeast section of Kansas City, exactly where the Head Start program is to operate.

Juniper Gardens is run by Drs. Montrose Wolff and Todd Risley. Both established authors and researchers in early childhood using direct instruction and reinforcement. Drs. Wolff and Risley show me around. The classroom looks like a typical state-of-the-art preschool with the latest equipment. The classroom is tiled with squares of bright red, yellow, blue and green. Designated areas represent a block area, dollhouse, water table, sandbox, children's reading circle, and singing area with standup piano, everything imaginable. At first glance, it looks likean ideal preschool classroom but on closer inspection an abundance of mirrors that seem out ofplace, surround the room. The mirrors turn-out to be one-way windows. Behind each window, sitting in booths are researchers collecting data and future teachers observing how to precisely use direct instruction and when and how to properly reinforce. Teaching is both an art and science. At Juniper Gardens they explore the science side.

Juniper Gardens is a model preschool and research lab nationally recognized and I get the benefit of learning how to build an exemplary Head Start program from professional researchers and master teachers. This is too good to be true.

Every morning I sit in an observation booth to observe master teachers and learn from researchers what to look for and how to assess teacher performance and children's learning.

In the afternoons I work with Mr. Burns on hiring staff and with the Purchasing Department, on ordering equipment and supplies. Drs. Wolff and Risley help select the right equipment and supplies. Dr. Caruthers introduces me to the ministers in the area and eight churches are selected, all perfectly located throughout the region to be served.

The first problem was to get the children to school. It was decided to start with 500 and gradually phase the others in. There are no available buses in Kansas City at this time. After a feasibility study and much discussion it is decided to use cabs.

On paper, cabs are a great solution. Limiting four children to a cab keeps the travel time short. In addition to being efficient they are safe. Also the use of cabs is cheaper than leasing buses.

The very first day I get a call from the lead teacher at Trinity. "Mr. Payne, Anthony didn't catch the cab this morning. The driver said his mother told him he had gotten on a bus."

"A bus. What kind of bus?"

"I don't know what to do. I'm at Mrs. Peague's house now. I'm worried."

"I'll be there in 5 minutes. Give me the address."

I get the address and arrive at the house. Mrs. Peagues is crying and the teacher is frantic.

"Mrs. Peagues, tell me exactly what happened."

"At 8:00 o'clock a yellow bus pulled up in front. I put Anthony on it."

"Not a yellow bus. A yellow cab."

"Cab? No. Bus. Yellow," she emphasizes.

"Do you remember anything about the bus?"

"I kissed him, he got on, sat in the front seat. As the bus pulled away we waved at each other."

"About the bus. A number? A sign?"

"It was yellow. For sure it was yellow. I didn't see a number. Wait. As it pulled away. A sign. A sign on the side, Billy Graham Crusade."

The police find Anthony six blocks away in a church basement singing with a handful of other children. 'It's the B-I-B-L-E. Yes that's the book for me.'

Immediately the teachers are alerted, notes are sent home with each child reminding, yellow cab. Not yellow bus. With CAB in big letters.

Other than that incident the cabs were fine. In fact, perfect. But, third week a call from the dispatcher, "Mr. Payne, we are going to have to do something. The drivers are threatening to quit. They plan to boycott Head Start."

"Wait. Wait. I'll be right down."

I drive to the main headquarters. I meet the dispatcher and a handful of angry drivers. The situation is; the times conflict with their regulars needing to get to work. Head Start only pays weekly and no tip is allowed. But the big problem is, some of the children are not toilet trained.

I meet with Dr. Caruthers and explain the situation. Before I blink, Purchasing will add a 10 percent gratuity, and plastic seat covers can be installed on the back seats of every cab.

That same day I meet with the owner and dispatcher. I proudly explain what can be done. The owner and dispatcher excuse themselves and go to an adjoining room to talk with the cab drivers' representative that handles complaints and disputes. In less than 5 minutes the owner apologizes, "Sorry. We will continue for two weeks. You have two weeks. That's it."

I call Dr. Caruthers, "No dice. We have two weeks."

"Jim, come to my office tomorrow. We'll have lunch. Be here by eleven thirty."

At lunch I find Dr. Caruthers is way ahead of me. He has a back-up plan ready. He got with the Director of Transportation. They found a company in the adjoining county to have extra buses they will lease.

Like magic. Problem solved. So I think. Getting the kids to and from school is solved but the kids being so young get restless and disruptive having to spend so much time riding.

I switch some of the teacher aides from the classroom to become bus monitors. Their job is to control disruptive behavior. Reports of fighting and crying trigger a crash course on behavioral management which results in children sitting perfectly still with nothing to do. The behavior management program worked but it isn't normal or natural for 3 and 4 year olds to sit for long periods of time doing nothing.

The teachers come up with the idea of teaching children while riding the bus. They initiate a 'Bus Rides are for Learning' program.

It starts out with the teachers teaching the aides songs and rhymes to use on the bus. The song 'Wheels on the Bus' and rhyme, 'Mary Had a Little Lamb' are the first. Next, aides read short stories to the children as they ride the bus.

Learning activities coupled with behavioral management techniques turned bus rides into classrooms on wheels. Concepts taught in class were reviewed on the bus like number and letter concepts, time-day, month, year, colors, shapes, weather. The key is to mix things up so the kids don't get bored. On occasion, pie tins, used to simulate steering wheels, are issued to each child as they get on the bus and as the driver turns the kids rotate the pie tins and shout, 'left' or 'right.' Giving each kid a bubble blower and a bottle of bubble soap causes onlookers to take a second glance as hundreds of bubbles flow out the windows of the buses.

It didn't take long for the aides to come up with their own ideas by pointing out common events occurring along the way. The bus might stop, letting the kids talk with construction workers working on the road. Mailmen and garbage collectors are big for kids to question.

The 'Bus Rides are for Learning' program minimized behavior problems, reinforced learning and is a hit with parents and community workers.

Just as transportation challenges evolved into superior learning opportunities, so did the food program. During the school day breakfast, lunch and snacks are provided.

Originally it was planned that the kitchens in the eight church sites would be used to prepare the food. A month before school started, I was stunned to learn less than half of the kitchens passed the required health inspection. Not because of cleanliness or sanitation but because of outdated equipment and improper provisions for food storage.

These problems were not anticipated nor budgeted for. The solution: we turned to an outside catering service. Each morning heating units, on wheels rolled into each center containing well-balanced, nutritious meals that exceeded all government standards.

The food program worked like clockwork but it didn't take long to realize much of the food wasn't eaten. Not because it was poorly prepared or tastes bad but because it was unfamiliar. Kids gobbled down hamburgers and hotdogs but wouldn't touch Salisbury steak or any type of casserole.

The first reaction was to fill bellies. Only serve familiar foods. Then it was decided the job was to get the kids to eat whatever was good for them.

Our parental instincts considered holding dessert until the plate had been cleaned. Or don't let them leave the table until every morsel was consumed. Maybe restrict play time. All might work but maybe a little too extreme for 3 and 4 year olds. It was decided to come up with ways to encourage, entice, stimulate, maneuver and con the kids into eating.

To determine the effect of any program initiated, each day, uneaten food was measured by the gallon. Uneaten food was scraped into a gallon bucket, then discarded into 55 gallon containers, later to be picked up by the sanitation department. The amount of garbage was recorded and within a short time it became obvious the kids liked hamburgers, hotdogs, French fries, chili, sloppy joes, peaches and surprisingly, spinach. Recorded high food waste: Salisbury steak, casseroles of any kind, chow mein, carrots, green beans, baked potatoes and apricots.

It was deceptively simple. A 'happy plate' program was initiated. A child cleans his plate, earns a 'happy plate' honor, selects a paper leaf the color of his choosing, pins it on a bare tree drawn on construction paper attached to the bulletin board. Within days the tree is covered with brightly colored leaves much to the delight of the children, resulting in minimal garbage, much to the glee of the nutritionist. Next, a turkey requiring colored feathers, then a snow man needing to be covered with cotton balls.

Upon close examination, the data indicated there were some days the amount of garbage remained high. Sure enough, on the days of high amounts of garbage, the 'happy plate' program was briefly suspended getting ready for the next 'happy plate' event. The 'happy plate' program got kids to eat some of the things they didn't like but the program did not change their food preferences. In other words, when incentives were not used, they would not eat Salisbury steak, casseroles, chow mein.

After displaying the data at the staff meeting, Peyton, a young, enthusiastic, full of him-self, male teacher suggested, "Let's teach foods through units on different cultures. Maybe that will do something. The data shows, by far, kids hate chow mein. Let's teach an exciting unit on China, the Chinese people, their customs and then introduce them to chop sticks and chow mein.

We could have them make coolie hats and wear them to lunch."

The teachers nodded, then right there on the spot, developed a unit on China. Ultimately, it was decided to divide the centers in half. Four would teach the unit and the other four would go with the regular curriculum. Then a few days later the programs would switch.

As hoped, on the first round, the four centers teaching the unit on China, zero or almost zero garbage of chow mein. The comparison group, lots of chow mein garbage.

Two days later, the programs switched, shockingly neither group had garbage. Days' later chow mein was served again, no garbage. The children had learned to like chow mein. The uniton China actually changed food preferences. They ate chow mein without incentives.

A unit on Mexico led to an appreciation for refried beans, rice and tamales. The AmericanIndian unit led to yams, succotash and corn. After the Black American unit, I learned to like chitt'lins, shortnin' bread and collard greens.

It was found, non-preferred food like apricots, when mixed in with a preferred food like peaches, resulted in zero garbage. When the amount of peaches was systematically and gradually decreased as the apricots increased within a short period, apricots served alone resulted in zero garbage. The same results with spinach/preferred and carrots/non-preferred. I was learning so much from the kids and the kids were learning so much from Head Start.

Half way through the first year, a half dozen kids were identified as gifted. Not smart. Gifted. One day a week the six were bused to one center for advanced instruction. The regular teacher for the gifted unexpectedly had to leave. I was in the building so rather than calling a sub I took over.

To me the gifted kids looked no different from the others. Nothing special. Seated in a small kids' chair with the six in a semicircle sitting on the floor with their legs crossed in front of me, I explain how the earth revolves and because of its huge size how difficult it is to realize it's actually round.

103

Spencer blurts out without raising this hand, "Da earth ain't no round."

"Ha. You think it's flat?"

"Of course not. Da earth's a truncated sphere."

I quickly change the subject. Finally it's break time. The six scurry off for snacks. I grab a juice, look up the word 'truncated.' The dictionary indicates truncated, as an adjective, refers to short. I don't know how that fits with the shape of the earth but I am in no position to argue with Spencer. I never really liked Spencer anyway. He always acts like he is smarter than anyone else.

At the close of the year, Ross and Herbert, two psychologists, provide information on the children's academic growth that is staggering. Ross and Herbert, two bright young men wholove to analyze and measure everything. They single handedly set up an evaluation system, second to none, in the country. They took a battery of tests that included two intelligence tests, a language test, an achievement test, a preschool inventory, a phonemic awareness test and a behavioral checklist; tested every child at the beginning of the school year, and at the end. Increases were recorded in every category including significant improvements in IQ scores. We were on to something special and we were proud until a team of outside consultants from the Regional Department of Heath, Education and Welfare paid a visit.

The HEW team, made up of four early childhood experts expressed concern about using teachers' aides as bus monitors. They wanted all food and snacks prepared by parents in the area and paid for their services. They were not impressed by the test results. They advocated a developmental program that is exploratory in nature. Direct teaching and blatant reinforcement techniques had no place with young children. Later I discovered community action agencies were preferred over Head Start programs administered by public school systems.

In an attempt to appease, teacher aides were removed from their roles as bus monitors. Kitchen equipment was updated and coolers and freezers were installed using Head Start funds. Parents were hired as cooks and the outside catering service was terminated.

Ross and Herbert continued with their stellar assessment program. All the teachers and staff stayed and dutifully attended staff development sessions on how to conduct a developmental

104

program.

Same centers, same teachers, same staff with the addition of hiring parents as cooks, the second year ran without a hitch. Enthusiasm remained high. The classroom curriculum became a little more traditional and the instruction a little less directive and the reinforcement methods more subtle. The major difference was the major push for parent involvement.

According to the Head Start Policies Manual, every Head Start program must have effective parent participation. There are four kinds: a) decision making, b) classroom participation, c) help with developing educational activities, and d) welcoming teachers and staff into homes to determine ways parents can contribute to the child's development at home.

During the first year, we prouded ourselves in having an active parent advisory group in each center that religiously met every month. The advising groups provided volunteers that helped in the classrooms and the community. They were an integral part of the program's success. I thought our parent program was outstanding until Awilda Salard was hired the second year as our fulltime Parent Coordinator. Mrs. Salard was the most active volunteer during the first year. She was a big, dark skinned, black woman that everyone loved. She was loud, robust and funny. Her smile displayed white teeth that were perfectly formed.

Shortly after she took over as the parent coordinator, parents volunteered as bus monitors. They considered the role important and performed as well as the first year teacher aides. She knew all the cooks that were hired and she helped the nutritionist with ordering and preparing interesting and tasty meals. She was a one woman whirlwind.

A major contribution was her getting an army of parent volunteers to help tutor individual students that needed extra help.

Students that are significantly behind in learning particular concepts need extra help in order to catch up. Over the years, prior to Head Start, early childhood research clearly documented concept milestones as to what to teach and the sequence in which to teach. With the help of Drs. Wolff and Risley we turned empty shoeboxes into tutoring boxes. A label on the outside identifies the concept to be taught. Inside contains the materials. The directions for teaching the concept are taped to the underside of the lid, not to be lost or misplaced. Over 200 tutoring boxes are sent to each center. The boxes address concepts like color recognition, number identification, counting, letter sounds, phonemic picture cards. The boxes are sequentially placed on custom built shelves located in storage closets. Each tutoring supply closet looks like the storage area in the back of a retail shoe shop.

Ross and Herbert conduct training sessions with the parent volunteers on how to determine what to teach to a specific individual child, how to present the material and what to do when the child responds correctly and what to do when the child struggles.

Ross and Herbert enter my office excited. Before either sit, Ross blurts, "We're on to something."

Herbert accentuates, "Something big.""Sit. Tell me what's up."

They sit. Ross leads, "These parent volunteers are excellent. They are professionals."

Herbert adds, "The children are catching up and they love being tutored."

Ross and Herbert lay a series of individual learning graphs on the top of my desk and point to a couple of individual charts that show concept mastery above grade level.

Ross and Herbert leave as excited as they entered. Head Start is blessed to have such talented and dedicated people like Ross and Herbert.

The second year's gains match the first. As before, most of our Head Start graduates enter the public school system functioning above regular kindergarteners. We are proud but HEW isn't.

The site team comes. They don't like Head Start being administered through the publicschools. They love Mrs. Salard as everyone does, but they hate me. I am labeled as a 'behaviormod zealot.'

During the third year, the parent participation component related to teachers going into the homes to determine ways parents can contribute to the child's development, is emphasized. Everything else remains the same.

Additional teachers are hired to visit parents' homes and teach parents how to teach their own children. Ross and Herbert accept the responsibility to assess the children's performance as was done during the first two years. I was interested in the program's potential for helping children learn so I decided to use the results as data for my dissertation. I drafted a proposal, 'How to Teach Parents How to Teach Their Own Head Start Children.' My advisor, Dr. Jerry D. Chaffin, agreed to serve as the chair of my doctoral dissertation committee. He helped me select five additional members. I presented the proposal to the committee before the third year started. It was approved.

The Director of Curriculum, Lucy Livingston and an outside early childhood consultant, Ida Feingold, develop materials to use. A series of booklets entitled, 'Project: Home Start' contain pencils, crayons, scissors, tape, paste, the works. Everything is provided. The booklets present similar concepts used in the tutoring shoeboxes.

All Home Start teachers are licensed and certified in early childhood. They attend a pre-service workshop on how to use the materials. The paperwork is completed, a list of the assigned parents is issued to each teacher and Mrs. Salard makes arrangements to show the Home Start teachers the area and introduce them to their parents personally.

Ross and Herbert, using a table of random numbers, select a little over 100 children. All attend the regular Head Start program while half receive the benefit of home visits.

Being the first and only program to randomly select parents, it is soon realized, a few of the parents do not want to be involved. These few complain they didn't have time. A couple of the teachers actually feel they are intruding and are uncomfortable visiting these homes. It is decided to form a subgroup, non-cooperative, and discontinue visiting these homes.

HEW gets wind the data from the Home Start program is a part of my dissertation. They demand the local Economic Opportunity Foundation inform me that I cannot use the data. I call Dr. Chaffin to explain. He responds, "Jim, you are not doing anything wrong or illegal. Call Joyce. Tell her, she will put Bill on it."

Joyce North is the social worker that worked with me in both the Haring project and the

Wyandotte project. Her husband is a law partner of a major firm in Prairie Village, Kansas. I call Joyce. Joyce puts me on to Bill. Bill listens to my problem. Somewhat familiar with the tension between HEW and EOF, he assures me, "Don't worry. I'll take care of this. Give me a week."

The following week Bill arrives at my office in Rosedale. He sits, "Damn. They really do hate you and they don't like Plucker either. You don't need to worry. They understand you have the right to the data."

"They haven't liked us from the beginning. What do I do now?"

"You go ahead. I'll contact Chaffin."

With the help of Ross and Herbert, the data is collected. We put it in the computer at the Office of Research at KU. The dissertation is complete after I write up the results. The results were disappointing. No differences. The results from each of the various tests showed no differences in the performance of the children in the Head Start group when compared to the Head Start Plus Parent group. All the time, effort and money seemed wasted. The saving grace was the Head Start children regardless of the group, showed significant improvement, similar to the gains of the children of the first two years. In other words, Head Start worked but teaching parents how to teach their own children didn't add to the children's learning or achievement.

Finally. Finished. I'm ready to defend.

After 3 years of service as the director, I resign to accept a faculty position at the University of Virginia. My defense is scheduled for the following week. The phone rings, Ruth Ann, my wife, answers, "Hello."

She covers the receiver with her hand, "It's the dean."

"Dean who?"

"Dean of the School of Education at KU."

I take the phone, "Hello."

"Jim, this is Dean Ridgeway. Sorry to bother you so early this Monday morning but I need to meet with you as soon as possible."

"Sure. What about?"

"Your dissertation defense scheduled for next week."

"Ok. When would you like to meet?"

"Could you get here by one today?"

"Yes. I suppose so."

"Fine. Come to my office. My secretary will give you a parking permit."

"Fine." I hang up, turn to Ruth Ann, "What do you think this is all about?"

From my house, it takes an hour and a half to get there and 30 minutes to park. To play it safe, I start at ten. I take the turnpike. The secretary hands me the permit. I put it on the dash and am in his office 30 minutes early. Dean Ridgeway immediately comes out. Shakes my hand. Shows me to his office. Motions for me to sit while he positions himself behind his desk.

"Jim, your committee has told me of your fine work. I skimmed through your dissertation and it looks impressive. You have obviously invested a lot of time and effort into it. I'm aware of some of the controversy surrounding Head Start with HEW and EOF. I hope everything blows over and you get on your way to Virginia."

"Yes. I'm excited. They have a great special ed. department at Virginia."

"Jim. Are you aware there are rumors, there is a plan to picket your defense?"

"Picket?"

"Yes, demonstrate. Protest."

"Dr. Ridgeway, I know the HEW people don't like me and through EOF I was told I couldn't do my dissertation using Head Start data. This got resolved. Last week I was accused of misusing Head Start money to do my dissertation. EOF sent a letter to Dr. Chaffin telling him to hold up my graduation but I think that also was taken care of. I don't know anything about a protest."

"It has been resolved. Sort of. According to your attorney everything has verbally been handled but there is nothing in writing. We don't want any trouble and we sure don't want anyone to get hurt. How close are you to defending?"

"It is scheduled for next week, Tuesday."

"No. I mean how ready are you to defend?"

"I'm ready now. I've been working on this for a long time. I don't think there are any questions I can't answer. I'm ready."

"Good. I've got your committee waiting in my conference room. We want you to defend now."

"Right now?" I don't have my notes. I didn't even bring a copy."

"I understand. But, it's best to do it now."

Ridgeway gets up and leads me to the conference room. Dr. Chaffin greets me, smiles. "Jim. This is it."

I'm seated at the head of a large oak conference table surrounded by heavy oak chairs. Dr. Chaffin sits to my immediate right. Three committee members line each side of the table. Each give a slight assured nod. I know each very well and they know me. I've had them in class and they have helped me navigate through the dissertation process. Somewhat nervous but not scared, the questions begin. Gradually, the intensity increases. Questions come from both sides, one right after the other.

I glance at my watch. I've been here over 3 hours. This is a bit long. I've been told most defenses last about an hour. Dr. Chaffin leans over, "Jim. That's it. Step out for a moment. We will call you back when we are ready."

I step out in the hall. I wait for more than 30 minutes. Maybe I didn't do as well as I thought.

Dr. Chaffin sticks his head out and motions for me to return.

I step in the room, each committee member smiles and one by one they shake my hand to congratulate me. I passed.

No one leaves. Everyone sits and motions for me to sit.
Dr. Chaffin turns to me, "Jim. We are very proud of you and impressed with your work. The decision to pass was easy. What took so long is we decided to pass you with honors. This isn't often done. Passing with honors will be designated on your transcript and any document requesting information regarding degrees earned, you are to indicate you earned your doctorate from KU with honors."

I couldn't believe it. As a group, we sort of mini-celebrated without anything to celebrate

110

with. Each committee member related something I did or said that they thought funny or meritorious. After another 30 minutes, Dr. Chaffin informs, "Dr. Ridgeway wants to talk with you before you leave."

I'm taken to Dr. Ridgeway's office. This time the two of us sit side by side on the couch situated next to the back wall.

"Congratulations. We are so very proud of you. Before this hits the papers we think it best for Ruth Ann and you to get out of the area. Let things cool down. I've called Ruth Ann and Dr. Carriker at UVA. When you get home, things will be packed to leave for Charlottesville. Dr. Carriker has made arrangements for you to be their guest for two weeks. While there, you can make living arrangements, set up your office and get acclimated to the area. I suggest you not tell anyone when you return to Kansas City to get your things, make your stay short. Jim. These people aren't nice. It is extremely important you get something in writing from EOF clearing your name. We have contacted your attorney and he assures us he will stay on the case until the matter is resolved – in writing. Again congratulations."

We stand. Shake hands. I drive back to Kansas City. Ruth Ann is waiting. A big hug. A big kiss. Bags loaded. Off we go to Charlottesville, Virginia.

Bill worked with HEW which resulted in the following letter on EOF stationary:

Dr. Jerry D. Chaffin   March 1, 1971
University of Kansas
Lawrence, Kansas

Dear Sir:

This letter is a follow-up to a letter you received from Mr. Walter Browne, Acting Managing Director of the Economic Opportunity Foundation, Inc., which letter was dated August 6, 1970. In that letter, Mr. Browne requested that Mr. James S. Payne's graduation be held up because of charges being alleged by Mr. Ralph D. Johnson, Acting Assistant Regional Director, Office of Child Development of the Regional Department of Health, Education, and Welfare.

Those allegations were that Mr. Payne expended Federal Funds to do research in the preparation of his dissertation. At that time, Mr. Payne was Director of E.O.F.'s Head Start Programs.

In that letter Mr. Browne stated he had no other alternative than to write such a letter until such time as those charges were either proved or disproved. We are fully aware that Mr. Browne's request was ignored in your reply in a letter dated August 7, 1970. You wrote that you wouldn't consider the matter further unless Mr. Payne was formally charged with illegally appropriating funds in the programs.

Well this letter is an attempt to clear up this matter. Please be advised that no such charges were ever proved. In addition, to our knowledge, Mr. Payne was never charged with illegally appropriating funds and there is no present or future intent by either 2our agency or the Regional Department of HEW to file such charges. This agency has determined to its satisfaction that no basis exists for such charges.

Yours very truly,

John L. Zumwalt
Managing Director
Economic Opportunity Foundation, Inc.

I shared the letter with Dr. Carriker. Over the semester we became dear friends. He read my dissertation and learned much of what was accomplished in the 3 years of Head Start. Upon his suggestion I wrote my first book, *Head Start: A Tragicomedy with Epilogue.* The book was released in 1973 and for two years, according the publisher, it was the best selling in early child-hood.

112

My first book.

Four budding authors, from left to right, me, my
wife Ruth Ann, Roxana Davison and Cecil Mercer.

My doctorate diploma.
My dissertation was, Teaching Parents How to
Teach Their Own Head Start Children.
I graduated with honors.

–Chapter 13–
UVA

—

1970

Graduated, Doctorate Degree, University
of Kansas (honors)

1970

Hired, Assistant Professor, University of
Virginia

(I learn how to lecture a large group)

I arrive in Charlottesville, Virginia as an Assistant Professor thinking I had beat out a bunch of applicants for the position to find out later I was the only applicant to meet all the criteria for the job. The department needed a person to teach a state-required course entitled "Rehabilitation Techniques." They needed a person with a doctorate in special education and experience in vocational rehabilitation. Most individuals with doctorates in special education have experience either with public schools or residential settings, not vocational rehabilitation.

The course, "Rehabilitation Techniques," a required course for a small select group of special education majors, could only be taken as an elective by anyone majoring in anything else. The first fall semester I had six students, the following spring semester I had eighteen, and the first summer session I had thirty two. During the second year, enrollment jumped above one hundred and by the third year, I was teaching one of the largest enrollments at The University of Virginia.

Registrations jumped so fast each semester that we needed a larger room. As a standard procedure, large lecture classes were over-booked much like the airlines over-book its flights working on the assumption not everyone would show up. Unfortunately, not only did everyone show up for my class, some of the students would bring a friend or possibly, if their parents were visiting, they would bring them as guests. Each class session, students would squeeze into the room. Marc, my graduate assistant, would keep an eye out and provide folding chairs for the aisles.

The rooms I taught in were tiered, auditorium style and I taught from a stage. Students would come early and fill up all the seats: Marc did his best to accommodate the guests; the overflow sat on the floor in front. Some students would sit on the edge of the stage facing the audience with their legs dangling down. Everyone was polite and the atmosphere was festive.

The students were respectful; they listened, took notes and laughed at appropriate moments. Test results indicated they actually learned something. However, during one lecture, something seemed different. The students were courteous, responded at the right times, took notesbut everyone smiled throughout the lecture, and seemed not as attentive as usual.

I ended class and Marc helped me clean up. Marc was unusually silent. He was always full of himself but on this day he had a half-ass grin on his face.

"Marc, are you ok?"

He nodded while returning the folding chairs to their rightful place.

"Marc, something was different today. Did you notice it?"

He kept picking up the chairs and replacing them.

"Everyone listened, but I felt they weren't with me. Do you think they were paying attention?"

"They were paying attention alright," Marc said as he continued stacking the chairs.

I wrapped up my lecture notes, re-organized my transparencies and re-wound the film shorts. I put everything in two boxes, each labeled Rehab Tech, set the boxes on the two-wheeler and Marc and I headed back to Peabody Hall.

On the way back to Peabody, I kept thinking about my lecture. "Marc, the problem was I didn't have good eye contact. The students weren't looking at me or the screen. They weren't paying attention."

"They were paying attention. Believe me, they were paying attention." We took a couple of more steps and Marc continued, "Did you see the blonde sitting on stage to your far right?"

"What blonde?" Marc broke into a huge smile, without looking at me, "The blonde whose boob kept falling out of her blouse every time she leaned over to take a note."

"Are you kidding me?"

"She'd lean over, one would fall out and as she took notes with her right hand, she nonchalantly tucked it back in with her left. Dr. Payne, it was a beautiful thing to watch. Pop out, put in, pop out, put in, pop out…"

I interrupted, "I get it. I get it."

We kept walking forward and the more we walked the madder I got. Abruptly I turned the two-wheeler over to Marc. "Take this to my office."

I made an about face without comment and headed toward the Registrar's office. That was the last semester "Rehab Techniques" was overbooked and that was the last class session anyone was allowed to sit on the stage.

My fifth year at UVA, the department hired a graduate assistant who always wore a spaghetti string blouse with no bra. Her eyelashes were unusually long and her skirt was unusually short, thigh high. She never wore hose or socks. In high school at Desoto, all the girls had worn bobby socks and the boys sweat socks. In Charlottesville, in the 70's, the women didn't wear socks or bras. I don't know if it was cultural or generational, but it was fact.

The graduate assistant had shapely, bronzed legs and she always wore clogs, blue leather tops with thick wooden soles that made a unique, loud clomping sound as she walked down the tiled floors of Ruffner Hall. When she walked, as her clogs clomped, her blouse would swish back and forth causing her nipples to project out like two small raisins. Whenever she walked toward me those raisins seemed to stare straight at me.

My office was situated three doors down from the departmental office. One day, I'm sitting at my desk with the door open when I hear the familiar clomp, clomp and just as I look up, the graduate assistant passes my door with those raisins pointed in the direction of the departmental office like seal-beamed headlights from my Chevy Impala.

I pause and look down at my crotch to discover an erection. Not a ninety degree erection, but a real blood-induced one. Presently, at eighty three, I wear boxers, back then I wore briefs and I can verify that my Fruit of the Loom Jockeys were no match for that erection. Although I was alone in the privacy of my own office, I was embarrassed. What blood I had left flushed my face, leaving me a little dizzy from my blood deficient brain.

From that day forward, I always closed the door. Unfortunately, the doors in Ruffner Hall were purchased from the lowest bidder; they were thin as paper and far from sound proof. Every morning I'd hear the clomp, clomp, clomp and every morning, involuntarily, up he rose. I tried putting fingers in my ears, no good. Humming out loud, no good. A size smaller jockey short, too painful. I tried a lot of preventives, too intimate to share, all to no avail. One day while pondering my dilemma, my mind regressed back to my psychology days at Washburn.

I imagined how Pavlov's dogs must have felt every time that bell rang. The bell would ring and as the dogs salivated they would think, "Where's the food." Academically and theoretically, I understood classical conditioning, but until I experienced it, I really did not get it. That student provided me an opportunity to gain a greater appreciation for classical conditioning. When she graduated, I was relieved.

To this day, when I pass through the women's section in a shoe department and I see clogs on display, I smile involuntarily but quickly move on.

CORKS AND CURLS INTERVIEW.

JAMES PAYNE

Mr. Payne is an Associate Professor in the School of Education. In particular, he teaches Special Education and is best known for his Rehabilitation Techniques class.

Q. Dr. Payne, your Rehabilitation Techniques class has the reputation of being one of the biggest guts. Do you have any qualms about your percentage of A's and B's and the current issue of grade inflation? I don't want to put you on the line like this . . .

A. No, that's fine. The grade distribution in my class has been about the same as when I started seven years ago. Seven years ago, though, I started the class out with, I think, twelve students. Well, I taught a lot differently when there were only twelve as opposed to four hundred. But the grade distribution probably has remained about the same. I did get in a bind one time when the class just bursted from eighty to a couple of hundred. I didn't have any help in the class, and it overwhelmed me. I got fouled up, didn't give a mid-term, and when it came down to the final time, everybody clustered at the top. I wasn't able to discriminate well, and I gave a very large percentage of A's. But I have probably paid that price, because the average student that enrolls in the class thinks he's going to get an A. That means you've got 50% that are going to get something other than an A. 70% that are going to be disappointed. That 30% has held for at least the last three years, yet the reputation is still there that it's an easy course.

Q. In a large class, a student often does not have access to the teacher in the lectures. Do you try to keep office hours or make appointments, or do you stay after class?

A. For myself, what happens is I have handled it in a variety of ways. I've found that where the class takes on meaning, is when you meet with students on a one-to-one basis. Toward the end of the semester, I will give the final exam and then allow people to come in and talk to me about the responses on the exam. I do this setting up appointment times anywhere from fifteen to thirty minutes per student. And I will, myself, run through no less than two hundred students

a semester. Now some people think this is artificial, and that you can't tell much meeting so many students in such a short period of time, but the majority of the students I've talked to, come in either to discuss the class, or to give some type of feedback about the class. Some, of course, want to haggle for grades. I enjoy this too. Because I'm through, grades to me are insignificant. To the students though, they're very important, so I have to be somewhat sensitive about it. As it stands right now, they pretty much have to take their grades the way they come. And it's a tough decision for me as it is for anyone when it comes to large classes.

Q. How did you ever get interested in this field?

A. I graduated with a B.A. degree in Psychology and upon graduation I found I wasn't employable. Nobody wanted a B.A., especially a B.A. in Psychology. So I applied for a job in a restaurant. I started washing dishes and in a very short time had worked my way up to becoming the manager. It was a large restaurant chain in the mid-west and it was a time when it was difficult

"I've found that where the class takes on meaning is when you meet with students on a one-to-one basis.

"I hire handicapped people there, but not because I feel I owe it to them."

"It makes sense out of chaos; you can predict things beyond chance, and you can manipulate variables to bring about changes.

My course won 'the best lecture course' 5 years in a row. I was featured in the university annual, Corks and Curls.

Marc Columbus was far more than a graduate assistant. We later became business partners.

I later wrote the text to be used for my class.

REHABILITATION TECHNIQUES

Vocational Adjustment for the Handicapped

James S. Payne, Ed.D., Allen K. Millar, Ed.D., Robert L. Hazlett, Ed.D., and Cecil D. Mercer, Ed.D.

120

–Chapter 14–

Allen Miller

—

1970

Hired, Assistant Professor, University of Virginia
(I learn how to build a privy)

I'm sitting in my office at the University. A person enters unannounced. No appointment. He sits down and explains he is principal of one of the rural high schools in the surrounding area and has a special education teacher he would like me to observe. The teacher is Allen Miller, who has a degree in animal husbandry, not special education. Before I can ask any questions the principal clarifies that the parents like him, the kids love him, and there are no disciplinary issues. But his teaching techniques are a little unusual. The principal wants me to pay a visit, observe Allen, and evaluate his teaching.

I am busy at the time but I committed myself to visit the following week. The next week, I drive way out in the country, with no idea the school is so far away from the university - a typical country high school behind a large gravel parking lot.

I enter the building, report to the main office, and explain my presence. I ask where Mr. Miller's room is. The receptionist explains, "It's Tuesday so he will be teaching outside his room in the back of the building."

I report to the back of the building to find Mr. Allen Miller working with five adolescents. He is five foot nine, and his overweight belly protrudes over his belt. He wears dirty jeans, a red and black plaid shirt with the tail hanging out, and he is sweating like a hog. The five students are severely, very severely mentally handicapped and all are working, putting together what looks like a privy. I watch while they work. Then Allen turns to me, while holding up the back side of the edifice, "Hand me that hammer, will ya?"

I hand him the hammer and he and his five workers continue to assemble the structure.

In the middle of the construction, I explain who I am. Before I explain why I have come, he replies, "The principal told me you were coming to observe me. We have to make delivery of this by eleven. Could you just watch for now? We can talk later"

Before I reply, Allen is backing up his beat-up, blue Dodge Ram to the privy, while the five students guide him. Allen gets out of the truck and the six of them tilt the privy and slide it onto the truck bed. The next thing I know, the five students jump onto the truck while Allen motions me to get into the cab.

I step up into the cab, only to see a full-sized black lab on the seat beside me. Allen gets behind the wheel, pulls the dog close, while I settle into shotgun. Each kid in the truck bed yells one at a time, "Safe," "Safe," "Safe," "Safe," "Safe." The truck heads out.

Allen introduces me to the dog. "Ringo, this is Dr. Payne from the university. Tell him hi."

Ringo, on cue, lets out a little yip, and turns his head to glance at me, only to look back immediately to the road straight ahead.

As we bounce along, Allen gives me a rundown on each of the five students, not just family background but skill level. He explains how proficient each is with hammer, saw, crowbar, screwdriver, pliers, etc. He knows each student's ability to count and make change. He describes each student's psychological makeup as reported in their individual file. He does this from memory. No written notes. No report to examine.

"What's the deal with the privy?"

"Many of the folks out here still use privies. We build 'em and they buy 'em." Do you know what they had these kids doing before I got here?"

"What?"

"Making pot holders. Can you imagine? How can you make money making pot holders?"

We get to the farm where the farmer and his wife are waiting. The five students guide Allen as he backs the truck next to an old dilapidated privy. Allen, the students, the farmer and I easily slide the new privy from the bed of the truck and lay it sideways against the side of the dilapidated privy. Each student gets a hammer and a crowbar and begins tearing down the dilapidated privy, throwing the old wood into the back of the now empty truck. Then they tilt up the new privy and place it where the old one was. The students strut around their newly erected privy, admiring their work.

As the kids climb into the back of the truck, the farmer pays Allen in cash. Allen takes the money, parcels it out to each worker and promises to take them to town on Friday. The kids stuff the money into their pockets. The farmer's wife hands each a sack. Containing a baloney sandwich, an apple and chips. Before I know it, an old blue igloo cooler is popped open and each kid takes a drink. Allen hands me a Coke and the two of us get back into the cab. Allen gives me half of his sandwich pulls out a second sandwich, for Ringo and we drive away.

We get back to the school, the kids clean up the boards that can be reused; the rest are discarded in the bed of the truck. The good wood is slid through the window of the classroom. Three students inside the classroom stack the lumber while two students outside feed the lumber in through the window. The classroom looks like a lumber yard. Lumber stacked neatly in piles according to length and width. A fourth of the room is allocated for typical classroom instruction, whatever typical is for this astute teacher.

At the close of the day, the kids get on the bus to go home. I have to get back to the university to teach my evening class, but I ask Allen if I can come back the next day. He responds, "Yes, come early. Tomorrow we complete our work for Mr. Sullivan. We leave at 7:30 a.m."

The next day I get there a little before 7:30. The kids get off the school bus and immediately report to the Dodge Ram, where Allen and Ringo await. Everyone piles into the truck; Allen drives, me in shotgun, and Ringo in the middle. We arrive at Mr. Sullivan's farm to find a good-sized barn gutted. The roof is somewhat intact except for a few gaping holes. The outside walls have been stripped away. What remains is held up by four corner posts that serve as pillars.

Two old faded Allison Chambers tractors are parked on each side of the gutted barn facing outward. Allen and the kids attach chains from the tractors to the two closest corner posts holding up the roof.

A student climbs onto each tractor while the three remaining students get the blue Igloo cooler and place it on the side of the hill facing the barn. The cooler is popped open; each student gets a Coke, Ringo gets some water in a dirty old bowl. Allen hands me a Coke and signals the drivers to pull away.

Effortlessly, the tractors move in opposite directions to collapse the roof before the de-lighted eyes of the on-lookers.

The kids, with Cokes in hand, walk down the hill to admire their work. After consuming the beverages, everyone, including me, begins to disassemble the roof, being careful to save the good lumber. Allen had worked out a deal with the farmers in the area: let his class tear down old barns and shacks for a small fee plus the reusable lumber. The class then produces privies and outdoor furniture to sell back to the farmers.

Allen also negotiated with the county commissioner to paint all the dumpsters in the county. Every student learned to spray paint, build things and wait 'til Friday to spend his money.

I report my findings back to the principal and strike a deal to use Allen and his class as an observation site for my student teachers. In exchange, I get Allen enrolled as a graduate student in special education.

That next semester, we had one of the finest, teaching sites for practice teachers interested in dealing with severely handicapped adolescents. And the most creative teacher I had ever witnessed was now enrolled as a graduate student at the university and assigned to me as his advisor.

I will never forget Allen,
he was a prince of a fellow.

–Chapter 15–

Buddha Woman

—

1971

Born, 2nd child, Janet

1975

Promoted, Associate Professor, University of Virginia

(I learn from Buddha Woman)

Over the years Allen and I became very close friends. I want to believe I helped him but in reality he helped me.

There was a time I felt the need to be closer to God. Some personal turns were not going well. I had been turned off by formalized practices of traditional religious denominations. In a moment of reflection and questioning, I turned to Allen. "I'd just like to see God."

"Do you want to see him or get close to him?" Allen asked.

"I don't know."

Allen advises, "You need to meet Buddha Woman. She is about as close to God as it gets. What are you doing Thursday?" Not waiting for a response he says, "I'll pick you up at six."

Thursday, the blue Dodge Ram and Ringo arrive and before I know it, I'm in front of a small mobile home, on cinderblocks out somewhere in the woods. We pull up where another truck and two cars are parked. We enter the trailer without knocking. Three fraternity boys are sitting on the floor. They were so engaged they never even noticed Allen and me.

A parsons table is centered against the wall, and just above it is a two by three foot picture of a bald pot bellied man sitting with his legs crossed and his hands, palms up, on his knees, his thumbs touching his middle fingers. Later I learn this is the lotus position. On the parsons table are two lava lamps. Other than the table, the room is empty.

Allen and I sit on the floor beside the three guys.

Before I could get comfortable, Buddha Woman emerges through a curtain from an adjoining room. Tall, with unblemished dark skin, and long black hair that reaches the middle of her back, she is wearing eye makeup as heavy as Elizabeth Taylor's in "Cleopatra." She is barefooted. A ring circles the index toe of her right foot. She is wearing a flowing gown of yellow silk.

She lowers herself to sit in a lotus position with the grace of a goddess. She speaks of love and harmony. Suddenly she rises and exits through the curtained doorway returning with a pillow for me, "Sit."

Next, she shows me how to cross my legs and position my hands. The others watched patiently. She pats me on the knee. "Be patient, my friend, be patient."

She positions herself in front of us and after about five minutes of espousing the value of love and harmony, she instructs each of us to stare at a single point between the eyes of the man pictured on the wall in front of us. "Close your eyes. Inhale through your nose and exhale through your mouth. Gently position the tip of your tongue behind your front teeth." She tells us when to inhale and when to exhale. We follow her instructions on cue and catch the rhythm. She chants lessons of goodness, righteousness, and forgiveness.

I begin to feel light headed.

The next thing I know, she is getting up. I look at my watch. We had been meditating for over an hour, experiencing a semi-hypnotic state of unconsciousness.

But it's not over yet. Buddha Woman disappears behind the curtain to return with a kitchen chair made of golden oak, with a straight latticed back. She sets the chair directly in front of us. As its four legs touch the floor, music sounds from behind the curtain -- soothing, and rhythmical, with the sound of soft bells, tambourines, and a Kenny G-like clarinet. Had the chair been replaced by a ceramic vase, I could have imagined a snake emerging from within.

Suddenly, Buddha Woman begins to dance around the chair. She swings her leg over the back and spins around. Her yellow silk robe flows to the soft rhythms. She seats herself facing us and dramatically crosses and uncrosses her legs back and forth, back and forth. Then, she spins around, lifting one leg high above the back of the chair to position herself backwards. The back of her dress is cut low revealing she is braless.

Buddha Woman's chair dance resembles pole dancing, not sexy, but seductive. I can't speak for Allen or the boys but I was aroused. That night my sexual performance with my wife, according to my wife, was enhanced. My wife, Ruth Ann, never met Buddha Woman but she was delighted when Allen and I decided to continue to visit her.

After a couple of months Buddha Woman suggests we participate in a Buddhist retreat. So Allen and I attend a three day Buddhist retreat in Maryland, actually it is more of a Buddhist cult than an authentic Buddhist retreat.

The two of us leave on a Sunday. The retreat, which begins the next day, is held on a camp ground. As a group we sleep on the floor in individual sleeping bags. During those three days we are given brief instruction for perfecting our meditation techniques and enhancing our feelings. We are fed very little and allowed only water to drink. By the second day, I am very hungry and very tired. That morning we are taught a chant "Namo Myo Rengge Kyo." The chant originates from a 17th Century Buddhist Master and the experience is profound. After chanting "Namo Myo Rengge Kyo" hundreds of times while sitting in a lotus position staring across a pond, I begin to see flashes of bright colors - florescent, orange, yellow, green. The colors come in flashes. The more I meditate, the more I chant, the wilder the flashing and the brighter the colors. By the third day I see a light that speaks to me, a dialog. At first, scared, I begin to realize it is a semi hypnotic physiological condition caused by lack of food and sleep, half conscious and half subconscious. I experiment with manipulating the colors and my interaction with the bright light. It reminds me of the psychology course at Washburn where we hooked ourselves up to a psychogalvanometer that measured perspiration in our finger tips. By thinking about something hot I could move the needle back and forth. At the retreat, through meditation, I can also manipulate the colors through chanting. I can alter my responses to the bright light. It is like reliving my undergraduate psychology days all over again. I possess power I didn't know I had. Mental power; mind control.

That Wednesday night I collapsed in my sleeping bag, only to be awakened by Allen early morning, anxious to get back to Charlottesville and with Ringo.

I had called my wife to explain we'd be home around seven. When Allen drops me off at my house just a little before seven, my wife greets me with a kiss. Much to my surprise, dinner awaits. I'm starved. Ruth Ann has prepared a meal fit for a king. Two candles adorn the sides of the table. We sit side by side. I realize we are there to dine, not to eat.

We clear the table, put the dishes in the dishwasher, and get ready for bed.

As I enter the bedroom I notice a kitchen chair placed at the foot of the bed. Golden oak with a straight latticed back. Having endured three days without much sleep, being exhausted, suddenly, my heart begins to pound. I don't recall exactly what happened that night but what I experienced was next to godliness.

My obsession for wanting to be close to God stems from my inability to solve problems

130

for a loved one. Talking, counseling, teaching, lecturing, punishing, scolding -- when nothing works, -- what does one do? It is tempting to become angry or depressed or to give up. But if there is a God maybe, just maybe, there is another way to help.

Everyone experiences injustices. Life isn't fair; things can go wrong. It's bad enough when you're the victim but when catastrophes happen to a loved one it is more hurtful. You cannot control the situation -- you are powerless. I need God to help me help loved ones overcome or combat an injustice they will not admit is dragging them down.

I was nineteen. The "amens" were like verbal projectiles exploding throughout the sanctuary. I was outside myself, shouting and singing. Suddenly, the congregational bombardment drove me into myself to reflect. And, for the first time, drowning in the muck and mire of my own misdoings, I realized my sin reverberated in my belly.

My sins were sucking me under.

Then out of nowhere I heard, "Sinners repent. Come forward. Salvation is within your grasp."

In a trancelike state, I moved forward to confess my sins before God and before every wide-eyed parishioner issuing the roar of "amens."

I cried, then wept, then fell on my knees. I was sweating and shaking. Suddenly, I felt empty, cleansed. I had let God into my soul. I vowed never to forget that feeling, that feeling of God possession.

I don't remember my parents ever going to church but both my mom and dad were believers. On special occasions, my mom would say a blessing before we ate. She introduced me to a Presbyterian. Before I knew it I was attending the First Presbyterian Church. In retrospect I knew my mom wanted to go to church but for some reason didn't or couldn't herself. So she sent me.

I attended regularly and now saved at nineteen, I became even more active. I was respected by the minister and members of the congregation. The church was growing. A new wing needed to be added. A building campaign was kicked off. I prayed for guidance and volunteered to help seek donations and pledges. I constructed a pledge thermometer on poster board which was displayed in

131

the foyer. My responsibility was to color in the increments moving toward the funding goal.

Initially, the donations and pledges rolled in and I enjoyed coloring in the amounts on the thermometer. Less than half way to reaching our goal, giving slowed and abruptly came to a halt. It was decided to seek assistance from an outside firm skilled in running financial campaigns.

Two men from New York arrived to train us how to raise money. The two men didn't look like anyone I'd ever seen. Their shirts were heavy starched, French cuffed. They wore unscuffed shoes that glistened and suits with a slight sheen. Each wore a pinky ring sporting a diamond. I liked their enthusiasm and their positive outlook. We learned from them how to conduct ourselves in people's homes. We memorized scripts and learned how to overcome objections. I was doing simulations. I was the star. Just as I began enjoying it, the training became more advanced. It focused on the vulnerability of older members. After getting a commitment, we learned how to, as they said, "bump" them to a higher level.

Even at just nineteen, I got very good at securing pledges and the New Yorkers were right. Older members could be "bumped." When you did it right the bump worked. It was easy but it bothered me. I felt uncomfortable, even guilty. I prayed about it and finally went to the minister. He was more interested in the campaign for a new wing than he was about my concern for trickery and the deceiving of older members.

I quit going to church. My mother never asked me why. My mother was a smart woman. She knew things I was just beginning to learn.

Line drawing, as I remember it, of the picture of Buddha we looked at in Buddha woman's trailer.

–Chapter 16–

Baptist

———

1975

Promoted, Associate Professor, University of Virginia
(((I learn how to fight negative Forces)

Ruth Ann and I had dated for eight years. We had never had sex, but we didn't need to. We perfected foreplay to such an Olympian level that when we finished, our clothes needed to be washed and our bodies needed to shower. No two people could have been more in love. And no two people could ever have been more horny.

She was a Baptist, and I was a former Presbyterian. After our marriage, I became a Baptist, devoted to both Ruth Ann and the church, a small country church. Everyone knew every- body and what everybody was doing with everyone else. I loved going to that church. Ruth Ann played the piano and although I was not in the choir, I loved to sing. Over time, I became the layleader and every once in a while, I'd deliver the sermon.

A couple of years later attendance began to drop. Reverend Stuckhouse and I talked about it. We formed a small prayer group. The group met every Sunday before church services to pray for help and guidance. I took it upon myself to send a thank you note to everyone who attended church. I did this for six months, and frankly I enjoyed writing those individual notes. All hand written, most said the same thing.

Despite our efforts, attendance kept dropping.

As lay leader, the minister and I attended a retreat each year. The retreat was a big deal. I looked forward to it and when I got there I got into it. I'd sing, pray, socialize. I was a good representative for our church. Reverend Stuckhouse was somewhat shy -- maybe humble might be a better description -- but regardless, we made a great team.

The retreat always featured the Bishop. I worshiped the Bishop, older, handsome with gray-white hair, who wore a custom-fitted black robe with a dark blue collar. One day, his concluding remarks inspired me. I jumped out of my chair, ran down the aisle, and hugged him. "We are a dying church. We need you to come and save us. As a conduit to God, you are an inspiration. You must come. We are in dire need," I told him.

The Bishop tried to pull away but in my exuberance I had a death lock on him. "Son, Son, things will work out. God will come. Give Him time."

Not letting go of him, I pleaded, "Time is the problem. We are at wits end. You have to come. God is calling you."

A couple of bystanders tried to pull us apart. I dropped to my knees and grabbed his left leg, "I will not let go until you agree to help us."

"I've got a full schedule, son. I'll pray for you. I'll pray for the church."

I squeezed his thigh. He tried to push me away. I prayed louder, holding on for dear life, "Oh, God, speak to our beloved Bishop. Let him know how desperate we are." I continued to hold tight, going on and on, until, finally the Bishop kneeled down and through clinched teeth, "I'll come. Now let me go. Let me go, now."

When I released him, he immediately turned to Reverend Stuckhouse. "Come to my office next week. And bring him."

I am pleased with myself and happy for the church. As Stuckhouse and I drive back to our little town, to our little church, Stuckhouse seems to be in shock.

"The Bishop is coming.," I say over and over.

The next week Stuckhouse and I go to Kansas City. The Bishop's office is a shrine, big and ornate. The receptionist sends us to the secretary. The secretary asks us to wait. So much velvet and walnut, I'm overwhelmed. Stuckhouse is not only silent, he seems distant. Before we know it, the secretary had escorted us to the Bishop's office. I rush forward to embrace him but he steps backward and offers his hand, then turns to his chair behind a walnut desk bigger than our dining room table, and motions for me to sit. The Bishop addresses Stuckhouse and runs through our declining attendance figures and other financial stuff I have not been privy to.

Within a matter of minutes, a date is set for the Bishop to come save our church.

Three weeks to prepare. The Bishop had written five books. I bought all five and displayed them in the foyer for all to view. I placed articles and announcements in all of the surrounding towns' newspapers. I rented a van from a nearby radio station equipped with a loud speaker system.

The morning of the big event I cranked up the van at seven a.m. drove up and down every street multiple times "Wake up. Wake up. The Bishop is coming. The Bishop is coming. First Baptist Church nine o'clock. First Baptist Church at nine."

Much to Reverend Stuckhouse's surprise and delight the church began to fill. Soon all the pews were packed. Folding chairs were placed up and down the aisles, along the back of the church and down front. People kept coming, so we opened all the windows for people on the outside to hear the Bishop's message. The Bishop delivered the same sermon he had presented at the retreat. I was disappointed but the congregation was thrilled.

After the sermon, everyone who could squeeze in reported to the basement for the meal --cafeteria style. I gave the blessing. The Bishop, Reverend and Mrs. Stuckhouse, Ruth Ann and I sat at the head table. I looked at the people gawking at us, an imperfect facsimile of The Last Supper.

We finished our meal and I leaned toward the Bishop to remind him. "Now, we go into the kitchen to thank the ladies who prepared the food."

He turned to me and said, "I'm running late. Not feeling well. I need to go."

I looked at him in disbelief, "We need to thank the ladies."

He was reluctant, but the five of us filed into the kitchen. Although most were senior citizens, I'd describe their behavior as giddish.

We led the Bishop to the side door where his chauffer and, his big black Buick were waiting. The Bishop was whisked away and we all waved in appreciation. As I watched the back of the big black Buick depart from our small church, from our small town, my heart ached. The Bishop had not been worth the trouble. He was a fake. Ruth Ann and I quit the church, never to return.

Several years later, we were greeted by the Methodist minister in the church near our new home. The three of us attended and we liked it. This church was the largest of any church I had joined: two ministers, one male and one female. The sermons were fresh and inspiring, facilities and accommodations more than adequate. Most important, it met our spiritual needs.

A year later, my daughter Janet came home from high school to announce that Reverend Scott, the Methodist female minister, had been fired.

"What?"

"Dad, she has been fired."

"Why?"

"They say she is a lesbian."

"What's that got to do with anything?"

"I don't know."

"I'll check into it."

Sure enough, Reverend Scott had been fired. All that preaching about love, forgiveness, compassion, and they fire the minister because she's a lesbian. We never darkened the door again.

I know I shouldn't judge a religion by a single church. Churches by their very nature are various and fallible, even in some cases corrupt. But deception, pomposity, prejudice?

Presbyterian, Baptist, Methodist, Buddhist dropout. Damn. Today I continue to face a real problem with a loved one who is experiencing an injustice. The situation is beyond my skill level, beyond my spiritual level.

I sit in my office in anguish. I don't know what to do or where to turn.

I respond to a soft knock on my door, "Come in."

It's Tom Kergel, a student in one of my large lecture classes. I motion for him to sit down. A religion major, he occasionally drops by and we explore concepts I cover in class. Tom is extremely bright. He has studied higher level thinking. Our relationship is not professor-student, it is more of a brotherhood. We respect and admire each other and stimulate each other's thinking.

Tom knows my turmoil regarding the injustice confronting my loved one, yet not the specifics of who or what. He knows the situation weighs so heavy on my heart. "I've made arrangements for you to see Dr. Wright," he tells me.

Dr. Wright was Tom's main spiritual teacher. He had tutored him in understanding the mysterious workings of the supernatural. Tom tells me he has made arrangements for me to meet Dr. Wright, for a two hour conference.

Tom and I drive to a small house outside Washington D.C. We enter a dimly lit dining room. It smells musty. Dr. Wright greets me and the two of us sit at one corner of the table while Tom sits on the opposite side.

During the first hour and a half Dr. Wright says little but asks questions. He enters my world.

"How do you know there is a God?"

"What did you learn from your Buddha experience?"

"Why did you leave each of the churches you served?"

"What have you tried to do regarding the injustice inflicted on your loved one?"

"Describe your feelings about your turmoil?"

After questioning me for an hour and a half, he touches my arm and embraces me with his eyes. "There is an answer to your problem Dr. Payne. There is a solution. Consider altering your view of God. Rather than thinking of God as a person, a person that is all powerful, a person who solves problems, think of God as a limited Force. A Universal Mind of all knowledge and of great power but not all powerful. Think of you, me, Tom as being a part of this Universal Mind and power unidimensional. Not a separate part added to the Force but an integral ingredient of the Force, dimensionally separate. All our knowledge and a great deal of our power springs from a Universal Source. Many great thinkers have believed in unit consciousness, that information stored in our brains is not limited to our own memories of past experiences or acquired information. One mind common to all. When we tap that Universal Mind, wonderful things happen. Some theorists have explained that our individual minds are like inlets in an ocean of Universal Mind. Many great ideas may come from a source outside of ourself, but in reality they

140

are a part of Universal Mind, just as an inlet is a part of the ocean."

Dr. Wright continues, "You, me and Tom are integral parts of this oneness. All knowledgestems from it. A person must tap eternal truths from this Universal Source. You know there is a God. You have experienced His presence when you were saved. You vowed never to forget.

You had and still have a personal relationship with God. I want you to see God as a somewhat limited Force. To overcome an injustice inflicted on a loved one you must help the Forcecombat all negative energies. Your relationship with God must become more intimate and personal."

It is hard for me to explain but, at this point, Dr. Wright and I are connected in both mind and body. He is not just talking and I am not just listening. He is not there and I am not here; weare everywhere but nowhere at the same time.

Dr. Wright's tone gets more intense. "Throughout our lives negative Forces surround us. They are ever present. They seize opportunities to influence us when we show signs of fatigue or weakness. To combat them, we must connect with the Universal Self. When the negative force affects a loved one, however, our only choice is to obtain the aid of the Universal Self. This is truth. Mamby-pamby prayer won't do it. We must fight the negative Forces mono-to-mono. Now,I want you to go outside while Tom and I put together a weapon that is spiritually nuclear. Once you are in possession of this weapon you must use it with all the vigor and intensity you can muster."

I get up from the table and I walk outside. The air is still. The sky, medium dark blue and cloudless. On the horizon, just above a pond, there is a horizontal strip of mellow yellow. Above the yellow is a swath of orange that blends into the dark blue. I had never seen such a spectacular array of colors. I had never learned such a profound lesson.

Before I know it, Tom motions to me. Dr. Wright places an envelope in my hand and says, "You won't need me anymore, Dr. Payne. Tonight when you get home open the envelope and follow the instructions to the letter." Somewhat jokingly he ends, "May the Force be with you."

That night before going to bed, I open the envelope.

****

BEWARE OF IMPENDING FORCES

There are times when things go bad for individuals we care about. These are the injustices of life. These are the times that try our souls. These are the times we get confused, depressed, disgusted...

We must be ever mindful to leave all punishment to the Force. However, to help marshal the positive forces that will ultimately combat all negative forces, I present to you the following prayer to fight negative forces. Consider this prayer a weapon that is spiritually nuclear. At a minimum, say the prayer three consecutive times with conviction and determination every morning and every evening in times of need. Insert the name of your loved one in the blank space provided.

Omnipotent One:
Surround_____with abundant love and care. Command the angels to attend in Your name. Crush, defeat, nullify, undo, reverse, obliterate, destroy, discredit, redeem all of the evil, the evil effects, the evil intentions, the evil purposes, the evil angels, the evil agents, the evil agencies, the evil influences against_____,we ask in Your name.

****

That night and the next morning I follow the prescribed program. By the third day I actually feel empowered. At least, I am doing something of value, something of purpose.

Within three months, the situation with my loved one resolved itself. The problem disappeared. It seems like magic.

I have shared the Beware of Impending Forces process with others of various faiths and they report similar results, a satisfaction with self, a belief the negative forces were actually combated and a blessed resolution of the problem. Furthermore, they tell me the prayer has even a greater effect when it is connected to their specific religion. They substitute, "we ask in Your name," with "we ask in the name of Jesus, or in the name of Buddha or Krishna." This has had such a profound impact on my life I unconditionally pass it on to those searching for an answer.

Tom Kergel knows more about religion than any person I know.

Dr. Wright, spiritual leader par excellence.

As a struggling reader, Dr. Wright's book, *From Cult to Cosmos*, was worth the time and effort to read and study.

144

–Chapter 17–

Redskins

—

1975

Promoted, Associate Professor, University of Virginia
(I learn football)

I was, waiting at the National Airport in Washington, D.C. for a flight on Piedmont to go home to Charlottesville. I was returning from a meeting in Dallas with the National Association for Retarded Citizens. The connections were not good. To pass the time I picked up a discarded *Washington Post*. As I skimmed over it an article in the sports section caught my eye. George Allen, Head Coach and General Manager of the Washington Redskins was considering retirement.

At this time in my professional career, I was developing a motivational theory based on my previous work experiences. My initial research indicated the theory was effective, even powerful. The theory was not only practical in motivating both children and adults it could also be used to predict group outcomes. I discovered I could apply the theory to beating the point spread beyond chance on professional football games. The Redskins were of particular interest to me because they were predictable. Simply put, the Redskins seldom beat the point spread when they were favored and usually beat the point spread when they were the underdog. When I applied my theory to understanding the motivational strategy of the opposing team, comparing it with the Redskin strategy and coupling it with the favorite/underdog historical trend, betting on a Redskins' game moved from a gamble to an investment opportunity.

The next morning I called Coach Allen's son George, Jr. George, Jr., had completed my class at the University of Virginia and knew of my theory and its predictability aspects.

"George. Jim Payne from your Rehab course last year. I read your dad is considering quitting. I don't want him to quit. I've studied him. I've studied the team. I can help him."

"He is not going to quit, Dr. Payne. He isn't even thinking about quitting. He is totally focused on this season. That news article was a farce."

"Good to hear. I understand you are in law school now. How is it going?"

"I'm buried but I'm loving it."

"Great. If you are ever over by the Education building, look me up."

"I will."

I hang up the phone and for some reason I wrote Coach Allen a letter and mailed it the next day.

January 3, 1977

George Allen
. . . .

Dear Coach Allen:

Over the holidays I read that you may be considering retiring as coach for the Washington Redskins. I phoned your son, George Allen Jr., to find that the newspapers had distorted the story and in fact you do not plan to leave. I was glad to hear this. You are one of the finest coaches in the game today.

In previous conversations with George Jr., I discovered you have a degree in psychology and know a great deal about motivational theory. About 5 years ago, I came across a motivational theory by Clare Graves that has virtually changed my life. I have researched his theory. I've developed a couple of assessment instruments that would allow a manager to better understand what motivates an individual: prayer, money, praise, fellowship, esteem, religion, stickers, etc. As George Jr. knows, I have applied the theory to football, studying coaches and coaching styles.

I have convinced myself I can predict football outcomes beyond chance. As a management tool I have used it in teaching counselors how to approach employers in order to secure jobs for the handicapped. I have even used it in my own Furniture Stripping Business.

I believe this system would be invaluable to a football coach. If you are ever in the Charlottesville area visiting your son I would welcome an opportunity to share this theory with you. I am particularly interested in you and the Redskins. According to the theory, your team is in a transitional stage of rapidly changing motivational needs. A team in transition may become confused, disorganized and disenchanted. On the other hand management may capitalize on the transition and revitalize the workers through what I now call Differential Management Theory.

I can be reached at my home, university office or furniture stripping shop.

Hope to meet you sometime,
James S. Payne

Within a couple of days I receive a response on Redskin stationary.

January 5, 1977

Dr. James S. Payne

....

Dear Jim:

I appreciated your letter on January 3, 1977.

I am very interested. If you could take time to visit Redskin Park, we will take care of your expenses. If you could arrive around 10 AM we could meet, have lunch and you could be on your way before the heavy traffic starts.

Let me hear from you.

Sincerely,
George Allen
Head Coach and General Manager

At this time we were experiencing some of the worst weather in the history of Virginia. I hesitated to set up an appointment because I felt I couldn't get to Washington as a result of the ice and snow. However on January 14th, I received a call from Bill Hickman, First Assistant to George Allen. Bill asked me if I had received Coach Allen's letter. When I responded that I had, he wanted to know why I hadn't called or written. I explained about the weather and he quickly assured me that Coach Allen was serious. He wanted to see me soon regardless of the weather conditions. He then connected me with Coach Allen and he explained he would like to talk with me personally, at my earliest convenience. We set up an appointment January 17. Before hanging up Coach Allen said, "Be here at nine and plan to spend the day."

On January 17th, I drove to Redskin Park. I was a little behind schedule so I stopped at the Mobil Station in Centerville, and phoned Coach Allen's secretary to tell her I was running a little late. One of the service attendants overheard me. After I hung up, he asked if I was going to see Coach Allen. I said yes, and he replied, "You must be one of the luckiest guys in the world."

Later I told the story to Allen while we were eating lunch at the Marriott and he gave me an autographed picture to return to the filling station attendant. It read, "To our friends at Mobil."

It was about six degrees above zero as I pull into the parking lot and parked in a Visitor's slot. Snow covers the ground but the parking area, containing less than a dozen cars, has been plowed clean.

Redskin Park, a few miles from Dulles Airport, is located in a yet to be developed industrial area. I felt I was in the country, far from any major business center. The wind whistled around my body and the short distance I walked from my car to the door left my hands and nose cold. I was entering a multimillion-dollar football training complex. The two story building contained a multitude of offices, meeting rooms, a weight room, locker room, equipment room, medical room, and heaven knows what other. It reminded me of a military building, big and bulky.

The building sits adjacent to two football practice fields, one covered with artificial turf, the other with natural grass. A half a dozen observation towers sprout up from the ground resembling the oil rigs you see in Western movies.

I enter the building to find stairs leading upward. As I climb, I am surrounded on both sides by large abundant pictures of football scenes, and plaques. At the top of the stairs is the trophy case. I turn right and enter the secretary's office. She snaps up to greet me and quickly directs me into Coach Allen's office.

On top of a large executive mahogany desk in place of a name plate is a black sign with gold letters shouting, "No One Ever Drowned In Sweat." I take a look at the room. A brown leather couch. Its back against the wall, two matching leather chairs, a coffee table is proudly displaying a Redskin football helmet. A bar with matching mahogany cabinets, sink and a refrigerator. In front of Coach Allen's desk are two additional leather chairs. Coach Allen's chair is an executive high back. Behind the massive desk is a window that overlooks the practice fields. Below the window a mahogany credenza displaying pictures of the Coach's family and dignitaries.

When Coach Allen enters - bigger than life, just under six feet tall wearing a white short-sleeve sport shirt with a Redskin logo. His face is nicely tanned with full eyebrows that resemble those of a handsome movie star. Newspapers report he is in his mid-fifties and uncomplimentary articles make fun of his hair, indicating, that Grecian Formula hides the gray. I find his hair to be immaculately, razor trimmed, if however, he uses Brillcream advertised as "a little dab will do ya," he uses two dabs. His brown eyes have a slight squint to them. As he grabs my hand I can tell he is a fine physical specimen.

"Jim. Sit. My son has told me much about you. I'd like to take your class. He said it is the best."

"Thanks."

Coach Allen moves to his rightful place behind the desk, sits, leans back, puts both hands behind his head and says, "I want you to teach me your Differential Management Theory."

"Fine. When would you like to do it?"

"Now."

"Now? You mean right now?"

"Yeah. Right now."

"It's involved. It takes time."

"Didn't Bill tell you to plan to stay the day?"

"Yeah. but…"

Coach Allen cuts me off and says "I've blocked off the entire day. Let's get started." Without notes or visual aides I begin with the history of how I got interested in the theory. Coach Allen took out a pad from the top desk drawer. Periodically, he would jot things down. By noon we were into the basics of the theory. Suddenly, we were interrupted by a buzzer. Allen punched a button, "Yes."

Over the speaker, "John is here for lunch."

"Thanks," Coach Allen gets up, "Let's go to lunch."

He leads me down the steps to the parking lot where his chauffeur, a good sized beefy guy, stands beside the opened rear door of a white Lincoln Continental limousine. Allen steps aside, motions for me to get in and Allen slides in next to me. We head toward the Marriott at Dulles. On the way, Coach Allen tells John to slow down, and points to where a dozen or so birds are frozen in the water.

"A tragedy. All of them frozen to death."

I nod but say nothing.

"Two years ago I was in Egypt and witnessed loggers demolishing trees," Allen turns to me. "This huge tree that existed years before the Birth of Christ. When that tree fell a part of me fell."

I lowered my head, and nodded to indicate I understood.

After a quick lunch we came out and a guy in a car passed us with long hair, a hippy looking character, wearing a Dallas Cowboy stocking cap. George hit his hand on the hood of the car and in a loud joking voice yelled, "Hey, where can I get a hat like that?"

The guy was startled, jumped a little and the three of us laughed. The guy had no clue who had hit his hood.

When he returned to his office I witnessed a different person. Allen was getting the hang of the theory. Instead of being silent as he had been during our morning session, he would stop me from time to time and read something to me, from a letter or off of a plaque. He never asked any questions but his contributions supported and reinforced the theoretical concept I was referring to. He was getting it. He could identify with my theory. He could relate to it. At times he paced the floor while I continued to teach and instruct. At times his excitement turned to anxiety. When he read words to me, he would point to each as he read. Often, he omitted words or inserted words that weren't present. He couldn't read any better than I could and this made me comfortable and increasingly confident. I began to wrap it up at around 8 p.m.

"Jim. My son was right. Your theory is brilliant. I want you to teach it to my staff. Can you come tomorrow?"

I was stunned. I couldn't believe it. "We are still on break at the university. I can come any time."

"Tomorrow it is then. Be here by 9 o'clock. We will meet in my conference room. Plan for thirty. Bring visuals if you want. My son tells me you use videos. We have all the equipment you need."

Allen showed me to the door. Then suddenly, he turned to the bar to open an upper cabinet, inside, were small boxes of Sun-Maid raisons, stacked neatly. There must have been over hundred boxes. He handed me two then opened the refrigerator and pulled out half a pint of milk and gave it to me without comment. He patted me on the back as I left his office. I didn't get two steps out of his office when he called to me.

"Wait a minute."

I walk back in to his office. He was at his desk scribbling something down. He handed me a note.

January 17, 1976

To Jim:
1.   How to get everyone ready each day to win?
2.   How to improve in the off-season?
3.   How to avoid let down when we are favored?
4.   How to improve practice?
5.   What do we need most to win our Division?
6.   How can you help us most in the least possible time?

George Allen

Notice, he dated the note 1976, not 77, which it was.

At 8:30 a.m. on the 18th I arrive and set up my equipment in the conference room. By 9 a.m. the room is packed.

The large mahogany conference table seated six on each side and one at each end. An additional sixteen chairs lined the walls. A portable movie screen was positioned at a forty-five degree angle for the use of my overhead projector. Immediately behind me was a jumbo TV screen hooked to a VCR to accommodate my tapes. For six hours, without a break - which included a working lunch - I let them have it, Differential Management Theory. No one ever left the group. Everyone took notes. During the final hour we discussed specific Redskin situations. Allen thanked me, dismissed the staff, and the two of us retired to his office. Before I could sit down he shocked me, "I need you to come February 14, Jim. I want to introduce you to the players. Eventually you need to interview each player and draw up a motivational profile following your Differential Management Theory. Draw up the profiles as you would for any employee and I'll show you how to apply it to professional football."

Before I could respond he retrieved another two boxes of raisons and a half pint of milk. Just as I was leaving he said to wait a minute. He went to his desk, pulled out a sheet of paper as before and with a felt pen wrote:

Jim
1.   What is our problem?
2.   How about 1977?
3.   Estimate how you can help?
4.   Cost?
5.   Time?
6.   When?
7.   New players?

George

He handed me the note and said, "Respond to these by written letter before the end of the month."

A few days later, I called to inform Coach Allen's secretary that I would be returning February 14th. She mentioned I was to stay with the players for four days and asked if she should make overnight reservations. I explained I could only stay two days, the 14th and 15th. She would take care of it she said.

On January 24th I responded to the seven questions.

January 24, 1977
George Allen
. . . .

Dear Coach Allen:

Needless to say I very much appreciated the opportunity to share my ideas pertaining to Differential Management with you and your staff. I was particularly impressed with the interest shown and the openness conveyed. I returned to Charlottesville with a new perspective on your problems as they relate to motivating and inspiring the people that surround you. My mind was firing ever so fast and I am more confident than ever that Differential Management, when conscientiously applied to football, will in fact assist in winning games.

I plan to return February 14th to pursue this matter in more detail; however, when called to notify your secretary, she indicated you might be expecting me to stay several days. After reviewing my schedule, the best I can do at this time is to arrive early on the 14th and stay two nights.

You asked me to respond to several questions. Here is a brief reply. Sometime in the near future we can discuss the items more fully.

1. What is our (Redskin) problem?

One basic problem is; man for man you probably have less talent than most of the teams you play. The solution to that problem is better recruiting. At the same time, manage existing players in such a way that they will work as a unit and perform beyond each players' single ability. The performance of the team as a whole is more than the sum of each individual player's ability. Up to this time you have done admirably. You literally led the Redskins to victory over teams with more talented players. The problem this year is that, your players have grown psychologically and their motivational needs and expectations have changed.

By determining each player's motivational needs and by slightly altering management strategies to meet these needs, it is possible not only to motivate the players to perform beyond their single abilities but it is equally possible to inspire a nucleus of players to carry you to the Super Bowl.

2. How about 1977?

There is no reason why you cannot incorporate Differential Management into your preparation immediately. It is not drastically different from your present approach – it is a refinement, a concise and precise refinement.

3. Estimate how I can help?

You know the theory well enough to apply it once you know how each player prefers to be motivated. First, decide how much to involve your coaching staff. If you decide to get your coaching staff up to speed it will be necessary for me to work up motivational profiles on them and determine their specific coaching styles. Whether or not you involve the coaching staff I will need to know the players and observe firsthand how they are handled. It is imperative we carefully decide how you explain my presence. Also, I need to discuss with you in detail my role with the players. All management and inspiration must come from you and your coaches. In order for the system to work, I can only advise. I cannot tell you how to coach. The coaches and players must trust me but they must not expect magic. Also, when I suggest a strategy you must determine if it is appropriate and advisable. What will take time is meeting with each player to identify appropriate coaching techniques and creating motivational profiles.

4. Cost?

How much you involve the coaching staff will affect the cost. I insist on being placed on an incentive plan i.e., bonuses set for reaching the playoffs, reaching the Super Bowl, and winning the Super Bowl. I am in this to demonstrate Differential Management can win ball games. I will learn a lot and it will be fun but Differential Management is a serious business. When misused it could injure an organization, but when placed in competent hands, it is powerful.

5. Time?

I am available 1 to 2 days a week beginning the middle of March. When I meet with you I will present a recommended schedule.

6. When?

NOW – I want to begin meeting with the players immediately.

7. New players?

I definitely want to talk with the new players individually and share my reactions. I cannot evaluate their football ability but I will be able to advise you how they can best be managed and motivated.

George, I am excited as a new high school student. I hope we can get together. I know I can learn a great deal from you. In return, I am confident my ideas, knowledge and concerns will be of benefit to the Redskins.

See you on the 14th,

Jim

P.S. It is not wise to cut butter with a chain saw. Differential Management is evolutionary rather than revolutionary. Differential Management can blend into your present motivational system, supplement and complement.

After some back and forth calls with Allen's secretary I ended up in front of the Marriott at Dulles on the evening of February 13th. Carrying a brief case and a small bag. I arrived at the front desk. "Reservations for Payne."

The gentleman thumbed through a series of papers, "Professor Payne?"

"Yes."

He quickly responded. "Redskins?"

I nodded and he said, "follow me."

I was escorted to the far end of the counter where he explained that everything was paid for - all I needed to do was sign. I was given a key for room 125, a regular room, nothing special. But I must admit, everywhere I went people seemed to be staring at me.

Just before 8:00 a.m., the next morning I met Bill Hickman in the lobby. We went directly to the restaurant and waited for Coach Allen. Bill was a graduate from the University of Virginia, so we talked about Thomas Jefferson, the Rotunda, and the controversial honor code. Soon, George entered, shook my hand, and we ordered breakfast. He explained there would be about 14 players coming in - either new, injured reserve, or had been injured during the last part of the season. Three individuals would be making presentations before the group. One person would deal with weights, another on stretching the muscles, and I would talk on motivation. About this time we were joined by Lou, the weight lifting instructor, a beautiful man, deeply tanned, light hair, and possibly, late 40's, maybe early 50's. His suit was all leather. I would estimate over $1,000.00 worth. He wore a ring with two diamonds, each the size of my little finger nail. Later, I found out he was the U.S. Olympic Weight Lifting Champion and presently held a world's record set at the age of 36 or 37.

Shortly after I was introduced to Lou, Jim Curzi joined us. Apparently Jim joined the Redskins full time as a stretch and flex coach. We decided to give short introductory talks to the players, after which the players would be divided in half, one half going to Lou and the other to Jim. A player would be rotated out of these groups to me for a 30 to 45 minute interview.

We left the Marriott and went to Redskin Park. I went with Bill Hickman upstairs while George, Lou, and Jim went downstairs. Suddenly, in came Coach Allen, dressed in burgundy from head to toe - a Redskins cap, a windbreaker with matching pants, a gold stripe down each leg and his shoes were his regular athletic shoes, black leather, low cut with white laces. George psychologically towered over me. He murmured something then asked, "Do you think we ought to put you in uniform?"

I responded, "Whatever you think."

He turned to ask Bill. Bill replied, "I don't know, what do you think?"

I looked at Coach. "If you want me to I will be glad to change." He was probably concerned how I would come across to the players. Finally he pulled open his windbreaker and said, "Well, maybe you could wear a Redskins tee shirt like this one."

"Look, I will do whatever you want, -- but look at you, Redskins cap, all in burgundy, striped trousers, athletic shoes – I'll never look like you. I'm bald and bearded."

I looked at myself - gray pants bought at Kmart, a red sweater with a small hole in the left sleeve, and a blue Woolco blazer.

Suddenly, in popped Lou all in white, the Olympic insignia over his heart, a red, white and blue stripe running up and down each pant leg, blue tennis shoes. Had I had homosexual tendencies I would have jumped all over his body. I couldn't believe my eyes. I looked at Bill and Bill just grinned. Next, in came Jim all in cardinal red, from head to toe, a rainbow running up and down each leg. His tennis shoes were bright red. I couldn't contain myself. I burst into a big belly laugh and George laughed and said, "What the hell, come on."

The three of us followed George Allen into the lecture room. The players were seated, some quiet, some joking with each other.

Pictures of football scenes were plastered at random all over the walls. At the front was a large chalkboard with x's and o's, revealing football plays. An American flag stood in the left corner and a Redskins flag in the right corner. Above the chalkboard, in big bold print, a sign read, WHAT WE DO IN THE OFF SEASON DETERMINES WHAT WE ACHIEVE DURING THE REGULAR SEASON.

The room was half-filled with players. All wore white tee shirts and white boxer shorts. No crew cuts, no shaved heads. It was the 70's when men's hair had to be fashionable. A disgusting amount of hair covered their legs and arms. Later I found they had hair on their backs as well. I was intimidated by their bulk; their arms were more muscular than my legs.

George stood before the players and welcomed them to a new season. He explained that he had invited three men to help Redskins win games. The three of us were introduced and I began. For five or so minutes I explained why I thought games were won and lost on the sidelines, in the heads of players. Obviously you have to be physically in shape and know football, but mental preparation makes champions.

After I finished, one player sitting on the front row remarked, "If you think you're so damn smart, why don't you help the University of Virginia football team?"

Everyone laughed. Allen smiled and shook his head. I retorted, "They are too smart. Smart people don't play good football."

Everyone laughed again.

I sat down and in charged Jim Curzi from the back of the room. He was holding a stick over his head like a javelin thrower. The stick looked like a broom handle with the straw bristles cut off. He put his butt on the floor in the front of the room and pointed to two players. "Jump on my back."

They looked at one another, shrugged their shoulders and jumped right on his back.

Sitting directly on the floor, his legs stretched out in front of him to form a V, down went his head and chest until his forehead was touching the floor between his legs. The two players got up. Jim continued to lie on the floor, doubled over, flat as a pancake. I thought he was dead. I'm sure the two players thought they had hurt him, but as they leaned over to get a better look, Jim jumped straight up into the air and came down on his feet, and shouting, "I taught Terry Metcalf how to do that. That's why he'll never get hurt, never have a hamstring problem."

He then proceeded to demonstrate more elasticity. I knew if that wooden stick was the key to flexibility, I wanted to get one.

Next, Lou presented. As a distinguished middle-aged man he talked about the importance of strength and weight lifting. His theme was "Athletes Retire Too Soon." Within thirty seconds, he had the team eating every word.

I was beginning to wonder what the hell I was doing there. I felt a little out of my class. I'm

158

certain some of the players felt the same.

For two days, I interviewed players. Over the next two months, I interviewed thirty more. It took me about six different trips to complete the process.

After interviewing about a dozen players I responded to the questions Allen had given me on January 17th, at our first meeting.

1. How to get everyone ready every day? – To win? Use tempo. Try not to get everyone up all the time. If you get some players up too soon, they run out of psychological steam and let down.

2. How to improve in the off season? Integrate football related activities with off season programs. Definitely set priorities as to essentials (i.e., weights, physical therapy, etc.) and supplement essential activities with activities that meet the psychological interests and needs of the various players. For instance, Traditional players may wish to get involved in learning more about martial arts. Cognitive players may wish to get involved in one-on-one games like handball, squash, or tennis. Cerebral players may wish to be exposed to psychocybernetics. Psychocybernetics, for Cerebral players, improve concentration, assist in playing more heads up football, and also train them to fumble less and drop fewer balls.

3. How to avoid let down when we are favored? I love to bet against the Redskins when they are favored. They seldom beat the point spread. I suggest you approach each game with a different twist. Don't use the same old motivational tactics. For example, when you play Seattle or the Jets try to win through mechanics. Don't try to pump the players up. If you have to pump the players up emotionally to beat these teams, it will take off some of the psychological edge from future games. When you play St. Louis, get with some of your Cerebral players and ask them for some creative surprise plays. Developing plays will involve them, help them become thinking players, and a different breed from responding players. When you play the Dallas Cowboys, you will probably be in the game up to the very end. The

end gets agonizing.

I would suggest you not tell your team to explode or out-hit Dallas. The Redskins are older, not as physical. The veterans can probably stay with them for about three quarters, but the fourth quarter they weaken. With Dallas substitute a lot. You must develop a strategy of darting and dashing. Try to make the Dallas Cowboys try to outguess you. Use the "shot gun" offense every fifth time against them. Sometimes on defense don't rush at all, or do a staggered or delayed rush. At half time, if the Cowboys are ahead, they will still be trying to outguess you. This will be to your advantage. Get Dallas thinking. It will throw them off guard and you can beat their tails off.

Watch out for the New York Giants. Unless you change your motivational tactics they will beat you at least once this year, if not twice. When you play the Giants play all your players and keep them fresh. You stand a better chance of beating the Giants if you play the second team rather than the first team. The first team will go in confident, but not motivated. The less experienced second team, will be highly motivated. By interweaving both teams you should be able to beat them easily. The Giants have figured out the Redskins. They know exactly how you plan the game. They know exactly what you tell the players before the game and during half time. If you remain predictable, they're going to be tough to beat if not impossible to beat.

4. How to improve practice? With some of your more intellectually slow players I recommend a remedial type of teaching involving videotapes and imitation. For the other players I would use an inquiry method rather than a stimulus method. Eliminate dead time in your schedule. Practice how the team should conduct themselves on the sidelines. Actually, video tape players on the sidelines and show them what they do and explain to them what they should do. Even cover how they stand for the National Anthem.

5. What do we need most to win our Division? Review numbers 2, 3, and 4 carefully. Initiate a Differential Managing system, a type of precision management effective

in motivating and inspiring players. Create a mindset of winning the Super Bowl; put less emphasis on the Division.

6. How can you help us most in the least possible time? Teach the management techniques to your staff. It would take three days of introduction one day of interviewing, one day to report findings to you and one day to discuss all the findings with the staff. It might be faster and more efficient for you to show your staff what to do. At this point in time they have tactics and strategies on their mind, not psychological jiujitsu.

As May was coming to a close, I wrote the following:

May 25, 1977
George Allen
....

Dear Coach
Allen:

I am in the process of completing my motivational and management review of the Redskins. I plan to submit a motivational profile for each player I interviewed by the second week of June. I have been pressured for time. However, I have analyzed my notes and thoughts about alternatives. I am writing this letter to share with you my general thoughts on motivation and management.

You have consistently leveled with me, encouraging me to be straight-forward and critical. In fact during our last discussion, you specifically said to me, "Don't be afraid to be critical." George, if I had heard or seen anything to be overly critical about, I would not have hesitated to tell you. The truth is your players as a whole respect you and are willing to sacrifice for you. This is the ultimate achievement of "manage." After interviewing over thirty players, talking with you and your staff, observing you operate from time to time, I believe you are a winner as a football coach. You would be a winner selling hotdogs. You have all the ingredients of a winner.

Yet without some alteration in you present managerial style you will never be a Super Bowl champion. You are operating at one psychological level while the majority of your players are operating at another.

In my first letter to you, January 3, 1977, I mentioned the team was in a transitional stage of rapidly changing motivational needs. Your players are changing, yet your coaching strategies have basically remained unchanged. You will continue to win because you have excellent management hygiene, i.e., effective rules and charts, good money, a sound religious base, and heated competitiveness, but in my opinion you will not be a Super Bowl champion because you view these hygiene factors as motivational.

Lou may help your team become stronger, and Jim may help your team to be more flexible and agile, but only you can assist the team in becoming more motivated. I wonder if you have the time, knowledge, or expertise to gain that motivational edge. To be "the" champion, you need something extra. That something extra can be brought about through differential-precision management.

If in fact the head slap is taken away from the defensive unit or at least minimized as an effective defensive weapon, you will need to stimulate your offensive unit to new heights. At present, you win through good sound defense. But the next Super Bowl champion will have an explosive offense. Your veteran defensive players, as a whole, differ psychologically from your offensive players. Your offense basically just goes through the motions, they are not what I call motivated players, and they are far from being inspired players. Your defensive players give it all they have. Too bad they don't have the physical qualities to compliment their psychological effort.

To win the Super Bowl you will have to do a better job motivating the offense. This means a different approach from the one you use. It means a change in the daily schedule, a change in grouping (cluster management), and significant alterations in your present motivational terminology. Turn to a few of your key offensive members and meet with them for the explicit purpose of soliciting their ideas. They need a stake in the game to feel they are a part of the team that makes important decisions. Your three Cerebral offensive players need to believe they are important to the team, not only offensive stars, but thinking, calculating partners. This will position their mental framework as inspired players. Not all of your players want to be empathically involved or a part of the decision making process. Your Traditional players want to be told what to do and cheered on. Your Cognitive players want to be shown, reasoned with and patted on the back. Only the Cerebral players feel the need to be partners.

Also, you have some players that need someone to talk to occasionally. You can't always be available to all the players all the time. A staff confidant would help a few of the players. You might want to use Skinner.

A few players have heard you say the same things over and over again and consequently get bored. A phrase like, "This may well be the most important game of your career" is no longer motivating to these players. Ease off some of these phrases, or have someone teach these bored players how to cope with your repetitious statements.

George, in the locker room you have a sign showing a thumb and forefinger almost touching with a caption, "The difference between winning and losing is this much." Change it to read, "The difference between winning and being the best is this much." Between the thumb and forefinger insert "motivation makes the difference."

I will have the individual motivational profiles available for you whenever you are ready.

Jim

At Allen's request I reported to Redskin Park on June 10th. I was greeted by Coach Allen's secretary who promptly showed me an article from *The Washington Star* entitled "Allen hires a Psychiatrist to Probe Those Upset Loses." She asked if I had seen the article. I had not. She suggested I read the article before meeting with the Coach.

I sat in the chair next to her desk. Parts of the article caught my attention. I read:
(Allen) quickly added a new dimension to the Redskin's drive to the Super Bowl for the upcoming season.

Normally this would entail trading what the Redskins have left for the future for immediate help. However, this time Allen's first aid program took an entirely new direction. He chose a psychiatrist. He brought in help to probe the minds of players and coaches. Psychiatric assistance is not a new sports development, but it is new to the Redskins. It was an astonishingly radical departure from Allen's first six seasons, when he relied exclusively on a checkbook to sign the most expensive players, guile and his own know-how to sail them over troubled waters.

ALLEN'S MOVE in the field of psychiatry must be interpreted as an admission that he is not the perfect answer man, not the quintessential coach he sometimes credits himself as being, that he is mortal.

The mission of the psychiatrist was to discover why the Redskins often fail to beat teams they are supposed to beat. The most recent example of this heretofore unexplained letdown which has plagued Allen and disgusted fans was last November's shocking loss to the winless Giants.

. . . .

The more Allen thought about the past and projected the 1977 schedule, the more he became convinced that he should turn his puzzling disappointments over to a shrink who might be able to solve the problem. Allen is so perplexed by the jinx the Redskins apparently have against so called pushover teams that he is not even confident his team can whip Tampa Bay next October. Tampa Bay was winless last season, its first in the National Football League.

THE FACT that a psychiatrist got behind the locked gates of Camp Allen is a big, hush-hush topic, surrounded by secrecy which would make the CIA envious.

However, some details have managed to slip through Allen's iron fence. There were several mass sessions as well as separate meetings with coaches and players. There were also a number of one-on-one meetings, but it was learned that the patients did not have to stretch out on a couch. Which is unusual, considering Allen's fanatic attention to detail.

"It was shocking what went on in there," one source told The Star. "Some people are still talking to themselves about it. It was real weird, some of the things brought up and discussed. I have never heard anything like it."

One veteran who has played well, often spectacularly, without artificial assistance of any kind, treated the whole bizarre sequence as a joke.
"The doctor asked me what motivates me to play so long," he said. "I told him money, what else, and if he didn't believe me he could ask my banker."

………

I struggled through the article several times and although, far from being a psychiatrist, I realized the article was about me. I kept going back to the statement about hiring a shrink. The word "shrink" didn't set well with me.

George stuck his head out of his office and commanded, "Get in here."

Before I could get through the doorway, George was already seated and launched, "Who did you talk to?"

"I didn't talk to anybody."

"Where did they get the information?"

"I have no idea. I don't think it was just one person."

George nodded, got up from his desk, went out to talk to his secretary. I could hear him but I couldn't makeout what he was were saying.

When he returned, he said, "I've got one hour. Go through each profile as fast as you can, alphabetically. Tell me everything."

I took out the profiles from my brief case and reported my thirty some findings as instructed. It took a little less than an hour.

"Let me make sure I've got it."

Much to my astonishment, George repeated everything I had told him about each player in detail. He did this without a note. He remembered and recalled the motivational findings and used the Differential Management terminology accurately and precisely. I was impressed. Really flabbergasted.

Again he reported to the secretary and returned giving me a 4" x 7," black, six ring notebook filled with blank pages that included index tabs.

"Condense each profile to one page. At the top of the page put the players name, last name first. Next, put the motivational type and a phrase indicating the specific motivational keys. Under that put a line graph indicating motivational tempo and intensity. Four lines: name, motivational type, key phrases and intensity graph. Follow this with a single space narrative I can use as a quick reference. Keep each profile to one page, one side only. Jim, I need this quick."

I walked out the door with two boxes of raisons and a half pint of milk and headed back to Charlottesville. That night I drafted the abbreviated profiles and the next morning they were neatly typed and inserted in the notebook as instructed. I called George's secretary and informed her that the profiles were ready. She put me on hold and the next thing I knew Allen was on the phone, "Great. Can you get them up here tomorrow?"

"I can."

"Bring it by noon. We'll have lunch."

The next day I delivered the profiles. At lunch Allen explained he didn't want any bad press and he didn't want any distractions.

"I am intrigued by your theory, Jim. I only wish I had known of it earlier. It is hard to teach an old dog new tricks but I get it. I'm not sure I can do it. From here on I'll contact you by phone. Feel free to call or send a letter if you come across something you think I should know or could possibly use. Do not" he repeated, "do not talk with the press or anyone else about this. This could become a big problem for me." He repeated with emphasis, "A big problem."

We returned to Redskin Park. I got out of the limo, went directly to my car and returned to Charlottesville.

During pre-season Coach Allen never called or wrote. An article did appear in the paper indicating Coach Allen had made at least one change. The article quoted Allen: "I never believed in giving them water because I felt it disrupted practice and it also helped improve their mental toughness. But in this type of weather they need it, they need fluids, so I've changed."

I photocopied the article, circled the "I've changed" and in long hand with a felt pen wrote:

George:

Alter, refine, innovate, surprise, variety. These are tickets to accelerating motivation.

Keep it up

Jim

During the first regular season game, the Giants beat the Redskins as I predicted. The Redskins won over the Falcons but failed to beat the point spread. On September 26th I wrote:

September 26, 1977
George Allen

. . . .

Dear Coach Allen:

Congratulations on your win over the Atlanta Falcons. In both the Giants and the Falcons games the Redskins were favored and in both games the Redskins failed to beat the point spread. In Charlottesville the Redskins were favored four points against the Giants and nine points against the Falcons. If you remember, in January I suggested the New York Giants would probably upset the Redskins if motivational alterations were not made. I also predicted St. Louis would beat the Redskins ditto. The key to beating St. Louis is to get your Cerebral players involved. Listen don't tell.

Jim

On September 29th Allen called me. He shared his concern about St. Louis and asked for suggestions. I explained I needed to look at player profiles and to call me Saturday morning.

On September 30th during breakfast, the phone rang. George Allen. He said I had ten minutes.

"Tell your defense that despite injuries they are playing great. What little bit they do today will not make the difference between winning and losing against St. Louis. Have them do their stretching, weights and jogging. Then tell them to go home and relax. Do not get them emotionally high too soon. Wait til Sunday to motivate them. Even then, keep it low key. "Meet with your offense separately out on the field. Have them sit while you stand. Tell them you are concerned.

166

Explain it's an important game and they know it. Tell them they are intelligent, experienced and know the Cardinals; they know what it will take to beat them. Tell them they need something different, a different wrinkle, a couple of new plays to catch the Cardinals off guard, to make them think, and while they think, we Redskins, will knock the hell out of them. You want them to talk. What do they think will give the Redskins a motivational edge? Break up into small groups while you are still on the field. Do not take them inside. The assistant coaches are not to lead the discussion, they are to listen and take notes. At the end of 20 minutes form a circle in the center of the field. Have each coach summarize the discussion. Then take a break. Retreat to your office and look over your notes. Select six to eight ideas to use. Practice them and go home. Do not come across as anxious or desperate. Seem concerned and sincere."

This terminated the telephone conversation.

On October 2nd, I watched TV. Washington dominated St. Louis, 24-14. Both defensively, offensively, and with special teams. They also got the breaks. I couldn't tell if Coach Allen had used my ideas; however, I did notice in one short instance that Allen was kneeling with two Cerebral players. They were holding a clipboard between them and the players were pointing to the clipboard. In the past it was always Allen pointing to the clipboard talking to the players. I honestly didn't know if Allen altered his approach, but I sure got excited when I saw the three of them talking while the players pointed.

I wrote the following letter on October 3rd:

October 3, 1977
George Allen
....
George:

Congratulations – whether you used some of my ideas or not it was an outstanding display of Redskin football. It was artistic the way you put it to the Cardinals.

George, you now have a perfect opportunity to capitalize in every way on motivating both the offense and defense for the rest of the season. DO NOT make the mistake of preparing for Tampa Bay by over working the veterans. Bring in fresh blood. It was a great win now capitalize on it by altering your management style and motivational

167

techniques. In order to win the Super Bowl (the thought that just crossed your mind is you must win the Divisional title first – I know you George, you are predictable – forget the Divisional title for just a moment) you must get your team thinking and involved.

What you do over the next four or five days in my opinion will set the tone for the entire season. Think season not one game at a time.

Cheer down. Beat Tampa Bay with young blood. Play the veterans sparingly. Play Tampa Bay as if it is just a job. When you beat Tampa Bay with young blood you will be in a prime position to destroy Dallas with a fresh, healthy team and an inspired confident offense. I know you only plan and believe in preparing for each game one at a time. This will be a tactical error and you will run out of steam by the time you get to Dallas and the Giants will be a disaster.

How you prepare for Tampa Bay will determine the season. Think low key, young blood and use the veterans sparingly.

Jim

On October 5th, I got a note from the departmental secretary indicating George Allen wanted me to call. I called immediately and talked with Bill Hickman, who informed me Coach Allen was in a meeting and would call me at 1:00. Promptly at 1:00 the phone rang and sure enough it was Coach Allen. He was elated, even jubilant. He couldn't sleep Sunday night or Monday night because of the Cardinal win. He did not ask me for advice on preparing for Tampa Bay as I had hoped. He talked excessively for a good 15-20 minutes. Before hanging up, he bragged that former President Nixon had called to congratulate him. He ended the conversation with, "Jim, I'd do anything, I'd fly Fidel Castro in here, if I thought it would help the Redskins win."

After the call, I feared he was so excited he would return to his old ways and drive his veterans in the ground while de-motivating the rookies.

On October 9th, I watched the Redskins beat Tampa 10-0. Coach Allen for the most part played typical Allen football: defense. The game looked sloppy and I was disappointed more substitutions weren't made.

He over played the veterans. It was a motivational blunder.

With 3 wins and 1 loss one would think the Redskins were in it but I sensed it was all over. George would try to motivate the team with old clichés like, "This is the most important game of your life" and "the team that wants it the most will win" and "no pain no gain." This kind of talk would make the veterans trudge forward and the rookies would be turned off.

On October 16th the veterans played their hearts out against Dallas but stumbled in the end. Not even I could help them the following week against the Giants. Back in January I told Coach Allen the Giants would beat the Redskins if the management and motivation techniques weren't altered. Sure enough the Giants beat the Redskins and now they were going to do it again.

On October 22, I received a call from Coach Allen. I believe he knew they would lose to the Giants. The call was short. I watched the game and the inevitable outcome.

He called ten months later. "Jim. George here. I need your help. Come to Los Angeles."

At the end of the '77 season Coach Allen was fired and accepted the position of Head Coach for the Los Angeles Rams. According to the papers, his leaving the Redskins was controversial. As was his hiring to coach the Rams.

"What's up?"

"Jim, I need an expert in understanding dissatisfied and unmotivated players. Come and work up motivational profiles on the Rams. I've got some ideas I know you'd be interested in. Come and work for me full time."

"Coach, I'm an Associate Professor, tenured, well on my way to earning full professorship. My wife is Academic Advisor for the Athletic Department here. We can't leave."

"I will double your salary. You can research your Differential Management system. Take a one-year leave of absence. Try it out."

"I don't know. I'm honored to be asked. But I don't think so. Not at this time. Thanks any way."

"Jim, talk with Ruth Ann. Give me a shot for one year. At least, think about it."

George hung up. I sat dumbfounded. Ruth Ann came home and I told her what had happened. For two days that was all we talked about. We decided to talk to my Chair, the person who hired me, and my direct boss. He explained that because of my publication record and being tenured, it wouldn't be that difficult to get a one-year leave. Ruth Ann knew I wanted to research my theory and was supportive. This was a once in a lifetime opportunity. On Saturday, August 12th, I drafted

a "request for leave" letter and took it to my secretary's home to be typed. I called the Chair

to inform him of my intention. He said to bring the letter Monday by noon.

On August 14th, I woke up, got dressed and all morning imagined wearing a Rams sports shirt, cap, pants, sweat socks and black leather athletic shoes with white laces. Just when I was ready to drop off the letter Ruth Ann called, "Honey, I'm on my way home. Don't go to the university yet."

Ruth Ann walks in the door, kisses me on the forehead and hands me the Monday, August 14th edition of the sports section of *The Washington Post*. In big bold letters it reads, RAMS FIRE ALLEN, subtitled Hiring Called Serious Error.

GEORGE ALLEN's
GAME PLAN for SUCCESS

SET GOALS...dedicate yourself to immediate and long range goals and sacrifice to reach them.

COMMITMENT...make a total commitment to achieve success...regardless of any adversity.

WORK HARD...talent alone is not enough. Only by hard work can you become a winner.

CONDITION...discipline yourself into superb physical and mental toughness.

TEAMWORK...work for team victory without the thought of individual reward.

ENTHUSIASM...be positive. Enjoy what you do and do it as well as you can.

IMPROVE...be better today than you were yesterday.

ALWAYS GIVE 110%...give more of yourself than you want.

George Allen

Coach Allen gave this to me along with raisins and milk after our meeting.

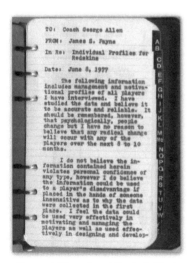

TO: Coach George Allen

FROM: James S. Payne

In Re: Individual Profiles for Redskins

Date: June 8, 1977

The following information includes management and motivational profiles of all players I have interviewed. I have studied the data and believe it to be accurate and reliable. It should be remembered, however, that psychologically, people change but I have no reason to believe that any radical change will occur with any of the players over the next 8 to 10 months.

I do not believe the information contained herein violates personal confidence of any type, however I do believe the information could be used to a player's disadvantage if placed in the hands of someone insensitive as to why the data were collected in the first place. I feel the data could be used very effectively in motivating and managing the players as well as used effectively in designing and develop-

George told me to put the individual player's profiles in this notebook.

The Washington Post **SPORTS**

MONDA

Rams Fire Allen

Hiring Called 'Serious Error'

LOS ANGELES — George Allen, who coached the Los Angeles Rams for the first two preseason games, has been fired and replaced by offensive coordinator Ray Malavasi, the team's owner, Carroll Rosenbloom announced last night.

Allen, hired to replace Chuck Knox as the Rams' coach last February, had lost both preseason games, 14-7 to New England in the opener and 17-0 to San Diego Saturday.

"It is my feeling that I have made a serious error in judgment in believ-

This article took the wind out of my sails.

171

–Chapter 18–
94-142

———

1975

Promoted, Associate Professor, University of Virginia
(I learn the litigation game)

By my tenth year at Virginia, I had published several books in special education and was fortunate that three were the largest selling texts in the field. The course Rehabilitation Techniques was voted the best lecture course several years in a row and I had served five years as chairperson of the Education Committee for the National Association for Retarded Citizens. I'm at my office and the phone rings, "Hello."

"Jim, this is Brian. We need your help."

Brian is the assistant to the director of the National Association for Retarded Citizens and he is the guy that makes everything happen.

"Sure, what do you need?"

"We need you to represent these parents from Richmond. Their child is severely involved and they want him removed from the public schools and placed in a residential setting."

"What! We've been spending all our time getting kids out of institutions and into the schools. Are these parents unaware of what's going on?"

"Jim, the parents believe the school setting is not safe. Their kid needs twenty-four hour care. They want him in a residential setting with close medical supervision."

"Brian, since 94-142 passed, there are cases all over the country demanding children be released from residential sites and placed in public school settings regardless of the condition or situation. I can't imagine anyone wanting their child taken out of a school and put in an institution."

Public Law 94-142, passed in 1975, states that all children are entitled to an appropriate education in the least restricted environment. Court case after court case have always and continuously favor removing the child from an institutional setting and placing them in the least restricted setting which is a public school.

"Brian, this isn't a case NARC should represent. It goes counter to what we stand for. I advise, don't take this on."

Brian returns a weak response, "Ok."

An hour later the phone rings, "Hello."

"Jim," Brian again, "the director needs your help on this one. We are being pressured to represent this case. You have to help."

"Brian, this goes against everything we have worked and fought for, 94-142 goes beyond a single case, 94-142 is for the greater good. For the first time, individuals with special needs become real players and not second class citizens. This is our ticket to inclusion."

"I know. I know. But the director…"

"You tell the director to get away from this thing, fast. Don't touch it with a ten-foot pole. NARC shouldn't get involved and I won't get involved."

Another weak, "Ok."

An hour later the phone rings, "Hello."

"Jim," it's the director, "we have called all over the country and we can't get anyone to take this on. Look, I'm just asking you to testify in the parents behalf. We know they can't win. We know they shouldn't win but they are good people. Just go and testify. I need a favor. I just want you to get them off my back. You don't have to observe the child or visit the parents, just show up and testify. I'm desperate. I don't have anywhere else to turn."

"Look, I'll take it on but at least I need to talk to the parents to warn them they can't win. I'll do it but my heart isn't in it nor should yours be."

"I know. I know. I'll have Brian call and give you the details. Thanks, we owe you one."

Brian calls and gives me the parents' names, some diagnostic information about the child and a run down on the case. I call the parents to set up an appointment to meet with them. Two days later, I drive to Richmond to meet with the parents in their home.

They live in a very nice part of town. I park in the driveway, ring the doorbell to be warmly greeted by the mother. The house is nicely furnished but I couldn't help notice in places the baseboard is scuffed up and in a couple of places there are actual holes in the drywall just above the baseboard.

I am invited into the kitchen for a cup of coffee. I sit at the kitchen table adorned with elegant placemats and a beautiful set of salt and pepper shakers. While the mother gets my coffee, I notice a dent at the bottom of the stainless steel refrigerator door that looks like it could have been hit with a sledge hammer.

While the mother and I have coffee, I learn the child, David, was diagnosed at birth as having the condition of severe/profound mental retardation and, although medicated, still has convulsive outbursts that are so violent neither the mother nor the father can control. David is in third grade and according to the mother, the teachers, aides, and the school in general, are doing the best they can but she is scared to death David might have a seizure one day that will be so violent he will do damage to himself or others that could be fatal.

As I am casually examining, with my eyes, some of the damage done by David's seizures, the father comes home. I immediately realize these parents aren't kooks. They know what they are doing, they are smart, informed and don't have anything against the school. They just want their son in a safe place.

I had originally planned to meet the parents face to face and explain they didn't really have much of a case but I'd do what I could to represent them. After meeting the parents and observing some of the damage in the home, I never mentioned anything about the case being difficult, if not impossible, to win. I told them in order for me to help, I'd need to see David both in the home and in the school. Preferably, I'd like to see him when he gets up, follow him through the day, and observe him as he goes to bed.

Arrangements were made for me to observe him Monday. In the meantime, the parents provided me with David's medical and educational records, various documents and a journal of the number and types of seizures experienced over the past years. As I examine the records, the school bus pulls up to let David off.

The bus is a typical small special education bus, yellow, that seats ten to fifteen students. I can see half a dozen students in the bus all wearing helmets and all slumped forward as if asleep.

The bus stopped. None of the students looked up, let alone looked out the window. The door opened and an adult helped David get out of the bus while the father took him by the arm and led him into the house. David moved as if he were in a daze or partial sleep. As David and the father passed me, I greeted him with a 'hello' that resulted in no response whatsoever. The mother turned to me and explained that he's medicated. David is taken to the bedroom to lie down. I gather up all the records and, as gracefully as I can, say goodbye and leave.

As I drive back to Charlottesville, I think how terrified David's parents must be and, at the same time, I admire and respect the school district for providing the best services they can.

I arrive at the house at 6:00 a.m. The mother and father are dressed. David is still in bed. At 6:30 the alarm goes off. David stirs and rolls over as if to go back to sleep. The father gently encourages David to get up. He is in pajamas with Disney characters on both the matching top and bottom. David is mobile but has touches of a cerebral palsied gait. He doesn't need a walker but as he walks, he lunges back and forth flopping each foot forward. He constantly drools. As he clumsily fumbles through freshening up, brushing teeth and getting dressed, his father remains close by to give assistance when needed.

The two go downstairs to the kitchen. The mother has prepared the four of us cereal with fruit, toast and orange juice. David can feed himself but he is sloppy. He is nonverbal but, on occasion, grunts or groans indicating sounds of approval when asked if he likes his cereal. In the middle of breakfast, the mother puts a pill in David's mouth. He downs it with a swallow of orange juice which merits a smile. After breakfast, he brushes his teeth again, and his dad helmets him before going out the door. His helmet is white and resembles a beat up football helmet of the 50s, no faceguard.

The bus arrives at 7:15. He joins five school mates. All special needs and all helmeted. Of the six, two are in wheelchairs and two use walkers. The bus arrives at the school at 7:45. Teachers and aides assist each student as they get off the bus. I am impressed with the care, compassion, and friendliness of each. They obviously care about each child as if their own.

The classroom is a typical classroom but is equipped like a first grade classroom. It is bright in color with an abundance of pictures and posters displaying cartoon characters and sports figures. The books scattered around are preschool books. There are tables and chairs to work from, no desks as would be found in a regular third grade classroom. There is a teacher and two aides for four children. A nurse comes in regularly with medication. She knows what she is doing and each

177

student knows when the medication is for them by going to her before their name is called.

The students are happy, well cared for and the educational practices are appropriate and carried out most professionally. Any parent would be proud to have their child served in this school by these professionals.

Unknown to me, today we are going on a field trip to the mall to visit Santa Claus. David's class and one other special education class is going. It takes some time to get everyone bundled up and on the bus. We pull up at the front door of the mall a little before 11:00. There is one adult for each child. Nine children, nine adults and me. After some maneuvering with the two children in wheelchairs, the nineteen of us stagger down the hall. We turn left and seventy-five yards straight down the end of the hall sits Santa Claus in a big chair flanked by two female elves decked out in red and white. Santa's area is festive with a giant decorated tree, garlands hang everywhere, and lots of boxes wrapped in dazzling colors. Background music of Jinglebells faintly fills the air.

As we struggle forward, I see a surprised look on Santa's face that turns to shock and by the time we arrive, there's a sign placed on his chair, 'Gone to Lunch.' He's not at lunch, this upsets me but I notice the adults are not affected and David's teacher asks the elves to help. The elves are both young and more than willing to help. One elf sits in Santa's chair while the other elf helps each child move forward and places the children one by one in the lap of Santa's substitute. Santa's replacement is great. She asks each kid what they want for Christmas. If the child is nonverbal, she runs off obvious possibilities to be responded with a nod or grunt. The children are ecstatic and joyful. We take picture after picture and as we leave the area, I couldn't help but think how glad I was that Santa left. The elves were better and the kids had a wonderful time.

We eat at the Food Court while passersby stare at us. During lunch each child in David's class is given their meds and as we get on the bus, three fall asleep including David. The medication knocked them out.

At the end of the school day, the vigilant care of getting everyone on the bus to go home was repeated. David is drowsy and is the first to get off. Greeted by his dad, he is escorted upstairs to rest before dinner.

The four of us eat dinner in the kitchen. David eats only with a spoon and is messy. As he finishes he and his dad go watch television while his mother cleans up. The news is on. David doesn't pay much attention. He rocks back and forth while drool runs out of his open mouth. The mother comes in and we switch to a sitcom that David is familiar with. I can tell he is following the story lines because he laughs, often times, before we do. At 9:30, his mom starts getting him ready for bed. Before going to bed he is medicated again, this time by the father. As David lays down, the mother reads to him. Within minutes he is asleep.

I thank the parents for letting me visit. I return to Charlottesville to try to figure out what to do next.

I have two exceptionally bright graduate students, Cecil Mercer and Jim Patton. I explain the predicament to them and ask for their help. Not only are they bright, they are problem solvers and they have lots of energy. They love life and are dedicated to helping special needs children and adults. The two agree to help.

"I'll contact our attorney and find out what she knows. I'll also get as much information about the judge as I can. You guys go to the law school and just find out the basics. We are not lawyers but we need to know how things work. We need to know something about the law."

They leave and over the following week, I find out our attorney just graduated and this is her first case. The judge is well known and highly respected. He was the judge that rendered the decision to bus children during desegregation. Decisions on a couple of other cases indicated in favor of the underdog. The judge is stern yet compassionate. By a reliable source he was described to me as a wise, no-nonsense, grandfather type of judge.

Jim and Cecil return. Jim leads, "Judges interpret the law. Justice is what a judge determines it is. Justice is the decision that stems from the courtroom."

Jim continues, "Judges are human. As early as the 16th century, Montaigne indicated a judge's mood or humor was often reflected in the decision. Attorneys have been trained in psychology and their job is to influence the judge to make a decision in their favor."

Changing the subject, Cecil says, "I read this paper by Brodsky. He describes the cross-examination process to be similar to Wonder Woman being attacked by enemies firing bullets. She moves her wrists with lightning speed so her bracelets deflect each of the bullets as they zing back at the assailant or harmlessly fall to the ground. In this case you are Wonder Woman."

Cecil continues, "There is this thing called the 'burden of proof.' In this case the 'burden of proof' is on us to prove the school doesn't provide an appropriate education and it is not the least restrictive environment. I've been told we must get the 'burden of proof' switched so the school district has to prove they provide an appropriate education and they are the least restrictive environment."

"What else?"

"One other thing." Cecil adds, "This case has been tried in moot court and it was concluded we don't have a chance. This case is a slam dunk for the school district."

"Great. Just great. Let's research past cases that are similar that involve 94-142. You guys do that while I find out what I can about the opposing law firm."

The law firm turns out to be one of the most powerful in Virginia. The lead attorney is a former Senator. Their track record for winning is most impressive. They have hired two expert witnesses that are regarded as top scholars in special education. I know both of them, read their work and know they are strong advocates for removing individuals from institutions and placing them in public schools.

Jim and Cecil return and explain they couldn't find any court case that wanted an individual moved from a public school to a residential setting. All court cases were the opposite, move the individual out of the residential setting into a public school. Furthermore, every case resulted with the individual being transferred to a public school setting. However, Cecil noticed something significant, "None of the decisions were made on an appropriate education. All were based on the schools being the least restrictive environment. Dr. Payne, some of the cases showed special needs individuals actually learned a lot or possibly more in an residential setting than in a regular school setting. But the school setting was always considered the least restrictive and the decision was always made to transfer the individual from an residential setting to a public school setting."

Before the trial got started, the parents, attorney, Jim, Cecil and I discussed how to proceed. The lawyer listened to the parents and was smart enough to know we were going to lose. Based on my theory, Cecil, Jim and I laid out a plan before the attorney and the parents.

Our immediate goal was to get the 'burden of proof' switched to the district so they would have to prove they were providing an appropriate education and they were the least restrictive.

We would assume the judge is a Traditionalist, matter-of-fact, sincere, open-minded, and compassionate. We knew the opposing litigation team to be Cognitives, confident, aggressive, smart, well informed and biased against institutions.

We would position ourselves between the judge and the opposing legal team as naïve, empathetic, powerless, and street smart.

Our position would be to play up safety and show David needing 24 hour care. Learning from the results of previous court cases, we would concede the schools are educationally doing a good job. In fact, we would try to get the opposition to focus on the educational benefits of the school.

The entire plan was based on provoking the Cognitive mindset of the opposition to take their strengths of being aggressive, confident and well prepared to an extended weakness of coming across as arrogant, insensitive and out of touch with the real world. We wanted the big guy to beat up on the little guy in hopes the judge would think, maybe, the little guy has a point worth exploring.

The plan was simple and the parents and the lawyer agreed to give it a shot. The format was simple for us, the parents would explain their concerns and I would follow as an expert witness in their behalf. It was our understanding the opposition would present the school districts case with testimonials by the administration, teachers and the two expert witnesses. We had a week to prepare.

I was preparing for the trial when Jim and Cecil burst into my office. Jim starts, "You won't believe what we found out. Get this. The judge is an ardent fan of the Washington

Redskins. He has season tickets and he goes to every game."

Cecil chimes in, "And he loves George Allen. He absolutely reveres him. This could be the edge we need."

"What are you saying?"

"Have Coach Allen call him and say you work together. Have him say something that shows you are a good guy. You are intelligent."

"You want me to ask Coach Allen to call the judge? Is that legal? Isn't that a little over the top?"

Jim interjects, "We are going to lose anyway. This might help a little."

"George would do it but I don't think it's right. It is too blatant, too heavy handed."

Cecil compromising, "Well then, when you are cross-examined when they ask you about your experiences, as you list what you have done educationally, simply mention your association with the Redskins as a consultant and personal advisor to George Allen."

"Guys, this is valuable information but let's think about it some more. I don't want the judge to get the idea we are trying to manipulate him. He is smart. We must come across as honest and sincere. We'll put the Redskin thing on the back burner for now."

Two days later I'm called into the dean's office. The dean greets me at the door, motions for me to sit in the guest chair located in front of his desk. He sits in his chair behind his desk. He begins, "Jim, you are a talented teacher and your books are becoming staples in special education. We value your service and respect you as a person, but we are a School of Education and we cannot be opposed to public schools. Next week, this case you are involved in, you will be testifying against the Chesterfield County School District. This makes us look bad. We can't have it. You may not be aware but the university has a morality clause that you signed in your contract. Any act which casts an unfavorable light upon the university may result in termination.

182

The President's legal council has notified me to tell you directly, when the case is over, if in fact you testify against Chesterfield, you will be terminated. This is not a negotiable issue."

"Dean, I can't get out of it now. The parents are counting on me. They have no other way to turn."

"I can't tell you what to do but I can assure you, if you testify, you will be fired."

As I get up to leave, the dean comes to me, warmly shakes my hand and apologizes, "I'm so sorry. Please consider not testifying."

The trial begins as scheduled. The court room is a typical court room one would see on the television series, Perry Mason. Dark wood, walnut floors, six chandeliers on a stem with tiered lights the shape of cantaloupe sized tulips, eight bulbs on the lower circular row and four bulbs on the top row. The walls are egg shell white with three giant windows, framed in matching walnut stain, stretching from the floor to the ceiling on each side.

The judge's desk sits on an eight inch elevated podium. The desk is massive walnut, paneled on the front with two rows of rectangular shaped frames, six inches wide by ten inches tall. The judge's chair is high back, black leather. Directly behind the desk, centered on the wall, is a round emblem, two feet in diameter, representing the state and an American flag on a 15 foot vertical pole on the left and a state flag on the right. Next to each flag is a door that supposedly leads to the judge's chambers. Everything perfectly symmetrical.

On the far right of the room, next to the wall, is the jury box which will remain empty in this case. A boxed area on floor level adjacent to the right of the judge's desk contains a walnut wooden chair to be used by witnesses called before the judge.

The room is divided by a four foot high ornate walnut stained, picketed fence behind which observers sit. In front of the fence, in the judge's area, are two walnut tables, one on the right the other on the left. Each table has four walnut wooden chairs facing the judge's desk for attorneys and their clients. Behind the fence are rows of walnut benches that resemble church pews for observers. The observation section is slightly tiered so the observers have a clear view of the goings on. The benches are divided by a center aisle that leads to a gate in the fence for individuals to enter and exit the judge area.

The parents and our lawyer sit at the table on the right facing the judge's desk. Jim, Cecil and I sit on the front row bench immediately behind the fence separating us from them. The three opposing attorneys and the superintendent sit at the table on the left while their two expert witnesses sit on the front row behind them, separated by the fence. The two expert witnesses and us, are separated by the center aisle.

As observers file in, they all sit on the pews in the left section. It reminds me of a wedding where the brides relatives and friends sit on one side and the grooms, the other. The school districts side on the left is jam packed while our side only contains Jim, Cecil and me. For a brief moment, the seating situation made me feel small, awkward, inferior; then, I realize, this works to our advantage of the big guy beating up the little guy. The seating arrangement works in our favor.

The mother testified first. She was emotional and teared up from time to time. The father was more objective and detailed, emphasizing the severity of the seizures and the importance of medication. After the mother and father testified, a small break was taken.

After the break, I was up. I explained what I was presently doing, my past experiences and what qualified me as an expert witness. This took less than fifteen minutes. Then it was time to be cross-examined. Jim and Cecil had prepared me for this and we had rehearsed answers to the possible and likely questions and scenarios I would be confronted with. The beginning cross-examination of any expert witness is to discredit the expert in the eyes of the judge but not push it to the point the expert will be disqualified. It is nothing more than a psychological show for the judge. My purpose is to come across as sincere, honest and street smart. Not a know-it-all or an academic. The way I did it was to actually be sincere and honest and when an academic question was raised I would hedge or preface my answer with, 'to the best of my knowledge' or 'based on my experience.' As it got close to lunch time the judge interrupted, "That's enough, Dr. Payne is most qualified."

After lunch I explained what I had observed and why David needed 24 hour care. This took less than ten minutes after which I was cross-examined again. Much of the case hinged on how the judge viewed the cross-examination of me. Again I needed to come across sincere and honest plus I now needed to get the opposing team to look overbearing, arrogant, insincere, over-confident and if possible, brutal. If I could somehow get them to raise their voice, possibly get mad and better yet lose their temper.

Any questions regarding education, learning or skill development, I praised the school and credited the teacher. When this was done, it confused them, they expected me to criticize the school's educational practices or the teacher. When I didn't criticize the school's educational practices or the teacher, this became disconcerting to them. They got visually agitated.

When they brought up the subject of medical aspects. I quoted from the records. As anticipated, they would sarcastically ask, "Are you a medical doctor?" I would counter, "Are you?" The more questions they asked the madder they got. When it looked like they were getting tired and about to quit asking questions I would provoke with, "Are you kidding, that's the most stupid thing I've ever heard." When a Cognitive's intelligence is questioned, their first reaction is to strike back. After four straight hours of questioning, they actually lost their temper and eventually I was dismissed.

Our attorney, parents, Jim, Cecil, and I went to dinner. We concluded we had accomplished what we wanted. We looked sincere, honest and very knowledgeable of the situation. They came across frustrated, angry, disorganized and arrogant.

The next day the superintendent explained their side of the story, awards received, status in the community, nationally accredited. During cross-examination our attorney only asked two questions, how long had he been superintendent and had he ever seen David. He had been super-intendent for eight years and he had never seen David personally. The teacher was next. Through her cross-examination, our attorney focused on the education and skills of the teacher and got her to praise and brag on herself. Our lawyer had the teacher show educational and behavioral records which were impressive. This went 'til noon. The purpose was to keep the opposition emphasizing their superiority in education and learning. The teacher nor the school were never criticized, in fact, they were formally deserving of praise.

At lunch, we knew we had controlled the trial by keeping focus on the educational issues which we believed, based on the results of previous cases, would not be used in making the final decision.

After lunch, the two expert witnesses pontificated about the ethics of 94-142 and the history of abuse of institutional care. As expected, they were quite eloquent. They droned on and on without aids or visuals and succeeded in boring us and the judge. During the cross-examination, our attorney merely asked how many times they had observed David. Both of their answers were the same, none. They had never seen David. Their entire testimony was academic.

We went to dinner feeling the judge didn't like the opposition any more than we did, but to the credit of the school and teacher they were doing everything they could do – they were reasonably prudent. We needed to show the judge the severity of the case. I turned to the parents, "Tomorrow morning each side will summarize and although everything has gone as planned we will lose. We must show the judge the fear you live with every day. He must see this is a life and death matter. I'm going to ask you to gamble and do something terrible."

The mother responded, "Dr. Payne, this is the most important thing in our lives. What do you want?"

"Tomorrow I want you to bring David in to the courtroom unmedicated."

The father, "He'll have a seizure."

"Exactly. I want him on the front row next to the aisle. Jim, Cecil and I will sit next to him.

When he has a seizure, he'll fall into the aisle. Jim and Cecil will immediately attend to him so he won't damage himself. While they are attending to David I'll follow but as I kneel down as if to help, I'll back into the gate to open it so the judge can see how uncontrolled and violent his convulsions are.

The two expert witnesses sit next to the aisle on the opposite side. I'm betting they will temporarily be surprised and pull away. They know what to do. They are trained. But I believe the element of surprise will make them pull away and then it will be

too late for them to recover because Jim and Cecil will already be on the floor helping. In fact, I'll be surprised if they get out of the pew. This will make them look like they are afraid of kids. This will reinforce, to the judge, they are academics. Because we are anticipating a seizure we will have the upper hand."

"Do you think the judge will buy it?"

"Only if it looks real. And it will be. We don't want David to fake it and we don't want David to know we are setting him up to have a seizure."

The father responds, "When he doesn't take his meds we can predict within a reasonable time period when he will have a seizure."

"Ideally, we need it to occur between 9:00 and 9:30."

The mother replies, "This is terrible."

"Yes, I know, but the judge must see we are dealing with a very severe situation."

The two of them look at one another, "Ok." They embrace.

"I've got one other favor."

"What?"

"Hold on." I go to my car and return, "I want David to wear this."

I hand them a Redskin t-shirt, burgundy with the big Redskin logo printed on the chest. Jim and Cecil look at the shirt, look at me, and then smile.

The next morning at 9:10, David shoots out of the pew, lands in the middle of the aisle next to the gate, wails and thrashes violently, the two experts jerk back while Jim and Cecil pounce on David and attend to his needs. I jump and kneel with my back against the gate. Then, I move back opening the gate so the judge has a full view of the violent thrashing. The commotion exceeded our highest expectations and the impact was dramatic. Jim and Cecil took David out of the court room to recover. It took over a half an hour to get things settled down.

When it came time for our attorney to give the closing arguments, she never mentioned the seizure episode. She praised the district and the teacher for their work and effort and ended, "We believe the least restrictive environment must include 24 hour care for the safety of our client." The judge announced he would have a decision after lunch. After lunch, the judge switched the 'burden of proof' and gave the school district two months to prepare. They had to show the school district was providing an appropriate education and the school was the least restrictive environment.

During the next eight weeks, Virginia experienced one of the most severe winters in its history. The schools had to close 10 days. When the trial resumed, all our attorney did was show a record of the days the school closed and asked how could the school be a least restrictive environment if it couldn't and didn't open?

The decision, the school district had 30 days to find an appropriate residential facility, open 24 hours a day, 7 days a week, 365 days a year. The first time in the history of the United States in a court case a child was transferred from a public school setting to a residential setting.

In the ensuing months the school district was unable to secure an acceptable residential setting resulting in the district purchasing a separate facility providing full comprehensive services 24 hours a day, 7 days a week, 365 days a year.

I'm sitting in my office and the dean unexpectedly comes in, sits down, "Jim, you made us proud. Chesterfield isn't happy but you successfully defended the right of a special needs child. I don't know how you did it but I want to know more about that theory of yours."

Without the effort and intelligence of Jim and Cecil,
we would never have won. They believed what we were
doing was right and just.

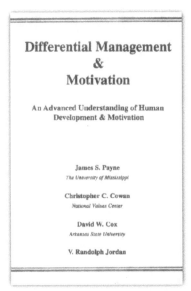

**Differential Management
&
Motivation**

An Advanced Understanding of Human
Development & Motivation

James S. Payne
The University of Mississippi

Christopher C. Cowan
National Values Center

David W. Cox
Arkansas State University

V. Randolph Jordan

I gave the dean a copy of the manuscript
before the book, *Differential Management and Motivation*,
was published.

189

–Chapter 19–

Cars

—

1975
Promoted, Associate Professor, University of Virginia
(I learn how to sell cars)

I finish my lecture. The students file out. This session I got on a roll. I was in the zone. Mark and Allen go through the routine of closing down; turn off the equipment, box up and file the lecture notes, straighten up the auditorium.

As I exit the stage by the side door I'm approached by a student. The student, in his early twenties, dark hair, lean, "Dr. Payne. Do you have a minute?"

"Yes."

"Your theory can be used to sell cars."

"And."

"And I want you to meet my dad."

"Mark. Allen. When you finish, turn out the lights. We'll be in my office."

As soon as we sit down the student spouts, "Differential Management can do more than just manage and motivate. It can influence people. It can influence people to buy."

"I'm listening."

"Our family owns a series of car dealerships. I told my dad about your course. He wants to meet you."

Before I know it, I'm in Savannah, Georgia being escorted through one of the largest dealerships in the southeast by Dale C. Critz, Sr. Mr. Critz is President and General Manager of Critz, Inc., and Chairman of the Board of SunTrust Bank. This particular dealership is impressive but not as impressive as Mr. Critz.

Junior is fast paced, preppy looking with khaki pants, light blue oxford dress shirt, brown penny loafers and hair long enough he keeps pushing it back with his hands to keep it out of his face. His dad, senior, is six feet tall, 210 pounds, suntanned skin, high cheek bones, big nose, bushy eyebrows, dark hair graying around the temples, white shirt, red tie, dark blue custom suit, shiny black shoes, puffing on a cigar as we move from one end of the dealership to the other. Mr. Critz is loud yet warm. Forceful yet empathic. Purposeful but not pushy.

The tour ends in Mr. Critz's office on the second floor overlooking the dealership that covers two blocks. His office is not plush, it is elegant. He sits behind a beautiful European style desk in a Herman Miller executive chair while Junior and I sit in two accompanying guest chairs. "Junior has told me so much about your theory, I don't need to take your course. I've read the text you've written and I want you to teach my salesforce. Dr. Payne, I want to know if you are available any Sunday of next month. We will fly you in on a Saturday and out late Sunday so you won't have to miss any work at the University."

The next thing I know I'm in front of eighteen seasoned salesmen in the executive training room at the SunTrust Bank. "Men, I'm excited to have the opportunity to share with you a theory I've been working on for fifteen years. Differential Management has been used to manage employees of one of the largest restaurant chains in the Midwest, used to persuade employers to hire the handicapped, inspired preschool children to learn and recently used with the Washington Redskins. This theory…"

"Dr. Payne. Sir. I don't mean to be disrespectful, but, just how many cars have you sold?"

I look at this gorilla of a man on the front row. Brown high-top shoes, white belt, dark blue short sleeved shirt stretches across a massive chest and a neck… he doesn't have a neck. His overly large pumpkin sized head sits square on his shoulders. I glance around the room to see seventeen pairs of questioning eyes, wondering why they are here and what will I do next.

Prior to this crew, I had been around some pretty tough football players and although I was scared at the time I knew I couldn't look intimidated. "None. But do you think I can't sell a car? Do you, for one minute, believe I don't know how to sell? Are you out of your mind?"

I step forward and get in No Neck's face, "I can out sell you any day of the week. You let me finish today's session without uttering a peep and this summer I'll take leave from the university. Set up a cubicle next to yours. And if I don't sell more cars than you in the first month, I'll kiss any bare part of your body you designate. Deal, no deal?"

Mr. No Neck. Stunned. Said nothing. I continued with a presentation on Differential Management that they never forgot and that summer I set up a cubicle in the Volkswagen showroom next to the gorilla.

I had an interest in selling. Earlier in my life I sold encyclopedias part-time and later graduated to vacuum sweepers. In high school, I tried Bibles and waterless cookware, but you can't count those because I was untrained and too young to know any better.

Through the encyclopedia and vacuum sweeper experiences I learned all selling is the same. Only the product changes; the process, the psychology, the system, all remain the same. Selling is simple once you crack the code.

My interest in selling happened three years after Ruth Ann and I got married. We had scraped up enough money to make a down-payment on a 10' by 55' Van Dyke mobile home. Two days after purchasing our coveted coach, that evening, what would ensue in 45 minutes taught us a lifelong lesson.

A knock at the door. I opened it to find a gentleman holding a black satchel about the size of two attache'cases placed back to back. He introduced himself and explained he had something that could enrich our lives. He was excited about it and, before I knew what had happened, he was seated in our small, spartanly furnished living room, explaining to my wife and me about the importance and joy of knowledge. From the time he knocked on the door to the time he left took less than 45 minutes and upon his exit, we found ourselves to be the proud owners of a set of encyclopedias.

Both working part-time, Van Dyke trailer – we needed a set of encyclopedias like we needed a hole in our heads. Momentarily we were proud and happy; later we couldn't figure out why we purchased a set of encyclopedias we couldn't afford, didn't need, and wouldn't use. We were both relatively intelligent, and not too naïve, yet we were sold something we didn't need – in our own home. Why? How? Simple: he knew more about selling than we knew about buying. He knew the psychology of selling and applied it.

Having a degree in Psychology, I was puzzled, confused, and frustrated. What did he know I didn't know? I got a part-time job selling encyclopedias and within one week I learned more about human behavior than I had learned in four years of college as a Psychology major.

The manager, Harold, taught me my first lesson by showing me a map of the city. He

194

instructed me to select any section of town and he would take me to that section and demonstrate how to sell. Somewhat confused but most certainly intrigued, I pointed to a low-middle-income area that I felt would be a challenge.

"Awe." East Topeka. My favorite place to sell. Easy pickins. Grab the stuff. Let's go get 'em."

I picked up the demo cases, put them in the company car and before I know it, we are in East Topeka exactly where I pointed.

Harold drives up and down a couple of blocks and then abruptly stops. "This is it."

It is 6:45 p.m. He knocks on the door. We enter. He presents, demonstrates, answers a few questions, and closes the deal. We are back in the car by 7:15 p.m.

I couldn't believe it even though I saw it with my own eyes. Harold smiled, "I knew we would make a sale before we ever entered. Did you see the fence? You can't buy that type of fence in a store; it had to be sold. Did you notice the gutters and siding? You can't buy that type of guttering and siding in a store; it had to be sold. Hell. I could have sold them my wife." He smiled, thinking he was funny.

It dawned on me; people reveal their susceptibility to sales by what they buy or by what they have bought. Flashback. Young couple, recent purchase of a Van Dyke. Shoot, to a profession- al salesperson, Ruth Ann and I were easy pickins.

Prior to my summer selling challenge, Mr. Critz had me study the entire dealership, develop motivational profiles on each employee, review each manufacture's sales program for each model and conduct a survey of the dealership's customers.

After analyzing over 100 questionnaires filled out by customers visiting the Volkswagen portion of the dealership, 70 percent were identified as Cerebral. Cerebrals are interested in ecology, good gas mileage, fresh air, organically grown food; they bicycle, jog, picnic and camp. While studying over 100 questionnaires from the Buick side, it was discovered 80 percent could be identified as Cognitive. Cognitive like luxury, are competitive and in extreme cases are full of themselves. The results from the used car lot showed an abundance of Traditional types. Traditionals are conservative, like things to be basic and aren't interested in fads or change.

Volkswagen of America developed a *Struktogrmm* to assist salespersons in developing sales skills. The *Struktogram* divided prospects into three colors representing three distinct personality types. Blue represented conservative-type buyers who were interested in safety, economy, and durability. They usually preferred domestic cars to imports. Red represented individuals who were interested in performance, handling, speed, pickup, style and comfort.

Green represented people who wanted roominess, excellent gas mileage, no luxury and non-pollutant devices. Volkswagen implied that not only did each of the types of individuals look for a certain kind of car, but the actual selling approach should fit their expectations. They advocated, for most, an individual's car was an extension of their personality; furthermore, individuals buy cars from salespersons whom they trust and with whom they can identify.

The Differential Management theory closely aligned itself with the findings of Volkswagen. The major difference was, Differential Management was more specific and detailed in how to optimally manage and motivate various types of people prescribing specific detailed methods and techniques. Much more precise than the *Struktogram*. Simply put: Traditionals want to be told and sold by an experienced professional that has a lot of product knowledge. Cognitives want to be shown, not sold, they want to experience performance and look good. Cerebrals are a different kind of buyer. They hate pressure and will only buy from a salesperson they like.

My cubicle is next to Mr. No Neck's in the Volkswagen showroom situated between the large used car lot and the Nissan building.

Our showroom displayed a bright yellow Beetle and a light blue Rabbit. All cubicleswere the same; walls five feet tall so everyone could see in, a small desk, salesman chair, and two prospect chairs. A rotating system was in place giving each salesperson a chance to address a walk-in. Each salesperson was allowed to sell anything new or used.

My very first sale ended up on the used car lot.

A man and his wife drove onto the lot in a plain, no frills, 5-year-old car. She was in a housedress and he in jeans with a plaid flannel shirt. They were walking around a two-year-old shiny black Cutlass. The Cutlass was placed out front-center, because the sales manager had made a mistake and bought two exactly alike from a car rental agency and needed to get rid of one of them quickly. Mr. Critz was somewhat perturbed because apparently one is not supposed to buy two used cars exactly alike – the same color – for resale. So one was displayed proudly on the front row, while the other was hidden on the back lot behind a fence.

No one wanted to wait on the couple, and even though I wasn't up, the other salespersons gave me the go-ahead. I greeted the couple. He was a trucker whose handle was "Tenderfoot."

He was called Tenderfoot because his feet were tender. She was a housewife who worked part-time as a waitress. Both were unquestionably Traditionals, hard-working, salt-of-the-earth types. I knew a lot about Cutlasses, and I knew they were both Traditionals. Thus, I knew I was to be direct, come across as very knowledgeable, and tell them everything I knew about the product.

I showed them everything. I talked about safety features, economy items, the history and development of the Cutlass. I talked about the advantages of the color black, the importance of a powerful engine. I was so good; I even impressed myself.

They listened and said very little. During the test drive, the two just sat, looked, and basically seemed to enjoy themselves while I pointed out every conceivable feature of the interior.

After the test drive, we all got out of the car and just stood around looking. At this time I was so new I didn't know enough to take them inside to draw up the papers, so we just continued to look at each other. Finally, I asked, "What do you think?"

She looked at him and he looked at her and finally she said, "I don't see how we could possibly do it. It's too nice, and Darryl might get envious."

I said, "Who is Darryl?"

She said, "Our youngest son."

I said, "Why would Darryl be envious?"

She said, "He thinks we are getting something more basic for David."

I said, "Who is David"

She said, "Our oldest son."

It took me awhile, but then I realized they were looking for a car for their oldest son rather than for themselves. Not knowing what to do, I suggested maybe we should go show the car to David. They assured me it wasn't necessary because he was working. Anyway, they were buying it for him. They weren't buying it for a birthday or graduation; they were just buying it for him, period.

I said, "Well, this is a great car; if I were David, I'd love it."

They confirmed, "He'd really like it, but Darryl would probably feel uncomfortable, and David maybe would be embarrassed because it is a little too showy anyway."

I found out that David was expecting a car something like his dad's and much less expensive than the Cutlass. Darryl was a year younger and was to get his own car next year. So I started showing them less expensive cars, but we kept coming back to the Cutlass. If I said it once, I said it a dozen times: "Let's go get David and see what he thinks." Each time they declined.

Finally, the wife turned to Tenderfoot and remarked, "Maybe we could just go ahead and get Darryl's car too."

Tenderfoot replied, "I don't know, he would want one like David's. Fair is fair. Boy, I like this car." Then Tenderfoot turned to me and asked, "Do you have one comparable to this?"

I hesitated, looked at him, turned and looked at her, whirled around, sprinted to the back lot, got the other Cutlass, and proudly drove it to the front lot. The Cutlasses were parked facing one another. I opened both hoods, both trunks, all of the doors, turned on both radios to the same station and, while the music blasted across the lot, I stood back to admire my work.

They said, "We will take them both."

Not knowing what to do now, I took the couple inside to draw up the papers. When I asked for a deposit, Tenderfoot said they had none. I did everything I could to get a deposit; that is what I was trained to do. But Tenderfoot insisted he would finance the whole thing.

Confused, not knowing what to do I look up out of my cubicle to see Mr. No Neck looking on from across the showroom. I get up. Go to No Neck, "I can't get a deposit. I don't know what to do." No Neck walks to my cubicle, I follow. He sits in my chair, I squeeze in behind him and remain standing. No Neck surprises me. He introduces himself to the couple. He is nice, warm, personable. Within seconds, he does a credit check to discover Tenderfoot owns his 18-wheeler, clear. It is used as collateral. No Neck escorts them, with me, to the finance officer.

Tenderfoot and his wife buy and finance both cars. Both Traditionals using a Traditional technique, with a novice salesperson and the help of No Neck make four people happy; Tender-foot, wife, David and Darryl. Five, if you count me.

I couldn't have done it without No Neck. When I thanked him he simply nodded, turned away, and returned to his cubicle.

The next day I was standing with the other salespersons in the showroom, looking out onto the lot when all of a sudden, a 25ish, longhaired, ear-ringed, individual drove up on a motorcycle. Before I could move, all the other salespeople disappeared; some went to their cubicles, some to the restroom, and one out back for a smoke. It wasn't my turn but, being the only person available, I was up.

Easy Rider parked his two-wheeler and walked around a Volkswagen van. I wandered out to introduce myself.

As I walked out, I noticed white lettering across the back of his navy blue tee shirt, "Save the Whales." An old beat-up bumper sticker was stuck to the left saddlebag, which read, "Split Wood Not Atoms;" it was just below a peace sign.

His name was Bruce; he liked to camp and was a skilled canoer. His eyes were blue, his hair hung just below his shoulders, he was wearing dock-siders with no socks and he had a leather friendship bracelet around his left ankle. Yes, no question about it – I had my hands on a real, whale-saving, one-worlder, you-are-the-children, anti-nuker Cerebral, if I ever saw one.

I didn't know much about Cerebrals, but I did know you can't sell a Cerebral; you let a Cerebral buy. I also knew Cerebrals don't purchase anything on their first visit. They reflect, think, shop and must like and trust the person they deal with. They hate authority figures and they are very consumer literate, i.e., they research the products before buying.

I asked a series of questions and, with my best body language and eye contact, I absorbed everything he said. I found out that he was interested in a truck to use for all of his friends to put their gear in while they traveled across the country. He had read *Consumer Guide* and *Consumer Reports* and knew exactly what he wanted, except for the size of the cargo space.

We went to a truck he had his eyes on. This was an interesting truck because it had been on the lot for over a year, was new –not used, but the cargo portion extended over the cab and was a little unusual. Frankly, the truck was ugly. Bruce liked the cargo area. He figured he could put a mattress in the cargo part above the cab and use it as a sleeping area. He said he had never seen a cargo area like that and the more he talked, the more I liked it. He knew everything about this truck. He even got under the truck to show me some aspects of the muffler. I'd never been under a truck before.

Although I was tempted to sell him, I knew better, so when he exhausted himself telling me everything he knew about the truck, I asked him if he had been over to the Ford dealership. He said, "No," so I suggested he might check them out. He shook my hand, mounted up, and drove off.

When I walked back into the showroom, the other salespeople snickered and No Neck avoided me as if I had the plague. The next day Bruce returned. I was in the back room at the time. No Neck opened the door and explained, "The wild one's back." As Bruce and I went to my office, he talked about a trip he was planning. We got out an atlas and chartered the trip to New Mexico.

We never talked much about the truck, but before leaving, he indicated that Ford didn't have any-thing he wanted and asked if I had any other suggestions. I told him trucks were a little out of my field, but I noticed some trucks on an independent used car lot about a quarter of a mile down the road. He left.

Two days later, Bruce returned to buy the truck with the unique cargo space. The following week he referred a friend who bought a van from me. Cerebrals are communal. They are attached as a group. When you let one Cerebral buy, when that Cerebral identifies with you, you will get a chance to help a fellow Cerebral.

Junior was right Differential Management could be used to sell cars. On that day, Differential Management morphed into Differential Selling.

By the third week, I'm leading the pack. I am beyond confident bordering on cocky.

A Buick LaSabre rolls on the Volkswagen lot. A dark skinned gentleman, maybe from India, enters the showroom. I'm up. I extend my hand, "Jim Payne. How may I help you – are you looking for a car for yourself or for someone in the family?"

He shakes my hand, "I'm Dr. Ophonospour. I want a diesel Rabbit. I'm trading in the LaSabre."

"Do you have a color preference?"

"I just want a diesel Rabbit. Show me what you have."

Gas prices are sky high. Diesels are hot. We sell them $500 above sticker. We have two. I show him both. He picks the black one and without driving it says, "I'll take it."
Before we go inside I question him, "Why a diesel?"

"Good gas mileage."

"What's wrong with the LaSabre?"

"Nothing. It's great. I love it."

"What do you like about it?"

"Its size. Its color. I like the leather seats. It's a smooth ride."

I find out Dr. Ophonospour is the Chief Physician at the hospital. He has been here less than a year. Upon coming to this country, he bought the LaSabre from us on the lot across the street. He lives in an upscale-gated community. The guy is a pure Cognitive. He is not a Rabbit person let alone a diesel person. Dr. Ophonospour is about to buy a car he will never like. He is hung up on the price of gas and I realize he doesn't know who he is. He ain't no Traditional. He ain't no Cerebral. He is a Cognitive. He doesn't want to buy, he wants to be shown, he wants to experience the sale but he doesn't know it. I've got to decide. I can make a quick sale knowing he will be disappointed or I can teach him a lesson in hopes of selling him something he will love and cherish.

We go to my cubicle. As I write up the buyers-order I explain, "I feel uncomfortable selling you this car. It isn't you."

Dr. Ophonospour looks on expressionless.

I lean back, look at Dr. Ophonospour. I slide the buyers-order off the desk and place it in the trash can. "I can't do it. You need an upgrade, from the LaSabre to a Riviera."

"A Riveria? I can buy two Rabbits for the price of a Riviera."

"Actually two and a half. But I tell you, you won't be happy with that Rabbit and I know you won't be happy with a diesel."

"Why?"

I reach down and remove my shoe. I slap it on the top of the desk." That ain't no Payless. That's a Gucci. I paid $310. Payless shoes are just as nice. Payless shoes wear just as long, maybe longer, Payless shoes fit fine. But when I wear my Gucci's they make me feel proud. They make me feel important. They make me feel expensive."

I get up, move to his side of the desk. While standing I grab his wrist. Hold up in front of his eyes. "This ain't no Timex. It's a Rolex. You can buy a whole lot of Timex's for the price of a Rolex. When you wear the Rolex it makes you feel important. It makes you feel like a winner."

I bend down close to his ear, quietly "See that guy over there," tilting my head toward Mr. No Neck. "He will sell you that diesel Rabbit or anything else but I know the Rabbit is not you and I know that Rabbit will not make you proud. It will not make you feel important."

Dr. Ophonospour glances at No Neck then he looks up at me. He says nothing.

"Follow me." I walk across the showroom, out the door, past the Nissan lot, across the street and stop in front of a black Buick Riviera parked on the front row. "Wait here."

I get the keys, hand them to him, "You don't drive a Riviera you experience it."

The two of us drive around the block. We get out. He circles the car one time. Turns to me, "Let's talk trade-in."

With LaSabre appraised, price agreed on, he writes a check for the difference. As he drives away I know I've made one Cognitive happy, proud and satisfied.

I return to my cubicle. Sit down and in comes No Neck. "How did you do that?" No Neck continues, "Let's go to lunch, I'll buy."

No Neck and I eat lunch. I teach him Differential Selling. In return, over the rest of the summer, he teaches me tricks on selling not written in texts or training manuals.

Friends, colleagues. At the end of the summer, not having to kiss any designated bare part of anyone's body I return to the university.

December. At the end of the fall semester the phone rings at my home.

"Payne residence. Jim speaking."

"Jim. Dale. I have a Mr. Ophonospour in my office. He wants a Mercedes 500. He insists on you selling it to him. I'll send Junior to get you."

Ruth Ann and I bought our first and only set of encyclopedias in our 10' by 55' Van Dyke trailer. A lesson we never forgot.

Dale introduced me to his dad.

PEOPLEWISE
Selling
the art of selling brain to brain

Dr. James S. Payne
and Dale C. Critz, Jr.

Dale and I coauthored a book on selling. The word, PeopleWise replaced the word Differential.

Dale and I got a kick out of writing the used car newspaper ads.

–Chapter 20–

Licenses

1975

*Promoted, Associate Professor, University of Virginia
(I learn about sex)*

Ruth Ann and I are approaching our 30th anniversary. We just paid off the house. Cars paid, no credit card debt. We are financially solvent. Kim was finishing high school as a straight A student and Janet is getting ready for middle school with track ribbons and trophies filling up her room.

Our house is perfect. Ranch style, situated in the middle of Charlottesville in a remote wooded residential area. We sit at the dinning room table. Ruth Ann and I celebrate the house being paid off. Ruth Ann with a glass of wine and I, two jiggers of Jack Daniels with Coke.

An open fireplace separates the dinning room from the front room. The fireplace is of large stones, expertly placed, scaling to the ceiling. The west wall of both the dinning room and front room is all glass. The back yard juts out 15 feet to a stoned wall 4 foot high. The stones are the same size and from the same quarry as the fireplace.

Beyond the 4 foot wall the yard slopes upward 20 degrees to a wooden fence 70 feet from the house. The incline is full of trees that attract squirrels and birds of all colors and sizes. This is a day of relaxation and joy.

Suddenly, without warning, Kim marches in followed by Janet with two, four-inch pig-tails sprouting out each side of her head.

Ruth Ann and I are seated at the dinning room table, side by side facing the fireplace with the massive window, displaying a magnificent view, on our left. Uninvited, unasked, Kim plops in the chair across from Ruth Ann while Janet slides quietly in the chair opposite me.

Abruptly Kim blurts, "Did you and dad ever get divorced?"

Saying nothing, Janet looks at me, then shifts her eyes toward Ruth Ann.

"No." Ruth Ann matter-of-factly responds.

Kim questions, "Then what are these," as two official looking envelopes are slapped on the table in front of Ruth Ann.

I start to get up as Ruth Ann stares me back down. Janet's eyes, more wide open than before, are glued on Ruth Ann.

Ruth Ann, motheringly picks up the two envelopes and without opening them, nonchalantly says, "These are marriage licenses. Your dad and I got married twice."

"What are you talking about?"

"Well, your dad and I dated all through high school and college. In fact, your dad was my first date."

Janet is now looking straight at me. She is looking as if she thinks something major is going on here.

Kim looks, dead on, at Ruth Ann with questioning eyes.

"Your dad and I were very much in love. We were infatuated with one another. We enjoyed each other. We had fun. We played with one another."

"Played with one another?"

At this point Janet's head turns straight at Ruth Ann. This is major.

"Yes. Augh. We played with one another. We fore-played with each other."

"Fore-played?"

Janet continues to look at Ruth Ann. I think she understands but I'm not sure.

"Your dad and I necked."

"Necked?"

"Yes. In fact, we necked for several years and…"

"And what?"

"And. We wanted to have sex so we eloped and got married."

Janet looks on as if to say, I get it.

Janet understands, while Kim continues in disbelief, "You didn't know you could have sex without getting married?"

Ruth Ann goes on as if babbling to herself.

"We knew we could have sex without being married but we chose not to. We wanted it to be special – legitimate. We didn't want it to feel like cheating. Your dad and I believed sex to be… I don't know. To be… saved. So we went to Bartlesville, Oklahoma and got married so we could be free to have sex. Yeah. That's it. We wanted to be free to have sex."

Kim looks at Ruth Ann dumbfounded.

Janet looks at both of us in wonderment.

"For a couple of years, after getting married, your dad and I had sex. Quite often, in fact. And we feared our parents were getting suspicious. So we got married the second time in DeSoto to please our parents."

Kim's mouth drops open. She slowly gets up, turns and exits followed by Janet. Just beyond the door, "Janet. Can you believe it? Stupid."

Briefly I mentally question if the actual act of sex is better than necking. I subconsciously transgress back in time. My mind flips through snapshots of scenes of fondling, French kissing, licking, arousement. Vivid mental pictures; embraced, entangled, pressed together in the backseat of the Ford, on a picnic blanket under a moonlit night, on the 18th green of the local golf course, standing up in her parent's closet. Nothing sacred. Nothing off-limits. As my mind reels off relived pictures of passion without sex, I mentally compliment us on our skill and dexterity.

Returning to the real world, in present time, I realize Ruth Ann is leading me away from the dining room table, through the door, up the stairs to our bedroom. And now at my age, experienced and knowledgeable, I can safely say; I don't know if the actual act of sex is better than necking but it is faster and more efficient.

I was her first date.

This made our parents happy.

No one ever knew we were already married.

This is an early photo of Ruth Ann,
Kim (front center) and Janet.

Kim and Janet questioned our
intelligence.

–Chapter 21–

Deaning

—

1985

Hired, Dean, University of Mississippi

(I learn Deaning)

I pick up the phone. "Get over to the Union. Now. Front. Outside. Steps. I want him removed." It's my boss. The Provost.

A small band of students gawked at John lying on the concrete slab to the right of the steps leading into the Union. Flat on his back. Kicking and jerking. Simulating a grand mal seizure or a bad display of the Saint Vitus Dance.

I pushed my way through the crowd of twenty five plus. Bent over, grabbed John's arm, gently but firmly lifted him to his feet, "That's enough. Let's get something to eat."

As we enter the Union, the onlookers dispersed without comment or incident.

We go through the cafeteria line. I grab a ham and cheese on white, he picks over several sandwiches and finally selects an egg salad on wheat. I get a Coke, he gets a Snapple apple juice. We sit at a distant table, by the big picture window, overlooking the Grove.

"John. If I've told you once I've told you a dozen times, you can't levitate. You are not going to levitate. You will never be able to levitate."

"Dean Payne. I was close. I was so close."

"John, you were not close. You flopped around like a salmon out of water."

I look down at my half eaten sandwich and mutter, "This can't go on. I've had it. We're going to talk with your parents."

We get in the car and drive 25 miles south to Water Valley. We turn off highway seven onto a graveled side road. After a quarter of a mile, we pull up next to his parent's house.

A weathered white, one story, farm house with a porch stretched across the front. The banister has two spokes missing and one of the three wooden steps leading up to the porch is loose. Nice house but in need of minor repair and a good paint job.

John steps ahead of me and enters without knocking while yelling, "Mom. Dad. I'm home." I follow and am immediately greeted by the father.

John introduces, "Dad, this is Dean Payne. Dean Payne, this is my dad."

We shake hands, the father motions for me to sit. Without comment I sit and then quickly rise to meet the mother as she enters the room. She nods and I return the nod. Without comment the three of us sit while John grabs an orange from a bowl of fruit on the table next to the kitchen. John leaves the room while the three of us look at one another in silence.

I sit on an old, but nice, couch facing the two of them. The father is seated in a matching recliner on my right while the mother is seated on a wooden kitchen chair to my left. An oak coffee table separates me from them. The two are elderly as is the house and furniture. As I look around, cluttered with knickknacks and magazines, I sense an atmosphere of love, caring and concern.

"I'm worried about your son. I like John and I find him fascinating to be around. He is sharp and a good student. But at times he acts odd. He draws attention to himself. It scares me. He thinks he can levitate himself. I'm dismissing him from school. I'm going to write up a disposition infraction. His behavior is not conducive to the profession of education. I don't want him around children. I'm sorry. I have no choice but I want you to know what I am going to do and why."

John's dad, hunched forward in his seat, looking down at his feet, slowly looks up at me and in a soft voice with a puzzled tone, "We wondered how long it would take before someone discovered he's gone a little crazy. Ever since he got back from California he hasn't been right. The damn kid thinks he can float. He got on drugs. They fried his brain."

The mother repeated, while shaking her head, "Fried his brain."

I felt terrible. I got up, left, and drove back to Oxford.

When I accepted the position as Dean of the School of Education at The University of Mississippi I thought I would be doing things that would change the world, revolutionize education, contribute to the greater good. I didn't know my job would require dealing with craziness. But frankly, I found craziness stimulating and invigorating.

After 15 years of service at The University of Virginia, I was offered, and accepted, the position of Dean of the School of Education at The University of Mississippi. My colleagues at Virginia questioned why I would give up a budding career at Virginia to go to Mississippi.

While at Virginia I had advanced through the ranks of Assistant to Associate to Full Professor. Full Professor is the highest rank a faculty member can attain and during the 15 years I had created, developed and perfected my own theory on Differential Management and Motivation. I was obsessed with advancing the theory. I wanted to know why people do things and how to help them do better. I had modified and honed my theory by consulting with a professional football team, developed a recognized method of placing individuals with disabilities on jobs and an effective selling system for products and services and served as an expert witness and advisor in an important law case.

Deaning would give me a platform to research my theory in an academic setting without having to consult. As a dean, I would spend 100% of my time applying my theory withstudents, faculty, staff and the administration. The timing was right and the situation was perfect.

My job was simple. As dean I was to improve teaching, increase scholarship and bring in money through federal grants. Improvement in teaching would be assessed by the university's course evaluations completed by students at the end of each semester. Increases in scholarship would be determined by counting the number of publications indicated on each faculty member's yearly activity report. Money would be determined by the number of federal grants awarded and the amount of money received. The effectiveness of me as Dean and the degree my theory worked would be determined on increases in course evaluations, number of faculty publications and amount of federal money granted to the School of Education. The goals were clear and the assessment mechanisms were in place. All I had to do was do it.

Two great universities, The University of Virginia and The University of Mississippi. Both comprehensive institutions, both flagship institutions for their states, and both located in beautiful university towns. The two universities enroll about the same number of students, 12,000. Both universities are smack dab gorgeous with the same nostalgic colonial style architecture. Virginia has the Rotunda, Mississippi has the Lyceum. Virginia has the Lawn, Mississippi has the Grove. From the outside one could hardly tell the difference but from the inside, the difference is magnified by economies. For starters, Virginia faculty are paid, on the average, $30,000 more per year and Virginia faculty teach no more than two courses a semester while Mississippi faculty teach four, and in some cases five. Because of the lighter course load Virginia faculty have time to publish and they publish a lot.

Generally speaking, students in Virginia are taught by published scholars while students at Mississippi are taught by Master teachers.

The School of Education building is located on the outskirts of university property. It is separated from the main campus by a bridge that crosses over the old railroad tracks.

The building, pre-integration, was the old white high school. The back part of the building runs north and south, two stories and built in the early 1930s. The front part runs east and west, one story, and was built in the mid-1950s. The floor plan forms a 'T' and the halls, wooden in the 30s part and tiled in the 50s part, are lined on both sides with metal beat up lockers, typical public school style. Neither section had been renovated since the original construction.

The school has one computer, a Radio Shack. None of the audio visual equipment works and in the middle of September, my third month, we run out of paper. In October all but one phone is removed because the phone bill can't be paid. In November, all the deans and mayors of each building are summoned to a meeting at the physical plant.

The physical plant building is like an old warehouse one would see in a 1940s gangster movie. Four giant boilers line one side of the room, pipes run everywhere, there is a constant gurgling sound in the background and the lighting, just above squint level, is limited by bulbs that haven't been cleaned or wiped off since being installed. In fact, a fourth of the lights are inoperable. There is about 50 attendees for 25 wooden folding chairs. Paul, the Director of Physical Plant, stands before the obedient crowd; microphoneless, he blasts out a message that ricochets, bounces and echoes off the dirty concrete floor.

"Gentlemen (there were no ladies present), if we have a severe winter we won't be able to heat the buildings."

I think: Aren't they first supposed to thank us for coming? And where's the coffee?

"The furnace was purchased during the Civil War... used."

I think: I'm the dean, what's this got to do with me? I know nothing about the Civil War or furnaces.

"And our Chief of Maintenance retired, and he is the only one who knows what to do when it breaks down."

I think: Have I fallen into a time warp?

"We have formed a committee to decide on a university wide plan for closing down. You will be notified of the plan shortly. In the meantime, notify your faculty and staff of this possible inconvenience and assure them they will continue to be paid if we have to close down. Thank you for coming and pray for a mild winter."

Spontaneously, those seated rise and everyone exits without comment in a calm and orderly manner. No one says anything and as I look around, I realize I am the only one surprised.

I began deaning July 1, 1985. The first month, I met with every faculty and staff member, individually, in their office at a convenient time for them. I wanted to know what they have done, are doing and would like to do.

Each individual is dutiful, loyal to the university, and proud to be a southerner. With the exception of one black faculty member, all are white, the majority aged from late 30s to late 50s, most graduated from The University of Mississippi and all are devout Christians. All offices are tiny, enclosing only one employee. I was told the architect that designed the 50s portion of the building, constructed the offices small enough they couldn't be shared. In most offices, a confederate flag or a picture of a confederate flag is proudly displayed.

Later, I find out during football games, confederate flags pepper the stands and the band plays Dixie after every touchdown, to a standing, clapping, screaming fan base. When I left Virginia, they had just banned confederate flags from the stadium and stopped the playing of Dixie. This gave me cause to reflect and process the culture I chose to further my career.

During the month of August I studied reports, documents of all types and the budget. It was clear the faculty and staff are underpaid and overworked. Reality set in. I went home to confess to Ruth Ann.

216

"I've made a mistake. My theory won't work here. I don't have the skills to help."

"Come on, you've helped struggling organizations worse than this."

"It's not the conditions. It's the faculty. The faculty are all the same, conservative, linear thinkers, close-minded, regimented, methodical, and believe what they are doing is not only right, it is the only way. Ruth Ann, they are Traditionalists. All of them are Traditionalists. Traditionalists don't like change. They don't even see any reason for change.

My theory relies on diversity, organizations filled with different personalities, different opinions, different viewpoints and the theory capitalizes on the differences so ordinary people, collectively, do the extraordinary."

"Honey, this is a diamond in the rough. It is perfect. You already have demonstrated you know how to help Cognitives and Cerebrals. But you haven't mastered Traditionalists. The Chancellor has identified success and how to measure it. Improve instruction, increase scholarship and secure federal funds. It can't get any clearer. Traditionalists have strong work ethic, they are loyal, and they have a strong belief system. I've met the faculty and staff. They are intelligent, mature, good solid people. For the first time you will be able to study and research Traditionalists 100% of your time without being distracted. And what you learn will be transferrable to other mindsets. Let's face it, we have landed in Utopia."

Prior to classes being started, my first address before faculty laid out my understanding of the situation that was before us and the limitations we faced.

"I appreciate having the opportunity to serve as the dean and I look forward to an exciting semester. I realize your respect for the position of dean and my wife and I appreciate your warm reception and hospitality. I assure you I have no hidden agenda and I did not come here to embarrass myself. The chancellor has made it clear he expects us to focus on teaching, publishing and writing grants. Money is tight and he instructed me to never come to him and ask for money. There is no money, but if and when there is, he assures me the School of Education will get its fair share. After talking with each of you personally it is clear you enjoy teaching and you value what you do. After reviewing records, documents and the budget I am under no

217

illusion as to the challenges that lie ahead. Unquestionably, everyone is underpaid and overworked. There isn't anything that can be done, at this time, about pay so I want to focus this first year on load. Teaching four and five courses a semester is excessive in a comprehensive university. As we start the semester, I want you to look at your schedule and the schedule of courses offered by your department. Look for ways we can reduce teaching loads without reducing the quality of instruction. It takes time to publish and write grants. You don't have time to write when you are saddled with four and five courses. Our goal is to reduce teaching loads and improve teaching performance. I have no mask and I have no magic bullet, but I have found, through previous experiences, the people in the trenches know more about how to run an organization than the administration does. All I ask is, as you go through the semester think about future course reductions and how to improve instruction. Think about it, talk about it and share with me any ideas you come up with. One last thing, my door is not open, I am busy and I am not just sitting in my office for you or students to drop by. But I am accessible, very accessible. All I ask is, call before coming by. Set up an appointment. I assure you when you come you will have my undivided attention. We will not be interrupted. What you have to say is important and you are important to this school. I am not going to address questions at this time because you are busy getting ready for your classes. As you prepare for your classes, think, talk with others and let me know what you come up with. Thank you."

The deanship came with many challenges but it also came with one undeniable blessing, Marjorie Douglass, Executive Secretary to the Dean. Marjorie is quick, to the point, no nonsense, matter-of-fact, blunt, knowledgeable and smart. No one messes with Marjorie and nobody messes with the dean because no one gets to the dean without going through Marjorie. Marjorie served the previous dean for 24 years. She was born in Oxford, graduated from the university and actually could run the school without a dean, but she respects the position and is loyal to anyone assigned as dean.

Marjorie is a mature woman, snappy dresser that adorns herself with rings on all fingers of both hands. A ring in Marjorie's nose or navel is unthinkable and disgusting, but she has a thing about dress pins in the form of butterflies. Every morning she arrives to work with a butterfly pin attached to her shoulder. Marjorie, 'Girl Friday,' a true blessing in disguise.

Within less than an hour after the first faculty meeting, Marjorie announces, "Dr. Cooper would like to talk with you."

Dr. Cooper is a professor in Counselor Education and based on his course evaluations he is an outstanding teacher. When I talked with him earlier in his office I was impressed with his enthusiasm and vitality.

"Dean Payne, I want to bring something to your attention. We teach a large course, Human Growth and Development, each semester. It has four sections and each section is taught by a graduate teaching assistant. None are trained to teach the course and the course has a bad reputation. It has been a problem for years. I'd like to teach the course. I'd like for you to consider letting me combine the four sections into two, give me two graduate assistants and use the remaining two to do anything you want. I will guarantee the course will receive high evaluations."

"When would you like to start?"

"I have talked with the chair and he believes we could actually try it this semester."

"This semester? Classes start next week."

"Yes. But he thinks we can do it."

"Do it. Let me know if I can help. This is great. Thank you so much. Good luck."

No more, than he gets out, Marjorie comes in and sits in the chair next to my desk.

"Dean Payne, you are not going to find this written anywhere but we require three more courses than are needed to officially graduate. Every time something new comes along, a trend, fad, state requirement, we add a course rather than fit the concept or idea into an existing course. Over time we have increased the number of courses needed to graduate and we are out of line. Look at the transcripts of our graduates over the past five years and you will see all of them have taken three more courses than they need. It costs the students money and it is unnecessary. If I were the dean I'd meet with the Chair of Curriculum and Instruction and tell her to reduce the number of courses to graduate immediately."

The Chair of Curriculum and Instruction is a good hearted person, quiet and has been with the university for over 20 years. She is liked and respected by the faculty. She is far from pushy. She likes to take her time to think things over. Marjorie thinks she talks things to death but as I study her actions and behavior, I believe she has excellent collaboration skills. She is masterful at getting a group of people to work together for a common cause.

When I talk with her she acknowledges three additional courses have in fact been added and she confesses this is an added expense for the students. Her solution, "I'll set up a committee to look it over."

The chair leaves and before the door is closed, Marjorie is in. I explain, "It's going to committee."

Marjorie looks at me with disappointment and a degree of disgust. She turns to leave the office and whips, "woop tee do." Marjorie is a "can do" person and isn't fond of committees.

The committee is made up of five faculty members. All of the faculty are experienced, each 20 years or more at the university and most are graduates of the university. All know more about the situation than I do. All realize the extra cost to the students is an unnecessary burden. All agree to reduce the requirements to graduate but surprise me by also showing how a significant number of course offerings can be reduced by initiating a rotation system. The system would offer each required course once a year rather than once every semester. Much to my delight, and Marjorie's surprise, the committee gets the faculty to officially agree to eliminate the three unnecessary courses, initiate a rotation system plus drop a handful of electives. As the second semester begins, no one is teaching more than three courses and a fourth of the faculty are actually assigned to just two.

Before Christmas, I receive a generic letter addressed to 'Community Leader' from David Horn, Area Supervisor Division of Vocational Rehabilitation, indicating interest in establishing a sheltered workshop in the Oxford area. Inexpensive space is needed. I write at the top of the letter, "Why not consider our gym," and return the letter.

The School of Education has an unused basketball gym that, on weekends, kids break into. Within a week, David Horn and the Director of Vocational Rehabilitation, John Cook, are in my office. They need a place to operate out of for five years. Within five years their plan is to build a facility in the Oxford-Lafayette Industrial Park. An agreement is made to use the gym at a minimum monthly fee. When Mr. Cook hears of my experience with Vocational Rehabilitation in Kansas and the system, using my theory I perfected in Virginia for placing handicapped individuals on jobs, he contracts me to conduct training sessions two weekends a month for six months. For each workshop, the School of Education will receive 10 cases of paper in exchange for the services rendered.

As we start the second semester, the rent from the sheltered workshop pays the phone bill so everyone has a phone. The training contract solves our paper problem and God blessed us with a mild winter.

Armed with phones, paper and reasonable teaching loads we are able to focus on improving instruction.

Because of the Chancellor's talent and effort with raising money, as the second semester starts, all of the audio/visual equipment is repaired, a TV monitor and VCR player are mounted on the front wall of every classroom, white boards replace chalk boards and funds are earmarked for training and travel.

At the start of the second semester, before classes begin, all faculty attend a three day retreat for the purpose of developing a strategic plan. Dr. Malcolm Provost, creator of the Discrepancy Model, orchestrates the training. The Discrepancy Model has been used by many progressive Schools of Education throughout the eastern part of the United States.

The training laid the groundwork for a comprehensive strategic plan spearheaded by the School of Education's first Vision Statement:

> To Be a Stellar School Dedicated To Providing
>
> And Developing Exemplary Instruction, Utilizing
>
> Research that is Relevant, Practical and Effective.

The Vision Statement was supported by four guidelines:

> Improve Quality of Instruction

> Make Economic Decisions

> Activate Writing and Research

> Invest in Faculty Development

The strategic plan, vision statement and supporting guidelines provided a blueprint to follow for the next five years, and for the first time in a long time faculty were allowed and encouraged to attend and go to workshops outside the state of Mississippi.

In the beginning, faculty chose to go to conferences and workshops they were familiar with but as a culture of superior instruction began to manifest itself, many faculty began to explore new and different concepts and methodologies.

Four faculty members spent a week in Kansas attending a Dr. Don Deshler training workshop designed to help university students take better class notes, increase writing skills, and improve study habits. One of our most highly respected faculty members attended a Skunk Camp workshop in California. The camp was conducted by Tom Peters, bestselling author of *Thriving on Chaos*. The camp emphasized teamwork and collaboration and used examples of real cases where a small group of employees band together to bring about major changes in large organizations. The faculty member was the only educator ever to attend Tom Peter's camp.

When the faculty member incorporated what he had learned in his advanced leadership course, two doctoral students got so excited that the doctoral students and the faculty member went for additional training in Denver Colorado. The excitement about the power of collaboration eventually led to the two students writing the first co-authored dissertation in the United States. Co-authored books and articles are common but a co-authored dissertation was unheard of. The two students went on to spread what they had learned, one as a superintendent of schools in Arkansas and the other as Vice President of a Community College.

Taking the lead from Dr. Cooper during the second semester, all graduate teaching assistants were replaced by full time faculty. Graduate students were not allowed to be lead teachers in any class. The graduate teaching assistants filled supporting roles with regular faculty or became graduate research assistants. Excitement about teaching and a curiosity to try different things permeated the school. Students could feel a difference and it dramatically effected the course ratings.

Marjorie sticks her head in, "The Chancellor wants to see you. He doesn't sound happy."

"When?"

"Now."

As I enter his office in the Lyceum, his secretary instructs, "Go on in. He's expecting you."

I walk in. He remains seated. He looks up from his writing and motions with a nod of his head to sit in the chair across the desk from him.

"We've got a problem. I've been informed we have an instructor teaching our kids how to put condoms on bananas. I want you to personally look into this. Find out exactly what is going on and get back here with the details."

"Chancellor, I'll get right on it."

The Chancellor returns to his writing indicating the meeting is over. I go back to the education building and Marjorie follows me into my office.

"Marjorie, who's putting condoms on bananas?"

"Dr. Swartz."

"Nancy? The gal in Home Economics? The nice gal that teaches the large lecture course, Human Sexuality?"

"The one and only. The whole town's talking about her."

Dr. Nancy Swartz is a very attractive young lady in her late twenties. This is her third year teaching. Based on student evaluations, she is an outstanding teacher. She teaches in the auditorium in Meek Hall. I arrive a little before class time and the room is already filled to capacity. I sit on the back row of the tiered auditorium that seats 100 to 150 students. Dr. Swartz enters the stage on the left to an appreciative round of applause. During the lecture, she augments her lesson with slides and a short film clip. The subject is venereal disease. She is captivating and the students are engaged. No snickering. No horse play. This is serious business. When it comes to Q and Atime, the room becomes electric. Students ask intimate questions which receive matter of fact answers sprinkled with humor. She finishes to a round of applause. This doesn't happen often in any university at the close of a lecture. Her teaching is stellar.

As the students file out, I move down front. She catches my eye and motions for me to meet her by the stage door on the right.

"You are something. Great lecture."

"Thanks."

"Nancy, I need to talk with you a minute."

"Let's go to my office."

Her office is in Meek, very small and barely big enough for a desk and chair. I ask about the class and how it is going. She shares her enthusiasm and shows me her syllabus. Then she shows me the text. I realize this isn't a course in anatomy or physiology. This is a course about sex. She is obviously excited about what she does and then she drops the bomb.

"You know these kids are so uninformed, so naïve, they don't know how to put on a condom. You know what I have to do?"

Without waiting for a response, she continues.

"I teach them how to put on a condom on a banana. Can you believe it?"

"Well, that's sort of why I'm here."

"Oh don't worry. The kids don't have to pay for the condoms. I get them free from the Health Department. They have to furnish their own banana though."

I couldn't think of anything to say except, "You are really good. The university is proud to have a person like you teaching such an important course."

I leave Meek and immediately go to the Lyceum. I tell the secretary I want to set up an appointment to see the Chancellor. She assures me he wants to see me and asks me to wait just a minute. The next thing I know I'm in the Chancellor's office.

"What did you find out?"

"I sat in on the class and Dr. Swartz is excellent. It is in Meek and ..."

"I know. I know. What's the deal with the condom thing?"

"Chancellor, there is nothing to worry about. The condoms are free. They are provided by the Health Department but the students do have to furnish their own bananas."

The Chancellor looks at me dumbfounded and after several moments of silence he dismisses me with, "Dean Payne, I think you've missed the point."

I return to my office followed by Marjorie.

"What happened?"

I explain what happened in detail then she responds, "He didn't mention Nancy is a lesbian?"

"A lesbian? What's that got to do with it?"

"A lesbian teaching Human Sexuality, putting condoms on bananas in the South. Don't you think that is a little odd?"

Marjorie gets up and as she exits the office says, "Toto, we aren't in Kansas anymore."

We finish the year and the School of Education course evaluations are the highest of any of the other schools. We went from the bottom to the top in one year.

During the summer IBM donated computers to the School of Education. The IBM computers along with computers purchased through the Chancellor's fund raising efforts were first issued to the secretaries, then a computer lab was created and before fall classes began, every faculty member had a computer. The university set up training programs on how to use computers for both faculty and staff. The secretaries took the lead and were the first to master word processing. With reduced teaching loads we looked forward to having time to write and publish. But publishing is different from teaching. Teaching is, for the most part, individually driven but publishing requires a strong infrastructure of support for typing, editing and the actual submitting of manuscripts for publication. Strong secretarial help forms a major foundation for publishing.

Just as the fall semester gets underway, Marjorie mentioned Dr. Main wanted to see me. Dr. Main is one of the most respected faculty members in the university. He is in his late 60s and

I would guess he is going to see me about retirement. I go to Dr. Main's office and after some small talk, Dr. Main throws me a curve. "Everyone is talking about improving the quality of instruction. I've been teaching the same courses the same way for over 30 years. I want you to help me improve my teaching."

"Dr. Main, you are a legend. You don't need any help."

"Yes I do. My course evaluations are embarrassing."

"What do you think the problem is?"

"I'm boring."

"You are not boring."

"Visit my class and I'll show you."

Arrangements are made for me to observe Dr. Main's class. He is right. He is boring. The following week we look at some options.

"I've been reading about this new concept, co-teaching. This is something different from team teaching. Team teaching has resulted into turnabout teaching. You teach for a while, then I teach for a while. We switch back and forth. Team teaching is a thing of the past. Co-teaching is the new thing to do. It requires two teachers to teach simultaneously. Simply put, both teachers play off of one another like you see two commentators do on the News, Weather and Sports shows on television. The research indicates it is best when the pair are different from one another, especially different in personality. Robert Garmston seems to be the front runner on co-teaching. Here is some information on it. Look it over and let me know what you think."

The next day Dr. Main returns, "It's like a Frick and Frack show. Abbott and Costello. Laurel and Hardy. Who would you pair me with?"

"I'm thinking June Horn. Dr. Horn is short, you are tall. She is a female, you male. She is fast paced, hyper, you are slow, steady and deliberate."

"Dean, see if she is willing. It might be worth a try."

Dr. Horn is hesitant but willing to try it. The semester just started but it isn't too late. Some teaching assignments can be changed. Both Dr. Main and Dr. Horn end up co-teaching one course and each has one additional course, keeping them both within the two course limit. Within three weeks, the students are buzzin about the Main/Horn duo. It became known as the edutainment course of the School of Education: informative but entertaining and far from boring.

Some nights after working late I see Drs. Main and Horn working together practicing their routine. They were perfecting their craft. A unique twist on their craft.

Through Marjorie, I found out Dr. Main had gone to Wal-Mart and purchased all the George Burns and Gracie Allen Tapes. He studied the tapes and, of all things, he decided to play the role of Gracie. An intelligent wise professor playing dumb and naïve. What a clever switch. George Burns played by Horn and Gracie played by Main. Together their course blew the top out of the student evaluations at the end of the semester.

Dr. Robert Brown came to visit. "Dean, you offered to teach us how to write grants if we were interested and had time. I am interested and with my new load I have time."

"Believe me, it's simple. The government sends out an announcement to tell you what they want. You respond with a proposal. To get funded you must show need and how you are going to do what they ask. It's that simple."

"How do I find out about the grant requests?"

"They send them to me all the time. Hold on."

I buzz Marjorie. "Pull the latest RFP for me. Dr. Brown wants to see what a Request for Proposal looks like."

Marjorie comes in with a RFP. "This just came in. It's about teaching math, science and foreign languages to impoverished high school kids."

Dr. Brown somewhat startled, "That's no good. I'm in Physical Education and my doctorate is in Forestry. I don't know anything about math, science and foreign language."

"Robert, it doesn't make any difference what it is about. I'm just going to show you what an RFP looks like and the process for responding."

We look over the request and it is a meg-a-million dollar grant, titled Star Schools. It requires the host institution to uplink courses for high school students located in impoverished areas to downlink satellite dishes to the school districts. The request encourages cooperation among universities. The more we look over the request, the more I get interested.

"Robert, let's use this to learn from. We can play up need.

Heaven knows we've got need. We will partner with another university that knows something about distance learning via satellite."

Within the week, Robert contacted the state department to secure the facts and figures on impoverished school districts within Mississippi. I contacted the University of Kansas, seasoned experts in distance learning. We formed a partnership and submitted a proposal.

A month goes by and unexpectedly the Provost comes to my office. He sits down and abruptly speaks in an angry tone. "What's this thing about Star Schools? The Chancellor was just notified by Congressman Whitten that we have applied for a multi-million dollar grant teaching high school students math, science and foreign language by satellite television. Don't you know before submitting a grant proposal to the federal government you have to clear it through the research people here? This has embarrassed the Chancellor. He was blindsided and I'm mad.

"I was using this proposal to teach one of our faculty how to write and submit a grant. The Star Schools RFP looked, to me, like a good place to start."

"Good place to start! We are talking big bucks here. This is out of your League. You know nothing about satellite TV. You are still using overhead projectors and the principal investigator has a degree in Forestry."

"We've partnered with Kansas. They are experts in teaching by satellite and ..."

The Provost interrupts, "Partnered with Kansas. How the hell did you manage that?"

"Called a friend on the phone."

"Let me see the damn proposal."

I give the proposal and without moving from the chair he begins to look it over. I watch as he thumbs through the document. The first couple of pages he reads quickly, then he slows

228

down and I see he is not just reading, he is studying it. He finishes, "It's well written. I'll give you that. But damn it, it's out of your League. You don't stand a chance. From here on, go through the right channels."

He gets up and just as he approaches the door, he turns and surprises me, "Jim, if by some miracle you get it. I'll be the first to congratulate."

He exits, Marjorie enters. "What happened?"

"He likes it. Marjorie, by damn, I think he is impressed. Pissed but impressed."

A month goes by and I get a call from my friend in Kansas.

"Jim, we made the cut. It is down to five. Our lobbyist just called me. Your Chancellor will be notified we are in the top five."

"A lobbyist? I didn't know we had a lobbyist."

"You can't land something this big without inside help."

"But a lobbyist? The Chancellor will be furious."

After the call, I run to my boss, the Provost.

"I just got a call, Ray." I never have called the Provost by his first name before. "Ray, we've got a problem."

"What problem?"

"We are using a lobbyist with the Star Schools grant."

"You are what?"

"We are using a lobbyist to help us with the grant."

"My God. This is illegal. As a university in Mississippi, the use of a lobbyist is forbidden. This can't be."

"It   is."

"Wait here."

The Provost leaves. He returns within five minutes.

"The Chancellor ain't happy. You are going to be written up on this. You should know better."

I leave. The following week, Marjorie announces, "the Provost is on line one."

"Jim, go out front and stand by the curb. I'm coming to get you."

I hang up and as I pass Marjorie's desk, "Marjorie, it was nice while it lasted. Hold down the fort."

The car whips up to the curb. I get in.

"By God, you got it. You won the freakin lottery."

We go to a small bar off the square. The Provost gets so drunk he falls off the stool.

Over the next six months, a studio is built in the School of Education building, enough downlink satellite dishes are purchased to serve over 80% of the school districts in Mississippi. Rather than a stationary uplink, the decision is made to buy a mobile uplink so some instruction can be produced from the field. The satellite system is state of the art interactive so the teacher and students can simultaneously see and hear one another. Star Schools received a lot of high profile press but I knew we hit the jackpot when the mobile uplink was used to transmit the University of Mississippi football games on local TV. You can't get any bigger than that.

As the second year ends, the course evaluations are sky high, a few articles are published and four faculty produced books, and the Star Schools grant reaped the largest economic benefits ever recorded in the history of the School of Education.

The third year positions itself for the crowning achievement by being scheduled for a reaccreditation visit from education's most prestigious accreditation agency.

During the first semester of the third year, written documents would be submitted to the accrediting agency.

During the second semester, a site team would visit the campus and assess the physical facilities and interview the students and faculty. After the visit, the results would be sent to the Chancellor.

During the first semester of the third year, while the documents were prepared and submitted, the faculty continued their excellent teaching and additional faculty members published. During this time, staff development training funds were awarded to the School of Education by the Mississippi Department of Education. The School of Education quickly became the largest recipient of state funding. The School of Education received more state grant money than all other institutions combined and the Star Schools program hit full stride.

During the second month of the second semester of the third year the site team came. There were six members, two from the South, two from the Northeast and two from the Midwest. They arrived on a Sunday for a working dinner. Visited the facilities and interviewed students and faculty Monday and Tuesday. On Wednesday they were gone by noon.

Things were uneventful Sunday and Monday but Monday night one of the fraternities initiated their pledges by stripping them down naked, printed the word 'Nigger,' in big black letters with indelible ink on their backs and chests and dropped them off in a black community 25 miles north of Oxford. As the pledges tried to get back to campus in the middle of the night things got out of hand. The police got involved and video scenes of the nude pledges were shown on national television the next day and photos of the students appeared on the front pages of major newspapers that evening.

The event disrupted the community and the university and it shocked the site team. As the committee prepared to leave Wednesday morning they briefly met with me. I was thanked for the hospitality shown by the university. The pledge situation was not mentioned but the chair of the team remarked, she had never seen so many confederate flags in her life.

The following week the chancellor gave me the bad news. We had failed and were put on probation for two years. The site team would return in two years and go through the whole process again. Never in the history of the School of Education at The University of Mississippi had the school failed.

Although we failed we were still accredited but we were on probation and had two years to get our act together. The local and state newspapers mistakenly printed we had lost our accreditation. Students graduating from a non-accredited institution cannot, legally, be hired to teach in Mississippi. For the rest of the year, I spent the majority of my time explaining to the news media, students and parents that we were accredited and only on probation.

The chancellor was disappointed, the provost was beyond mad, the faculty and staff were

231

in disbelief and I was puzzled. I couldn't understand with strong evidence of superior teaching, the number of publications by faculty and the extensive number of awarded state and federal grants, how the School of Education could fail regardless of a stupid fraternity prank and a proliferation of confederate flags. It didn't make any sense to me.

Once the written report was received I studied it to plan what to do next. The written report did not mention anything about the fraternity incident nor the preponderance of confederate flags but it did mention that our students were lacking in understanding basic principles of education and were unaware of the vision and mission of the school. This was bizarre for me because after graduating from The University of Kansas and serving 15 years at The University of Virginia I knew, deep down, our students were every bit as good as those in Kansas and Virginia. I was so upset I called the chair of the site team. She was nice and tried to dodge my questions about the students and then she confided, "Dean, I don't know how to tell you this but when we talked with your students some couldn't even answer the simplest of questions. They acted dumb. Members of the committee actually commented, they acted retarded. I'd suggest you look at your admission procedure."

After the call, I was even more puzzled. Our students are sharp and upon graduation not only got good jobs, the follow-up evaluations completed by their principals indicated our students were superior in both content and skill.

I went back to studying the report. With the help of Marjorie, we discovered the team was not impressed or interested in results, they were interested in process. They wanted documentation on when, where and how things got accomplished. They wanted to see minutes taken at meetings, voting procedures, grading rubrics for portfolios, grading mechanisms for comprehensive exams and how doctoral dissertation defenses were assessed. In the middle of this discovery, while getting a coke from the soft drink machine located down the hall from my office, I bumped into one of the clients from the sheltered workshop. He mentioned how much he enjoyed talking with the visitors last week. I looked at him and followed him back to the workshop. I talked with some of the clients and, I'll be damned, the site team grabbed students out of the hall for interviewing and they included some of the rehab clients from the workshops by mistake, rehab clients diagnosed as having the condition of mental retardation.

When the sheltered workshop got underway, we wanted everyone to feel a part of the school. The clients were encouraged to use the drink and snack machines and if they wanted, on breaks, they could sit in on a class.

When I explained this unfortunate situation with the chancellor and the provost, the provost wanted to contest the visit. However, the chancellor didn't want to stir up any more controversy. We were in damage control and he wanted to get everything behind us. He wanted us to focus on being prepared for the next visit.

Although hardworking and loyal, Traditionalists don't trust the administration. They respect the position of the boss but they will never trust the individual in charge. Traditionalists hate change. If the administration tries to force change, Traditionalists will dig in and refuse to budge. In extreme cases, they will engage in a work slowdown or possibly strike.

To accomplish everything the first three years, the school was run like a family rather than a business. Decisions were made by consensus rather than democratic vote. Portfolios, comprehensive exams and dissertation defenses were assessed by professional judgement rather than rubric or checklist. As the dean I never tried to be a part of the family nor gain trust. I did try to always do trustworthy things but never for the purpose of gaining faculty trust or becoming a part of the family. There was no pressure to do anything, only suggestions. Because things were run like a family it was considered a bottom up administration as opposed to a top down administration.

To pass accreditation it was necessary to turn the operation from being a family to moving toward a business model. We had two years to do it. However any quick changes would possibly result in resistance.

During the first three years, we met as a group once a month but notes were taken rather than formal minutes. Decisions were arrived by consensus rather than vote. Attendance was not required but there was always a full house. Attendance was never recorded.

In order not to disrupt the flow and interfere with the momentum of things, for the next two years, a secretary was assigned to take notes and convert them to look like standard minutes. They also would record those that attended. At the beginning of each faculty meeting, the notes from the previous meeting, listing those that attended, were distributed. After looking the notes over, the faculty was asked if anything needed to be changed. If necessary, proposed changes were made and the notes were typed up and carefully filed. When decisions were made by consensus, the faculty were asked if anyone seriously objected. The results were transcribed by the secretary and written to look like it had been voted on. Something like, "and it was unanimously agreed upon, or it was agreed upon with (blank) reservations."

Thankfully, at this time there was a national movement to assess student papers and projects by design. The 'measurement by design' movement generated ideas on how to list acceptable criteria for grading papers and projects and different types of entries sprang forward. Since the faculty had time to attend conferences and the desire to improve instruction, the development of checklists and rubrics were incorporated within the School of Education without resistance or fanfare.

Over the next two years, documents mushroomed, indicating the when, where and how things got done. The School of Education continued to reap superior results while documenting the process for how the results were attained. As dean, I was impressed as a theorist and researcher. I was learning a lot. My wife was right, we were in Utopia.

Jeannette Phillips presented a proposal for me to sign. The proposal was in response to a federal grant to establish a National Food Service Management Institute. The institute was to teach public school cafeteria personnel how to prepare nutritious meals using government subsidies. The Star Schools grant was big but this grant was huge. Star Schools represented millions of dollars, this one zillions.

Learning the appropriate protocol from the Star Schools grant, I informed the research people, they gave the ok, I signed it and Dr. Phillips submitted it. A month later Marjorie informs me the provost wants to see me.

"Jim, what are you sniffing over there? Star Schools is one thing but a National Food Service Management Institute is another. There is only going to be one and it isn't going to be in Mississippi. And if it did come to Mississippi it wouldn't come here, it would have to go to Southern. I want this squelched."

"I went through the proper channels."

"Jim, I talked with them before meeting with you. They have assured me they won't approve anything like this again."

"How can I squelch it? It's already submitted."

"I don't know. But don't encourage it. Let it die on the vine."

I return to the School of Education. "Marjorie, what's the big deal about Dr. Phillip's grant?"

"A couple of years before you came, the governing board decided to designate some of the programs to specific institutions. It was a way to economize. Home Economics was to go to the University of Southern Mississippi. We were to close down Home Economics. Jeanette got her cookie cutters together and they raised holy hell."

"Cookie cutters?"

"Those four seniors, teaching in Home Economics, behind their backs are referred to as 'the four, little old lady cookie cutters.'"

"I like those ladies. They've got spunk and they are crafty."

"Well Jeanette headed up the movement."

"Movement?"

"They picketed, wrote letters. They single handedly saved Home Economics but the administration wishes they would go away."

"The provost told me to squelch Dr. Phillip's grant."

"My advice, stay out of it."

A month goes by. Marjorie informs me, I'm to go to the provost's office. I walk into the provost's office, he says, "The chancellor wants to see you."

I go across the hall. The chancellor's secretary says, "Go on in."

235

The chancellor greets me, shakes my hand and offers me a seat. I sit in one of the guest chairs in front of his desk. He surprises me by sitting in the adjacent chair next to me. He moves his chair close to mine.

"Dean, I've been called by Congressman Whitten. He wants to talk about the National Food Service Management Institute. I want you to go with me Friday. We will fly up Friday morning, meet the Congressman and return Friday night."

"Chancellor, I've read the proposal but, really, I don't know enough about it to respond intelligently to any questions. Maybe you should take Dr. Phillips."

"Jim, let me make this clear. We are not going there to promote the proposal. The board has made it clear, we are not to be in the Home Economics business."

I leave the chancellor's office, go across the hall to the provost's office.

"Jim, when you are around the chancellor, don't mention anything that relates to those little old lady cookie cutters. It is a sore subject."

Friday we fly to D.C. At Congressman Whitten's office we are greeted by two of his assistants. We enter his office. The Congressman stands. The chancellor walks forward while I trail behind.

They shake hands. The Congressman takes his seat while the chancellor and I sit in the guest chairs in front of his desk. The two of them exchange pleasantries. The grant proposal is barely mentioned. The Congressman is aging and I can hardly understand him. When it is over, the two of them shake hands and we leave without me ever saying a word or shaking anyone's hand.

As we get out the door, the chancellor, without looking at me, mutters, "Thank goodness, it's over."

A week later, Dr. Phillips enters my office. "Dean, we are going to get it. It is down to three."

"Jeanette, it would be great but don't get your hopes too high. There is only going to be one in the entire United States."

"Dean, when we get it we won't have enough space. We will need to get some trailers. I think three to start with. Could you talk with the chancellor about putting the trailers on the empty lot across from the School of Education building?"

Without waiting for a response, Jeanette leaves in her excitement. I phone the provost and tell him what just happened.

"Jim, it isn't going to happen and we are not going to junk up the campus with trailers." He hangs up. Another week goes by. Marjorie informs me the chancellor wants to see me.

I enter the chancellor's office. No handshake. He points for me to sit. I sit.

"Dean, we are to meet with Congressman Whitten next Monday. We will fly in Monday morning, meet and return Monday night. Tell Dr. Phillips she is to go with us."

We fly to D.C. We are met by the same two assistants. This time when we enter, Congressman Whitten rises, comes forward and embraces Dr. Phillips. Clear as a bell he says, "Jeanette, I haven't seen you in ages. How's the family?"

The two of them walk side by side to his chair behind his desk while one of the assistants moves another chair next to his for Dr. Phillips to sit in. The chancellor and I sit in the two guest chairs opposite his desk. I sense the chancellor isn't happy and I am uncomfortable. The Congressman talks with Jeanette but the grant issue is never raised.

The Congressman gets up. Jeanette gets up. The two of them embrace again. The four of us walk to the door and before leaving the Congressman shakes the chancellor's hand and finally he shakes my hand. We leave without comment.

Tuesday morning the provost walks in my office unannounced. He sits in the chair next to mine.

"Jim, I don't know how to tell you this but the National Food Service Management Institute grant is going to Southern. The bill will be signed this week. I am so sorry. I think the board had something to do with it. I'm so sorry."

"Ray, this will kill em. Jeanette has her heart set on this. She has worked so hard."

"I'd suggest you break the news to Dr. Phillips before she hears the news."

The provost leaves. I go to Jeanette's office.

"Jeanette, the provost just informed me the National Food Service Management Institute is going to Southern. I am so sorry."

"Dean, it isn't going to Southern. It is coming here."

"But the provost said…"

"The provost knows nothing. The bill hasn't been signed yet. Believe me, it's coming here and we are going to need a place to park three trailers. I've already sent out for bids."

"Ok. I hope you are right."

"Believe me, I am."

I leave. Friday the provost enters my office. "Cha-ching. It's coming here. Can you believe it?"

The next thing I know, just like Star Schools, we end up at the bar just off the Square and the provost, just like Star Schools, falls off the stool.

We have one more semester before the accrediting agency pays the visit. I can't wait. If anyone's ready, we are.

Unexpectedly, Marjorie tells me to go to the provost's office and he ain't happy. I enter his office, sit and before exchanging pleasantries, "Dean, what's this deal about a secretary selling cosmetics in your building?"

"What secretary? What cosmetics?"

"I don't know who and I don't know what. But, it is illegal for any employee in the university to double dip."

"Double dip?"

"Yes, work two jobs at the same time on campus. You can't be employed here and at the same time work another job at the same time. Find out who it is and let her go."

"Let her go?"

"Yes. Fire her."

I go back to my building. "Marjorie, who is selling cosmetics?"

"Shirley."

"Shirley Messer?"

"Yes. She has been selling Avon for years. Even before you got here. She is big volume. Everyone in the university buys from her."

Shirley Messer is by far the best typist in the school. She is fast, accurate and smart. Shirley prepares all our accreditation documents and types most of the faculty manuscripts. Without her we wouldn't be where we are. We wouldn't be ready for the accreditation visit and the faculty wouldn't be as productive as they are. Shirley is a dumpy, five foot two that doesn't own a comb and I'm sure she doesn't use her own products.

I go to her office. As usual she is sitting in front of her yellowing, nicotine stained computer. She has a filled ashtray on her left and a filled ashtray on her right with a half lit cigarette balanced on its edge. A haze of cigarette smoke permeates the air. She turns to me, looks up, with a second cigarette dangling from her lips, mutters without removing the cigarette,

"What's up?"

"Shirley, do you sell Avon?"

"Yeah"

She immediately turns, opens a top desk drawer, grabs a current catalog, whips back around and hands it to me. "We've got a special on men's cologne this week."

"Shirley, you can't sell cosmetics here."

"Really? I'm number one in the state."

"Shirley, there are rules. You can't work two jobs at once on campus."

She removes the dangling cigarette from her lips. "I can."

"I mean, I know you can but you can't. The university forbids it."

"You are kidding me?"

"I am not kidding. You have to stop or I've got to let you go."

"Go? You can't run this place without me. Go? Are you kidding? Where's the people going to get their cosmetics?"

"Look. You can't work two jobs at once. It is against the law."

Shirley looks at me as if I'm out of my mind and surprises me, "You need me. The School needs me. You've got a problem. You've got a real problem. You better figure it out."

She puts her cigarette back in her mouth, turns, and resumes typing.

As I walk out of her office I realize she is smarter than me and more important. I do have a problem. The accreditation team is coming and I need her more now than ever. I go to the provost to plea my case. The answer is to get her to only sell her products during lunch hour and she must sign a Form 9. The Form 9 assures the employee won't double dip, that is performing two jobs at the same time. I explain everything to Shirley. She signs the Form 9 and informs her customers they can only receive their products between noon and one. Lunch time is considered the employees time.

I come out of the bathroom and hear a lot of commotion from the end of the hall. I go down the hall to find a group of 20 to 30 people bunched outside Shirley's office. It is a little before noon. As I stand, looking, at twelve sharp, the door opens. Names begin to be called. I nudge my way inside. Shirley is sitting in her chair surrounded by small white Avon bags filled with products. The bags form a sea around her chair. She calls out names of each person, they step forward to pick up their order while simultaneously placing an order for the next week. She looks at me without getting up. "What now?" .

"Just checking."

I turn to leave.

"Dean, Here. Next week a special is on men's aftershave. Page nine." She hands me next week's catalog. I turn, pushing my way out of the office while glancing at page nine. The aftershave is in a bottle that resembles a golf cart. It is on sale. I turn around, wait my turn and order two bottles. One for me and one for my brother Dan.

The accreditation team comes. I am impressed with the quality of instruction, the number of faculty publications, the number of state grants, the national recognition of Star Schools and our prized gem, Jeanette's National Food Service Management Institute program. The accreditation team is equally impressed but revel in the voluminous documentation telling how, when and what we did. We pass. In fact, at the time we are the only School of Education in a public institution in the South to pass every standard.

During the remaining four years of my tenure as dean, the teaching evaluations continued to be superior, more state grants were awarded, Star Schools expanded and a multiple million dollar National Food Service Management Institute building replaced the trailers across from the School of Education building. It was erected next to Jeanette Phillips Drive in honor of Dr. Phillips and the building was named, of all things, after the Chancellor.

During the tenth year, my wife, Ruth Ann, was diagnosed with cancer. As she underwent chemo and radiation I was replaced by my Associate Dean. The next years as a full professor were difficult but I lived through them to experience another life.

No one messes with Marjorie
and no one messes with the dean
because to get to the dean you first
have to get through Marjorie.

Faculty published
books as well as articles.

Ribbon cutting for first sheltered
workshop housed in the gym in the
School of Education. I'm
positioned on the far left.

Five years later, breaking
ground for the sheltered
workshop to be built in the
Industrial Park. I'm the
bald one on the far left
looking down.

–Chapter 22–

Mrs. Goodrum

—

1999

Passed, Mrs. Goodrum and Ruth Ann

(I learn dying)

"Jim. Come quick," my wife, Ruth Ann called.

I was heading down the hall to the bedroom and as I turned around, this time louder.

"Jim. Help. It's Mother."

I ran to the front room. My wife was kneeling next to her mom. Mrs. Goodrum was lying on her left side, holding her right knee next to her chest. She had hit her foot on the coffee table. As I bent down to take a closer look I could see that the nail on her big toe was turning to a deep bluish-green. In real pain, her moans were raspy. She needed a doctor and fast.

Mrs. Goodrum has been a widow for many years. She lived with us, a spry ninety-two year old who seemed to be always in the way, in the bathroom, in the kitchen, around the house. Ruth Ann's job required her to be at work a little after seven. I went to the university much later so I could sleep in. On occasion, I would slip out of the bed to use the bathroom, only to return to find my bed made. Mrs. Goodrum had made that bed so fast, so perfect without a wrinkle.

Most mornings, I'd stumble around, shower, dress and report to the kitchen to find my breakfast laid out. Orange juice cold, eggs hot and toast buttered, but no Mrs. Goodrum. She was off in another room, cleaning. She would have excelled in the military but in her day women were not admitted.

My son-in-law, Randy, the first one, played Rugby for the university. He would bring home jerseys soaked in mud and grime. By the time Mrs. Goodrum finished with them, the jerseys were clean as new. One day, two of the other players' wives visited Mrs. Goodrum to find out her secret. I don't know what the secret was but the shelves in our washroom were better equipped than the chemistry labs at the university.

Mrs. Goodrum was five foot one. Wiry, weighing less than one hundred pounds, she wore white, Ked's tennis shoes with souls so clean they looked fresh from the store. Around the house she wore what I call a washwoman's uniform, light blue with buttons down the front. Mrs. Goodrum's hair was just turning white, relatively short and permed, never a strand out of place. Her face was hollow, neck wrinkled. She had beautiful hands, working hands.

In the afternoons, she would change into gray sweat pants and a gray sweat shirt to exercise barefooted in the front room. This day, she hit her toe on the coffee table doing some type of crossover exercise, while lying on the floor. Mrs. Goodrum took to exercising as she did to cleaning - all business, no non-sense.

I bent down, she gasped for air. I thought she was going to pass out. "Ruth Ann, call 911."

"The hospital is just a few blocks away. We can take her to the Emergency Room." Somehow my wife and I got her mother up and into the Silhouette. Riding to the hospital our patient continued to moan and breathe hard. By the Grace of God, at the Emergency Room door an attendant returning a wheelchair saw us, helped get Mrs. Goodrum in the chair, and wheeled her past the registration desk and directly to the x-ray unit.

While Ruth Ann filled out the paperwork, I parked the van. Within less than an hour Mrs. Goodrum was released and on her way back home. She had indeed broken her toe, which was bandaged securely enough to hold until Monday.

Driving home I murmured, "Can you believe my 92 year old mother-in-law broke her toe exercising to a Jane Fonda aerobics tape?"

"Yes I can," Ruth Ann whispered. "Yes I can."

Breaking a toe at any age isn't funny. During the next six months Mrs. Goodrum gradually reinstated her routine of making my bed, preparing my breakfast and cleaning. But suddenly, without warning, she suffered a stroke. From that day on nothing was the same.

Her mind deteriorated with her body. She lost her memory, control of her bowels, and her mobility. For two years, Ruth Ann and I cared for her as an invalid. Then Ruth Ann injured her back. Mrs. Goodrum was admitted to a nursing home in Belton, Missouri. For four years, she never regained full consciousness. For all practical purposes she was considered brain dead.

After her death, I found myself at night reliving isolated events during our care for her. These unsolicited flashbacks made it impossible for me to sleep. I would get up, take pencil to paper and set down these memories. After writing, I was able to return to bed for a good night's rest.

Flashback: Dessert

Ruth Ann had made stir-fry vegetables. We were seated in front of the TV - Ruth Ann,

Mrs. Goodrum and I were watching Mrs. Goodrum's favorite program, *Wheel of Fortune*. Mrs. Goodrum was having a good day. At that time, she could move from room to room unassisted. She could fork the stir fries and eat them by herself, only dropping a small morsel or two in her lap. Ruth Ann, without looking, automatically would pick up and return it to the side of Mrs. Goodrum's plate to be discarded later as garbage.

The scene was all too familiar and the movements habitual. I finished my dinner and went to the kitchen. After rinsing and putting my dishes in the dishwasher, I cut five, perfect two-inch squares of fresh-cooked brownies from the tin and placed them neatly on a saucer. Gobbling down three of the soft, sweet, chocolates. The frosting at least a fourth of an inch thick. Ruth Ann knew how I liked them.

I returned downstairs to the TV room. Neither Ruth Ann or Mrs. Goodrum had finished their meal. I placed two brownies on Mrs. Goodrum's TV tray without comment. Before I could step away, Mrs. Goodrum focused on the brownies. With her fork balancing with stir-fries in her right hand she simultaneously and efficiently, snatched up a brownie with her left and had taken a small bite of brownie before the stir-fries could get to her lips. Ecstasy radiated from her eyes. She returned the stir-fries to her plate. At ninety three, Mrs. Goodrum had the grace and agility of a seasoned performer.

Like a shot, Ruth Ann shouted, "Jim!" And although quick, was far too late, for now Mrs. Goodrum's first brownie was gone. Within a millisecond, a lot happened; automatic primal instinct, thoughtless yet innocent delivery, Pavlovian reaction, surprise, ecstasy, perturbment, and now encouragement. Ruth Ann turned with concern and caring and said, "Mother, let's finish the stir-fries first."

Without moving her head, Mrs. Goodrum rolled her wide eyes toward Ruth Ann. Without an utterance, without taking her eyes off Ruth Ann, her left hand moved with purpose, toward brownie number two. Within an instant, she had taken another bite. It was like a spin move in the NBA as one moves to the basket catching their opponent off-guard for just a split second. And, in this case, the opponent, Ruth Ann, knowing she had been beaten, leaned back and sighed. "Jim, I won't forgive you for this."

246

Mrs. Goodrum finished number two with the finality of a slam-dunk while Ruth Ann hopelessly looked on. Mrs. Goodrum's eyes never left Ruth Ann.

By this time I was already heading down court, up the stairs, and to the kitchen – fast break – Ruth Ann was no match for us on this day of the brownie. Brownies 5, Stir-fries incomplete.

Flashback: Cookies

The next morning, we were eating breakfast around the kitchen table. Biscuits, scrambled eggs, oh so warm, tasty. I finished first and started to get up from the table. Ruth Ann looks at me as if to say, "I dare you to leave."

I settle back down.

This was going to be another good day: Mrs. Goodrum can get the scrambled eggs to her mouth with a spoon, unassisted. She can drink her coffee unassisted without dripping it on anything. She likes finger foods and the biscuit is a pleasurable experience for her both in taste and in kinesthetic touch.

I'm restless, but know not to move first. After what seemed like hours, Mrs. Goodrum is finished. She liked her breakfast. She moved her lips and tongue indicating bliss.

"Mother, would you like a cookie to go with your coffee?" I jumped to my feet as Mrs. Goodrum smiled with anticipated joy.

We were in the middle of a major snowstorm, and we had just stocked up on cookies, candies, snacks, chips, dip etc. After quickly rinsing the breakfast dishes and putting them in the dishwasher, I proudly laid out an array of cookies that would make any eight-year-old stare in amazement and wonder.

As I held the plate in front of Mrs. Goodrum, I said, "Mrs. Goodrum, do you want sugar wafers, fudge wafers, pinwheels, Fig Newtons, Nutter Butters, or Oreos?"

Without hesitation, without any latency in her response, she responded in her crackly, frail, monotone voice, "No Fig Newtons."

Mrs. Goodrum knows cookies.

Flashback: Lunch

We are eating lunch in the dining room, and Ruth Ann has outdone herself: mashed potatoes, green beans, pork chops, rolls. Everything was prepared to perfection. Ruth Ann is involved in a mostly one-way idle conversation with Mrs. Goodrum. Mrs. Goodrum occasionally responds in two or three words that don't make sense. It doesn't make any difference; she is obviously in a state of culinary bliss.

I was absorbed by the accumulation of birds eating fresh seed I had scattered on the snow outside the dining room window. Two glistening red cardinals. A blue jay. A robin I didn't realize robins ate seeds; I thought they ate worms. Fifteen to twenty other birds, some with blue heads, some with white undersides, some yellow, almost like canaries. It was too bad Mrs. Goodrum couldn't see well enough to enjoy these gifts from nature. I was totally absorbed, when suddenly I heard, "Mother, would you like a brownie?"

A shot of adrenalin charged through my body. I looked around. Both had completed lunch. I wasn't even half finished. The birds, those damn birds, had mesmerized me.

Ruth Ann began to clear the table. I didn't know what to do, a bead of sweat popped through the skin on my forehead. I had an emptiness in the pit of my now half-filled stomach. Startled, scared, almost in a panic, I gracefully got up from the table and excused myself without comment. I walked crisply to the stairs, put on my coat, scarf and the hat stored on the stair rail and I began to leave to shovel the snow. As I started to close the door, I looked up the stairs, into the kitchen, just in time to see Ruth Ann remove the Reynolds Wrap from the tin, only to find that her husband had eaten the last brownie an hour ago.

As I ducked outside, she looked into the empty tin in disbelief. She was stunned, shocked; had she been wearing a supporter, she would have been jockless. Another spin move, and I was down the court, headed toward the shovel, smiling in contentment. "No Fig Newtons for me either."

Flashback: Cancun

We are downstairs. TV trays, black bean soup with sausage, sandwiches garnished with Dijon mustard. Mrs. Goodrum is a little shaky today. She can't feed herself, so Ruth Ann feeds her a spoonful at a time, a bite of sandwich at a time.

We are still in the middle of a record-setting snowstorm. Our eyes are glued to the Weather Channel. The phone rings; it is our youngest daughter, Janet, calling from Cancun. RuthAnn takes the phone, and I assume the position of Mrs. Goodrum's healthcare provider.

Ruth Ann hangs up, exchanges places with me, and explains that Janet and Todd are having a wonderful vacation. Then she asks, "Where is Cancun?" "I have no earthly idea."

Mrs. Goodrum peeps, "I think it is south." I quip, "I can't even spell Cancun."

Mrs. Goodrum replies, "I can spell canteen," and then proceeds to spell, "C-A-N-T-E-E-N."

Ruth Ann looks at me. I look at her, and I realize we are in one of those free-association days - Rorschach conversations that go everywhere but nowhere, all at the same time. "Where did Kim (our oldest) just return from?" I ask.

"Sidney, Australia," Ruth Ann replies.

"Gosh, can you believe it? This younger generation. You and I have never been out of the continental United States, and they have been all over the place. Where was our last vacation?"

"Tunica, Mississippi," Ruth Ann quips.

Mrs. Goodrum mumbled, "Clyde took me to the Ozarks once."

Einstein was right. $E = mc2$. Everything is relative.

Flashback: Hair Day

Every Thursday at 4 p.m. Mrs. Goodrum goes to the Hair Port. Ruth Ann andI get her in the van, and we can see this is going to be very tough outgoing. Our patient is moving very slowly and seems somewhat disorganized.

It takes us longer than usual to get into the salon. On close inspection, her snow white hair is getting thinner, but, it shines radiantly. After Hair Port magic, she looks like royalty, so proper, so reserved, so pristine.

We always eat out after Mrs. Goodrum's appointment. We begin to discuss where to go this day. Our thoughts turn to easy access and warm temperature. It is the middle of February and even in Mississippi, it is still relatively cold. We decide on Shoney's and enter the front door, Ruth Ann, holding both of Mrs. Goodrum's hands is walking backwards. I walk behind my hands placed firmly under her armpits. Slowly, left, right, left, right…

Hostess: "Table or booth?"

Ruth Ann: "Either, one, but please make it the warmest spot in the place."

Hostess: "How about here?"

Ruth Ann: "Too close to the door. There's a draft."

Hostess: "How about here?"

We start to help Mrs. Goodrum seat herself and notice the floor vent. For some ungodly reason, the air conditioner is on.

Ruth Ann: "Sorry, the air is on. Could we sit in that corner?"

We are seated at last. We get hot coffee down Mrs. Goodrum. We all keep our coats on. With a fork of chicken in one hand and a roll in the other Mrs. Goodrum, can't decide which is which. She brings both to her lips simultaneously. Instinctively, Ruth Ann takes over and begins to feed her. Mrs. Goodrum settles back - she doesn't have to think; she can just enjoy each slowly chewed morsel. After each bite, she smiles. You can see the delight in her eyes. The food is acceptable, but for Mrs. Goodrum, it is a delight.

Ready to leave, we try to put on Mrs. Goodrum's gloves, but she can't control her fingers. Ruth Ann works to get the gloves on as Mrs. Goodrum looks on, confused, unable to help. Her hands, seemingly, are not connected to her body. Finally, Ruth Ann settles for Mrs. Goodrum's fingers being bunched up in a fist in each glove. The fingers on the gloves, shoot out in random directions. Ruth Ann on the left and I on the right, each support Mrs. Goodrum as we exit. Mrs. Goodrum is having a hard time putting one foot in front of the other. As we walk out through the foyer, I glance up and see the three of us in the full-length mirror, struggling to walk-lion on the left, tin man on the right, and scarecrow in the middle. "Toto, this road definitely doesn't lead to Kansas."

Flashback: Kevorkian

Four straight days, Mrs. Goodrum has slept every moment, except for getting up to eat. She has to be fed every bite, and she has lost control of her excretion functions. She is just existing. I read in *USA Today* about the trial procedures of Jack Kevorkian and, although I would never consider taking another person's life, I wonder if I would take my own life under these conditions. Mrs. Goodrum's presence makes this mental exercise take on an uncomfortable reality. I probably would, pull the plug on myself under certain conditions. As disturbing as this thought is, however, I realize Mrs. Goodrum is not capable of making such a decision, nor would I.

Kevorkian provokes complicated thoughts that make me question. I know what is right for me but it takes courage to do. But when it comes time to do, am I capable of doing it.

Flashback: C.D.

For ten days Mrs. Goodrum has slept 21 hours out of 24. When awake, she is fed while in a senile state. Suddenly, on day 11, without warning, she rises from the fog and enters our world. All morning she sits or shuffles from room to room (with Ruth Ann's and my assistance) sits, watches TV, talks to herself in short sentences, sits. This is a good day, no, better than good - this is a very good day.

To celebrate, Ruth Ann decides we will eat in the dining room upstairs. She lays out our fine china, the sacred silver. Everything looks so perfect. Mrs. Goodrum is assisted into the dining room and is seated at the elegantly prepared table. A feast: roast beef, potatoes, apple pie, candles, even background music. Mrs. Goodrum feeds herself with very little assistance.

During dessert, she just can't quite master the fork. Halfway through her pie, Mrs. Goodrum looks up and asks, "What is that?"

Ruth Ann replies, "Somewhere My Love." We were listening to QVC's compact disc of Kenny Rogers. QVC, the shopping channel had run a survey to determine what people wanted to hear, and Kenny Rogers complied with the people's wishes.

After we finish eating, Mrs. Goodrum joins us in the kitchen. She sits at the counter while Ruth Ann and I clean the dishes. Out of the blue, Mrs. Goodrum utters with a clean crisp tone, "You Are So Beautiful." Sure enough it's, Kenny Rogers singing *You Are So Beautiful*. Ruth Ann turns up the volume, and as we finish the dishes, we notice Mrs. Goodrum is actually tapping her foot, to the music, in perfect time.

Mrs. Goodrum smiles and says, "Nice record."

Ruth Ann replies, "Mom, it is a ... very nice record."

Ruth Ann and I exchange glances. We smile as both of us realize she was about to explain it wasn't a record, it was a C.D. Compact disc or record, Kenny Rogers was making this a non-Kevorkian day. Our three souls were touched as "You Light Up My Life" filled the room. A Kodak moment, QVC rises to the occasion, much to Ruth Ann's delight. I have to acknowledge the shopping channel, on this day, has achieved excellence.

Flashback: Kind Word

We decide to take a trip to Memphis. As we speed along the highway, Mrs. Goodrum looks out the window with a look of great contentment on her face.

We get her in the wheelchair, cover her legs with a light blanket and wander through the mall. We decide to eat an Annandale's. Mrs. Goodrum loves Annandale's. Since it is very difficult for her to go down stairs, we must travel the long hall, past the restrooms, out the back, past the dumpster, down another dark narrow hall into the kitchen, past the dishwasher and the garbage, over the rubber floor mat, out into the dining room door to reach a table. Thank God for ADA. I wonder how many people really know how important the American Disabilities Act.

Thirty years ago, I worked with Ross Evans, a black psychologist. Intelligent, handsome, great personality. Oftentimes we went to lunch together. We talked a lot about race and cultural differences. I distinctly remember asking him how he felt when whites were forced to serve him in restaurants, when he knew they didn't like it.

He explained how he used to have to plan his trips around where he could eat and go to the bathroom. How his mother always packed something to eat for him whether he needed it or not. His comment was simple, "I really don't care how they feel. I like knowing I can go anywhere, knowing I can get something to eat and go to a bathroom. If they give me a kind word, that is a bonus."

I remember the joke about the guy that goes into a greasy spoon to order breakfast. The waitress saunters over and asks, "What do you want?"

He replies, "I'd like a kind word - and if it's not too much trouble, give me black coffee, two eggs over easy, hash browns, sausage, and a side of toast, white."

The waitress spins on her heels and goes to the kitchen. She returns with the coffee and places it on the table with a plunk that causes a little to slop on the table. Before anything can be said, she spins on her heels and goes back to the kitchen. She returns to the table, slides a plate to him, proudly announcing, "Two eggs over easy, hash browns, sausage with a side of toast, white. What else do you want?"

The customer looks up and asks, "Where's the kind word?"

Disgruntledly, she looks at him and then, after grabbing some composure, glances to the left, and to the right, then leans forward and in a low, matter-of-fact tone, states, "Don't eat the sausage."

Stairs, back doors, kitchens, garbage, thanks to ADA and Affirmative Action we don't have to worry about finding a place to eat. Yes, a kind word is a bonus.

Flashback: Criterion

I'm in the office. The phone rings. It is Ruth Ann, crying and muttering something about the nursing home. I hang up and immediately drive home to her. Her eyes are red, and her face is wet.

She explains the nursing home in Oxford has called, and Mrs. Goodrum's name has come to the top again. She can be admitted. This has happened before. Each time, Ruth Ann decided to admit her she changed her mind at the last minute. After each rejection, Mrs. Goodrum's name is placed on the bottom of the list, and the whole process starts over.

This time is different. For four months Mrs. Goodrum's condition has deteriorated. She doesn't even know Ruth Ann, her daughter, her own flesh and blood. How humiliating, how tragic.

For many months Mrs. Goodrum has been unable to remember who I am, but I'm only her son-in-law. I am in complete control of my mental faculties, and I get confused about my own sons-in-law. My youngest daughter Janet has been married less than a year and, on occasion, I call her husband by the name of the person she dated in high school. To make things worse, her older sister Kimberly has been married twice, and I'm hesitant to learn number two's name because I question if he's here to stay.

Ruth Ann is beside herself. Should she admit Mrs. Goodrum this time? All those papers to sign. Yet, she will be safe. Will they treat her with love and affection? We are growing tired, impatient; yet, she will be safe. What will Mrs. Goodrum think? Can we afford it?

How does one decide when to admit an elder to a nursing home?

Ruth Ann decides the nursing home is acceptable, the best thing to do. The question is "when?" Timing is important. It is decided, she will be admitted the following Monday. The decision is based on a daughter's need to provide safety for her mother.

Flashback: Admitted

It is Monday. Ruth Ann is strong but emotional. After much mental and emotional effort, we get Mrs. Goodrum to the nursing home in Oxford situated less than a mile from our home.

The place is clean, yet cold; organized, yet distant; too perfect, too businesslike. This is not home; this is a business.

Have we made the right decision?

Mrs. Goodrum says nothing. She acquiesces. She goes forward as if in a trance. Ruth Ann is confused. It hurts so much.

We return to the car, and Ruth Ann goes to pieces. Her whole body is sobbing. Neither she nor I were trained on how to handle this situation.

As we drive away, I tell myself, "Don't look back." I had mentally rehearsed what I would do: I would look forward. As I mistakenly look back, a tear came to my eyes, and my stomach turned. I was sick. I remember reading Orwell's *Animal Farm* when the truck pulled away with the horses in the back, and the sign on the back of the truck read, "ACME Glue."

Flashback: Phone Call

It is early evening. I'm staying at the Holiday Inn in Meridian. I take a long distance call from Ruth Ann. This is Mrs. Goodrum's second day in the nursing home.

Ruth Ann is crying. I have difficulty making out what she is saying. As she continues talking, I begin to understand that Mrs. Goodrum is terrified. She won't let go of Ruth Ann's hands when Ruth Ann visits. Ruth Ann has to tear herself away in order to leave. The word "terrified" paints a tragic picture, in my mind.

The next evening, after completing my work, I drive home as fast as I dare. I go to the nursing home. As I pull up, I see Ruth Ann's car. I go directly to Mrs. Goodrum's room. Ruth Ann is sitting next to her mother's bed. Mrs. Goodrum is lying in a fetal position, holding Ruth Ann's hand.

As I approach, Ruth Ann announces me, "Mother, Jim is here."

Mrs. Goodrum remains non-responsive. Her eyes are wide-open; she doesn't move. Her cheeks are sunken. I swear she looks like a wild, frightened animal. – she is *"terrified."*

Flashback: Five Days

Five days have gone by. Mrs. Goodrum continues in a fetal position, her eyes are wide open most of the time. Sometimes she covers up her head with a blanket. Ruth Ann visits 2 - 6 times a day, as often as she possibly can.

Every time I visit, I am caught off guard by the old people there - on the porch, in the day room, in the hall. Walkers and wheelchairs, everybody needs assistance of some type.

The odor crosses between Pine Sol and Clorox. The floors glisten. The staff all wear clean uniforms and greet me politely as I walk through the halls.

Mrs. Goodrum's room is 15' x 20'. It has two single beds, and a Mrs. Allen is Mrs. Goodrum's roommate. However, I've never seen Mrs. Allen. Ruth Ann explains that the minuteMrs. Allen wakes up, she gets in her wheelchair and rolls all over the complex. She doesn't talkto anyone; she just rolls, like a caged animal.

The room is exactly like a hospital room with a connecting bathroom. The beds are hospital beds.

Five days later, Mrs. Goodrum has lost a pair of slippers, a pillowcase, and a night gown and her glasses. Her name has been put on every piece of clothing with a laundry pencil, but wewere warned that things get lost. But, I can't help thinking she has never been out of that bed!

It is almost impossible to get Mrs. Goodrum to sit up, even to eat. When she is fed – she has not fed herself for heaven knows when – she takes small bites. There is no twinkle in her eyes, and she doesn't smack her lips together anymore. When I ask her, "How does it taste?" there is no audible response or any recognition that she hears my question.

The nursing home is a pitiful sight. Everyone in a wheelchair is either slumped forward or leaning way over to one side. The few who use walkers shuffle from place to place. All have sad eyes and many have open mouths that drool. Worse yet are those who are bedridden. They lie motionless, as does Mrs. Goodrum, and some constantly moan.

Mrs. Goodrum continues to be terrified. Ruth Ann admits to great guilt. I am shocked. Is this what it is all about? Is this what life boils down to?

It has been less than three years ago that Mrs. Goodrum broke her toe on the coffee table doing aerobics to that Jane Fonda video. Today she won't sit up in bed.

Flashback: Seventh Day

Enough is enough. Ruth Ann can't take anymore. Today, Mrs. Goodrum comes home.

Ruth Ann drives her car to the nursing home I drive the van. Ruth Ann signs the release papers and I go dutifully to Mrs. Goodrum's room to pack. She continues in her fetal position, not realizing something is happening.

All her possessions fit in one suitcase and one hanging bag. I take everything to Ruth Ann's car. Next, I'm met by two aides who help me with Mrs. Goodrum. Her dead weight is difficult for me to handle. Finally, the two aides politely crowd me out of the way. They get her up and into the wheelchair. Before I know it, we are next to the van. The back seat is tilted backwards and the two aides slide her in. Suddenly, I glance over my shoulder and see Ruth Ann staring at us.

We drive to the house and, after much effort and a few near drops, Mrs. Goodrum is backin her room, in her bed.

The phone rings. It is Kimberly, our oldest daughter. She knows this is homecoming day.She is calling to find out how everything has gone. Ruth Ann gets on one phone, and I get on theextension.

Kim asks, "How did it go?" Ruth Ann gives her a ten minute, blow-by-blow account.

Suddenly Ashley, our granddaughter, Mrs. Goodrum's great granddaughter, asks, "Are you OK, Mimi?" Apparently she is on Kim's extension.

"Fine, fine, Honey."

"Is nanny OK?" the six-year-old asks.

"Yes, fine, fine."

"Do you still have to feed her with that plunger?"

"Yes, yes, but it's OK. She is doing fine."

"Does she ever get up to go to the potty?"

"No, no. She is still in diapers, but it is OK."

"Is she ever going back there?"

"Probably not. At least not now."

"Does this mean Nanny is a nursing home dropout?"

There is a pleasant silence. I sense a slow grin – a light-glowing grin moving across the telephone wires – from both Ruth Ann and Kim. Then, from the lips of a troubled Ruth Ann, "Yes, Ashley. I guess you could say Nanny is a nursing home dropout."

Flashback: Live Heart in a Jar

For six uninterrupted months, Mrs. Goodrum lies in bed, expressionless. Every moment she is cared for, her every need attended to. We continuously and systematically roll her to prevent bed sores.

She can't see, she can't speak, she can't sit, she can't chew. What can she do? At this point, she can swallow without having to have her throat massaged. She urinates regularly in her diapers, and her bowel movements are moist. She makes a face when given her evening medication, even when we try to disguise it in chocolate or strawberry Ensure. Occasionally, her foot will rhythmically move when music is played. That is it. That is life in the world of Mrs. Goodrum.

"Ruth Ann, it is scary. We are doing nothing more than keeping your mother alive. It's too weird. It's as if we were scientists, keeping a body alive in a basement laboratory," I pronounce.

As Ruth Ann takes the filled syringe of Ensure and shoots it into Mrs. Goodrum's mouth, she responds without emotion, "A live heart in a jar."

Feed Mrs. Goodrum.

Wipe Mrs. Goodrum.

Roll Mrs. Goodrum on her side.

Flashback: Kiss

Janet, our youngest daughter, and her husband Todd came to share exciting news about the purchase of their first home. They show us the pictures, specs, and explain in unnecessary detail the procedure for closing, as if we had never bought a house ourselves.

I can't get over them: Janet looks so beautiful and Todd so handsome. Todd and I go golfing and Ruth Ann and Janet go shopping. Ruth Ann is so alive and happy.

The next morning, Janet and Todd get dressed, pack the car, and ready to go back to their new home in St. Louis. Before leaving, Janet goes in to say goodbye to Nanny. I stand in the bedroom doorway and watch.

Janet talks to Mrs. Goodrum as if she could understand. She holds Mrs. Goodrum's hand while touching her grandmother's forehead. Mrs. Goodrum lies expressionless, eyes open. She resembles an injured animal lying at the side of the road. Janet bows her head for a moment, bends over and kisses her Nanny on the forehead. Janet's eyes moisten.

The routine is familiar. I shake hands with Todd, he hugs Ruth Ann and gets in the car. As he starts the car, Janet hugs me, hugs and kisses her mother, and begins to cry. I open the car door. She gets in and they back out of the driveway.

Their visit is a happy, sad sort of thing, like caring for Mrs. Goodrum.

Feed Mrs. Goodrum.

Wipe Mrs. Goodrum.

Roll Mrs. Goodrum on her side.

Flashback: Smart Pills

Kimberly calls to give us an update on our granddaughter Ashley. Ruth Ann is on the kitchen phone, and I am on the extension in the bedroom.

Ashley has been diagnosed with Attention Deficit Disorder and has been put on Ritalin.

She is passing everything at school but not without a lot of effort.

Ruth Ann: "Can you tell a difference?"

Kim: "I think so."

Ruth Ann: "How is Ashley handling it?"

Kim: "Fine. Yesterday she asked if she could take one of those smart pills when she sat down to play at the computer."

Ruth Ann: "Smart pills?"

Kim: "Yeah, she believes it helps her concentrate."

Thinking to myself, I wonder if smart pills would help Mrs. Goodrum?

Feed Mrs. Goodrum.

Wipe Mrs. Goodrum.

Roll Mrs. Goodrum on her side.

Flashback: Intelligent

Just a few years ago, I invited Mrs. Goodrum to come to a freshman class of honor students I was teaching. We were discussing value differences and how values are formed over time.

Mrs. Goodrum came, sat up front, and started telling about when she was born, where she went to school, how she got married – much in the same fashion that a doctoral defense would begin. Next came the questions. She was asked about the first train she rode, followed by plane, and then she described her first experience with a telephone, a refrigerator, a television. I was fascinated. She explained in detail, with a sense of humor, the major events in her life.

She talked about drawing water from a well and putting butter in a bucket and lowering it in the well to keep it cool. She talked about preparing meals on a wood stove and how she ironed clothes. When the students asked about her wedding, I tuned out. I had heard about how she fell in love with Clyde many, many times. It always ended the same way – blissful. Boringly blissful.

Finally, I interrupted this monolog to take, I thought, a well-deserved break. As the class got up to stretch and secure refreshments, one student on her way out, turned to me and said, "Boy, do you realize how intelligent she has to be? I could never have lived like that."

I looked at Mrs. Goodrum and realized I'd never viewed her as intelligent. She had been intelligent, unique, creative, and precious, even without smart pills.

Feed Mrs. Goodrum.

Wipe Mrs. Goodrum.

Roll Mrs. Goodrum on her side.

Flashback: Wind

I had just finished changing Mrs. Goodrum. Cleaned, wiped, and powdered her. She was ready to be fed. Ruth Ann entered with the Ensure the infamous syringe and a couple of small containers filled with baby food, all laid neatly on a tray. As Ruth Ann began the feeding, I straightened the room. I emptied the trash, dusted the chest of drawers, wiped off the window ledge, and returned to my chair next to Mrs. Goodrum, directly across the bed from Ruth Ann.

I had eaten something that was building up pressure in my stomach and intestine. I momentarily stood up next to the bed, meaninglessly tugged and straightened the sheets, while simultaneously releasing an *almost* silent blast of repugnant air. I decompressed. Instantaneously, as the odor began to rise and permeate the room, my eyes met Ruth Ann's. With an expression of pity I rolled my eyes toward the patient, shifting the gastronomic blame on defenseless Mrs. Goodrum.

Ruth Ann reciprocated with an understanding glance, and I returned to my chair safe and comfortable.

Such actions in elementary school could never go unnoticed nor could the blame be shifted so easily. The culprit would immediately be identified with the question, "Who pooped?" All eyes would have shifted to me and I would shrink in embarrassment.

In junior high, now referred to as middle school, such an act would generate uncontrollable commotion until someone would shout "Slugs," followed by a hit to my upper arm. The room would fill with laughs, giggles and sheepish grins.

High school students would nonchalantly ask if there is a frog in here or some comment would be made about pulling one's finger, as if this action magically releases wind.

Only in adulthood can the emission of intestinal gas be passed off on an unsuspecting senior citizen with the ease and grace of a "slight of hand" trick.

Feed Mrs. Goodrum.

Wipe Mrs. Goodrum.

Roll Mrs. Goodrum on her side and...God bless her.

Mrs. Goodrum lived to be 99.

My granddaughter, Ashley, thought smart pills might help Mrs. Goodrum

This is Mrs. Goodrum 5 years before her stroke.

–Chapter 23–

Esim

—

2001
Married, Esim Erdim
(I learn romance)

It's after five. I'm in my office cleaning up some papers so I can go home for a relaxing weekend. Abby, a colleague, sticks her head in. "Jim. Esim and I are going to the Square for a drink. Come join us."

"Thanks, but I've got things I need to finish."

"Come on. You don't have anything important to do. Come with us for some excitement."

"I'll join you later."

"You say that every time but you never show. Come on."

"Abby look, I don't feel like it."

"For crying out loud. You won't feel any better staying here. Come on."

"Okay, okay. Give me five minutes. I'll meet you. Where are we going to do our drinking?"

"Meet us on the deck above Old Venice."

"O.K."

"Promise?"

"Promise."

"Don't disappoint us."

"I won't. I'll be there."

Abby, a dear colleague of mine, teaches in Counselor Education. She is a bit on the pleasingly plump side and cute as a button. Her mission in life is to socialize. She loves people. She adores groups of people. Her interpersonal skills are off the chart. That heart is golden. I don't think it possible for her to go any place by herself. She is always gathering people to her. She gets people together for breakfast. For lunch. For dinner. She throws surprise picnics. She can drink most of us under the table.

Esim's office is directly across the hall from mine. She teaches TESL, Teaching English as a Second Language. She has two doctorates, is smart as hell, and reads all the time. For the past two years our conversation has been limited to an occasional "Hi," which she responds, "Hi. How's it going?"

I don't know why I'm going to have a drink with these two people. I don't drink all that much. The Square, however, is nice consolation. Winston Churchill has been known to say, "We shape our buildings and afterward they shape us." The same may be said of towns. The Square in Oxford is nostalgic, Civil War restored and bustling with tourists, University students and townees. In the middle of the Square is a two story, neo-classical, white courthouse built in 1840, burned by Union troops in 1864, rebuilt in 1871, restored in 1981 and again in 2008. It is picture postcard perfect. On the south side of the courthouse is a statue of a Confederate soldier facing south. Tourists are informed that it is the only statue of a Confederate soldier facing south in the entire country. I don't know if that is true but it sounds good to tourists as does the tale that Oxford's hometown legend, William Faulkner, was a drunkard and fired from the postal service for discarding batches of mail: claiming no one was worth a two cent postage stamp. The two story courthouse is capped with a clock tower sprouting from the center of the building, accessorized with four Roman numeraled clocks, facing each direction, that, after being expertly renovated since 2010, ring every hour on the hour, signaling the time to the people on the Square.

On all four sides of the Square, facing the courthouse, are upscale boutiques, a few law offices, a variety of restaurants and three banks serving a state that has the lowest per capital income in the United States. There are no boarded up or vacant stores on this picturesque Square. No peeling paint or broken windows. The oldest business is Neilson's Department Store, established in 1839. Tourists, university students and townees repeatedly patronize it because of its fine merchandise, elegantly displayed and reasonably priced. The store has been caringly maintained, retaining the original wooden floors. Ten department store windows line the eastern sidewalks of the square, taking up half of the block. Behind each window, regularly changed, presents clothing, of the latest fashions that rival Macy's or The Selfridge.

In a state earning the highest rate of illiteracy in the country, the Square presents three bookstores, Square Books, Square Books Jr., and Off Square Books. All three are owned by the mayor. Each year Square Books is recognized for having the highest volume of any independently - owned bookstore in the U.S. Highest illiteracy, three book stores illogical, but true.

There are enough restaurants on the Square to feed an army, for those that are lucky enough to find parking. Most evenings, beginning around five, Square Squaters begin to park their cars in the coveted spots lining the entire east side of the Square in front of Neilson's, Square Books Jr., The Visitor's Center and City Hall. Square Squater's cars, expertly back into each parking space, filled with pesky high school students that sit and watch the tourists, university students, and a few townees drive around and around and around the Square searching for a spot to park so they can patronize the restaurants. There is a movement to install parking meters to limit the time cars can take up valuable space but it will never happen because the Board of Alderman is jam packed with has-been hippies of the long-gone-by 60's that fear meter pollution. Parking meters will detract from the natural beauty and ambiance of the Square and besides that each member of the Board of Alderman graduated from one of the two local high schools, Oxford High or Lafayette High. They once sat in those cars and have mentally and psychologically pledged to protect the adolescent rights of their successors.

Old Venice Restaurant, a quaint eatery serving Italian food, is known for its pizza and lasagna. Upstairs above Old Venice is the Burgundy Room Bar and Lounge. Basically, all bars and lounges are the same - especially after the third drink - but what makes the Burgundy Room such a draw is its deck that overlooks the Square and its old courthouse.

The Burgundy Room opens each day, except Sundays, at precisely 4:30 p.m. Knowledgeable consumers of alcohol who appreciate the Humanities congregate around the front door leading upstairs to the Burgundy Room in hopes of securing one of the deck's fourteen seats, of old wooden straight backs that Humanities people think have character.

As you step out on to the deck there is a table immediately to your right, one to the left and another next to it. Each table squeezes in two people and all three tables butt against the outside wall of the building. These are good seats but not premier because to see the cars go around and around and around you have to look over and past those seated in the premier seats at the tables next to the railing directly overlooking the Square. There are three tables jutted against the outside railing overlooking the Square. The middle table seats two while the two remaining

268

corner tables seat three each.

The seats at the three tables that directly overlook the Square would be a kin to sitting in a front row seat at the Gertrude Ford Theatre that is the cultural pride of the South. The seats serving the three tables adjacent to the wall would be equivalent to sitting in a second or third row seat at the Gertrude, nice but not premier.

I arrive at 4:45 and am shocked to find that Abby and Esim, somehow, hit the Mother Load by securing the Northwest corner table. Esim faces east, drinking a Castle Rock Pinot Noir. Abby faces Esim drinking a Cape Cod. They both look at me and motion with their drinks for me to join them in the Catbirds Seat with Esim on my left, Abby on my right and me facing directly at the Square, front row-center-Gertrude like.

The two of them never utter a word directed at me but carry on a conversation as if I weren't present. I consume a Bacardi Rum and Coke. The two of them talk I watch the cars go around and around.

I had planned to have a quick drink and get the hell out of Dodge but the cars circling the Square mesmerize me. By the third Rum and Coke I am a little light headed, and surprisingly I begin to listen to them ramble on. It isn't particularly interesting but it was more interesting than watching the parade of cars circling the Square counter clockwise.

Suddenly, in the middle of this verbal haze, I hear Esim say something about being from Turkey. I abruptly enter the conversation stopping the two serial talkers with a disjointed, out of context, "Did you know the Turkish Military is revered throughout the world? Do you know why?"

In fear of a response, I continue, "Because they can't be brainwashed. That's why. Can you believe it? They can't be brainwashed."

I punctuated again, "That's why."

The two of them, simultaneously, turn to look at me mouths wide open but, thank God, speechless.

Brainwashing is of great importance to me. I find the techniques and procedures to be devastating yet fascinating and much more interesting than the jibberish going on at our table. Major Mayer's description and explanation of brainwashing is graphic and profound. As a

269

professional speaker, I often site Major Mayer's work. It is nearly impossible to hear his story and not be affected. I turn to Esim and directly espouse a mini lecture.

"Major William E. Mayer a psychiatrist, conducted an exhaustive study of prisoners of war captured in Korea by the Chinese. The psychological methods used were deceptively simple, yet powerful and effective. Major Mayer referred to this brainwashing technique as a weapon, one as powerful as a nuclear device. The fact was, up to 4,000 Americans survived those years of captivity in 12 separate camps, often guarded by as few as one armed guard per 100 prisoners. Never, not once in the course of the entire Korean conflict, did a single American successfully escape from any established POW camp. No machine gun towers, no guard dogs, no electric fences, no search light, yet nobody tried to escape, They were actually imprisoned by their own minds."

I was on a roll and ordered a fourth Rum and Coke. Without note-one, without aide of a computer or Power Point I impressed myself by continuing.

When the prisoners entered the camp tired and scared, rather than being beaten, tortured, or interrogated, they were extended a hand of friendship by an individual who spoke their language. They were asked only to keep an open mind, listen, and not to try to resist.
From that point on, the prisoners went through an intense educational regime that required listening to long lectures on history, civics, politics, and economics. Following the lectures they were required to participate in discussion groups. They didn't have to agree with the teacher's point of view; they just had to participate. If they did agree, however, they were favorably recognized. The educational process was systematic, consistent, and continuous. As time went by, the prisoners were encouraged to write and give presentations supporting the teachers' viewpoints, even if they didn't believe. It was reported by Major Mayer that many of the prisoners saw this as a joke or sham, but did, in fact, write papers and give oral presentations, taking positions against their own personal beliefs.
Over time they talked themselves into acquiescing and gave up their will to escape. Shockingly, some gave up their will to live. Thirty-eight percent of those captured died, the highest death rate of Americans in any kind of captivity in any prison in any war since the American Revolution.They did not die because of mass execution or systematic starvation. Many just gave up. This type of death was termed "give-up-i-tis." These individuals would crawl into a corner, pull a blanket over their heads, and die within hours.
Not starve to death. No physical disease present. They were not psychotic. They were not insane. They knew what they were doing. They made the most profound of all human surrenders. They talked themselves into giving up to the point of death.

At this point, I realize I am on automatic pilot. I had given this lecture so many times I am speaking without listening to myself. Abby isn't in the picture any more. I have tuned her out or possibly she has tuned me out. My attention was directed at the beauty sitting three feet in front of my gawking eyes. Although well into my fourth Rum and Coke, my mental faculties were firing on all cylinders and my senses were at optimal pitch.

Esim's skin was a pristine light brown, soft like a high quality chammy. One that returns the feeling of purposefulness as you wipe down your beloved car. A chammy that for a moment in time connects the two as one. Her hair was sculpted with swirls the size of quarters. Just the right length, as one could imagine a Greek or Roman scholar of ancient times might display. Not snow white or silver but blending shades of gray like a penciled drawing created by a gifted artist. Her eyes were pools of brown, not chocolate, but deep beyond the third dimension. Her body was unaccessorized from head to toe. Ringless ears, fingers, toes and navel, which I was not privileged to view. Her hands and fingers danced around the wine glass rhythmically. Her fingernails, untouched by polish, cut and filed to perfection. Her body and face, perfectly proportioned and her demeanor overflowed with full-glass abundance.

It is at this point in my mini lecture I realize I am not trying to educate her, I am trying to get into her pants.

Her body language suggests interest and her eye contact approval. Her appropriate nods and ever so timely smiles indicate I am close to scoring.

I continue my oral wooing. "Esim." I say, putting emphasis on the second syllable, "Major Mayer reported over 400 Turkish soldiers were captured. All one hundred percent, returned home at the conclusion of the war. Not one could be brainwashed. Not one died."

I lean forward for the climax and repeat, "Not a single Turkish soldier could be brain-washed."

"They were villagers." She says matter of factly.

"Villagers?"

"Yes. Villagers. They were so poor and uneducated they thought they were in a resort with free room and board."

At this point I realize I have not impressed her. I would not be getting in anyone's pants tonight. I want to hang my head, unnoticed and hopefully soon forgotten.

Then suddenly, realizing there are more games to be played, I recover with a smile and a little blurp of a laugh, "Ha. Villagers. Major Mayers never mentioned their rank." A wide smile. "Ha Ha. I bet Major Mayers hasn't even ever been to Turkey." Followed by a belly laugh, "HA, HA, HA."

At this point she laughs, with an accommodating feminine smile.

I didn't get lucky that night but six months later I got very lucky: married.

My first marriage had lasted 32 years and ended with Ruth Ann's untimely death from cancer. For two years I experienced loneliness and a hollowness that resembled hell on earth. Returning to normalcy I was presented with a second gift of love, life and romance.

Undeserved and unearned two great marriages in one lifetime. Yes, the first marriage was great but it could have been better, had I known better? I was presented a second marriage even better than the first, for I had learned to listen more and preach less. I am one of a select few that has been presented with two great marriages in one life time. One marriage to learn from and one to serve from.

Reading is important but love, life and romance are to be savored.

We are clowning at the door of the Courthouse to make arrangements to get married.

A second romance.

The chapel we got married in.

In the chapel, they also sold Avon. Note Avon sign at top of the building.

–Chapter 24–

Fulbright

—

2004
Granted, Fulbright Scholar, Turkey
(I learn to be a scholar)

Esim and I have been married for three years. "Jim, do you think your management theory will transcend cultures?"

"What do you mean?"

"Do you think you could teach it in Turkey and they could relate to it?"

"Maybe. I don't know. I think so."

"Apply for a Fulbright to teach the theory in Turkey. You will meet my family and test the applicability of your theory to another culture. It will be fun."

Obedient, I apply and surprisingly am accepted as a Fulbright Scholar, assigned as a senior lecturer to teach my theory, for one year, at Dokuz Eylul University in Izmir, Turkey.

Never being out of the continental United States, I find getting a passport difficult but with Esim's help it happens. We arrive in Turkey. I encounter the Turkish toilet. No commode. Just a six inch round hole in the floor. You squat over the hole and do your thing. No tissue. A small water spigot is placed on the side, a foot above the floor. You put your fingers under the spigot, get a little water and wipe. Esim informs me, tradition dictates, eat with your right, wipe with your left.

After multiple bathroom instances, I complain, "Esim, I don't get it. You eat with your right and wipe with your left but the water spigot is on the right. You have to crossover. It is awkward."

"It is not. It is on the left."

"No it isn't. It's on the right."

"You are kidding. It's on the left."

"Maybe in the women's it's on the left but in the men's it's on the right."

"You're crazy. It can't be."

"It is. The next time we go, I'll wait 'til no one is in. Then I'll show you."

Downtown Izmir is by the Ferry Station. I go in, open the stall, sure enough the spigot is on the right. I squat. Go. Crossover. Get a little water. Wipe. Finished, check the stalls, all empty, I go outside. I grab Esim. Show her in. Open the stall door and point, "see."

She looks up at me with puzzled eyes. Steps into the stall, turns around, simulates the squatting position, "left."

No! All this time, I've been going to the bathroom backwards. I question if I'm Fulbright material.

All Fulbrighters go through orientation.

"It's not a matter of getting sick. It's a matter of when."

"Don't drink the water."

"Don't brush your teeth with water from the faucet."

"Watch your things at all times."

"Don't argue with the police."

I'm not so sure this is going to be as much fun as Esim led me to believe.

We attend a reception hosted by the Ambassador of the United States. Ambassador Edelman and his wife are more than cordial and the Embassy Residence is most impressive. Palacious furniture, like out of a Hollywood movie. Our breath is taken away by the grandeur and elegance. Dignitaries dressed as if pictured in Vogue Magazine. Magnificent portraits of landscapes, buildings and figureheads line the walls. Food comes in waves, served by armies of waiters dressed in tuxedos with tails. Alcohol flows as if from an Artesian well. The following morning Esim and I have a splitting headache and best we remember we had a great time. If not, we should have.

Two days later, in the evening, in our apartment in downtown Izmir, I decide to take a shower. No hot water. Stunned. Disturbingly cold. The next morning before going to the university Esim and I report the problem to the Kapici (building maintenance person.) I explain to the Kapici, using Esim as my translator, "Last night there was no hot water." The Kapici responds in Turkish which Esim relays. "It was Monday. We heat the water on Thursdays."

Esim, familiar with Turkey, being born here, takes me by bus to the university. Dokuz Eylul University sits in a mountainous region. I teach in the American Studies Complex. The building is two stories, U-shaped. The base of the U sports the front entrance. The base is 50 yards wide.

The two arms of the U shoot away from the base each stretching out 50 yards. In the saddle of the U, outside, there are picnic tables, umbrellaed round tables with chairs for faculty and students to relax, sip tea/cay (pronounced ch eye) and have snacks. Esim informs me the left leg of the U contains faculty offices, administrative offices and faculty bathrooms. The right leg is for the students; classrooms, copying room, and student bathrooms. The base of the U is used as a giant hallway to get from one side to the other although students are prohibited entrance to the faculty side.

"You mean the faculty and students don't mix. They are separate including the bathrooms?"

Esim responds, "Yes."

"Do the bathrooms, by chance have commodes?"

"Yes. But no tissue. Here." She pulls from her purse a pack of tissue, not on a roll, a pack, like a traveling pack of Kleenex.

I immediately place the prized tissues in my briefcase. Relieved.

The entire building is concrete and as we walk down the hollow foyer, our steps echo off the walls. The students are allowed to eat, drink cay and smoke during class. Next to the chairperson's office door is a large five-foot picture of an American Indian smoking a peace pipe.

Next to the picture, Ten Commandments:
1. Treat the earth and all that dwell thereon with respect.
2. Remain close to the Great Spirit.
3. Show great respect for your fellow beings.
4. Work together for the benefit of mankind.
5. Give assistance and kindness wherever needed.
6. Do what you know to be right.
7. Look after the wellbeing of mind and body.
8. Dedicate a share of your efforts to the greater good.
9. Be truthful and honest at all times.
10. Take full responsibility for your actions.

A touching and profound display of American history, but apparently the Turks haven't heard of the dangers of tobacco. Involuntary inhalation is inconceivable in Turkey.

A couple of weeks into the semester, while standing in front of the American Indian Ten Commandments a Turkish colleague comes up behind me smoking a pipe. Standing by my side, he asks me about the United States' involvement in Iraq and whether America is really for world peace.

"We are definitely for world peace. Our involvement in Iraq relates to weapons of mass destruction."

He draws on his pipe. Nods. "Is it true you can't smoke on your campus in Mississippi?"

"Well, you aren't supposed to. You definitely can't smoke in the buildings."

With eyes glazed over. Maybe from too much smoke. While exhaling, "Did it ever occur to you, without tobacco the peace pipe is dysfunctional?"

He turns, leaves, I think, "I hope like hell we find those weapons of mass destruction soon."

I remember during orientation, Don Cofman, executive director, Turkish-American Association of Ankara stating, "There are two types of people in the world. Ones that think with their heads and ones that think with their hearts." He concluded, "Turks think with their hearts."

The Chair of the department takes me to my office. The key won't work. After an hour and a half, I finally enter. It's more like a cell than an office. The walls made of concrete are light pale green and the floor, garage gray. A window overlooks the courtyard at the base of the saddle of the U. I find a year's supply of glue, stapler with two rows of staples, 6 pencils, an inch long plastic pencil sharpener like you'd find in an elementary kid's book bag, 6 pens, eraser, small bottle of whiteout, ream of paper, 6 sheets of carbon paper, roll of tape with no dispenser, computer that doesn't work and a phone with no outside line. There is one bookcase, a desk with one chair. The building is not air-conditioned but I don't care; the faculty bathroom is equipped with commodes and I have tissue in my briefcase.

I meet my class on the other side of the U. The room seats 25. I've got 35 students. I enter, and everyone jumps to attention. I put my papers on the desk, nod, 25 sit, 10 remain standing. All students can speak English, some better than others.

"Where can we get 10 more chairs?"

Three students scurry out, within minutes everyone is seated.

I am impressed with the students. I can understand them and they, me. They are smart. Only the top ten percent of the population are allowed to attend college. After an hour of class I go to my office. Put my things away. I'm assigned one class that meets twice a week on Tuesdays and Thursdays. Just before leaving, the Chair enters my office. I motion for her to sit in the only chair. She sits. I sit on the corner of the desk.

"Dr. Payne. After class students contacted me. You did great. They are excited. Would you be willing to teach all the students we have in American Studies?"

"How many?"

"One hundred-thirty six."

"The room barely holds 35."

"We would move you to a bigger room. The biggest we have holds 70. You would have to teach two sections."

"Could the sections be one right after the other so I don't have to move my materials or equipment?"

"That can easily be arranged."

Arrangements were made. Tuesdays and Thursdays. Back-to-back.

After the first week, Esim and I celebrate by going out to eat. We select a restaurant 10 blocks from our apartment. Delicious food, professional service, ambiance, and classy. The bill of fare comes. 30,000,000 lira, not counting tip. I stare at the zeros. Esim laughs, it's $24.

One U.S. dollar equals a little over 1,300,000 lira. Esim explains, "The Turkish government plans to remove six zeros from the currency within the next two years."

Turkish people are kind, courteous, friendly and helpful. However, put them in a car and they drive with their foot to the metal and a hand on the horn. They do drive on the right side of the road but the lanes are unclear so everyone tries to out maneuver one another. Picture 3,500,000 NASCAR drivers. It looks like chaos. During orientation it was emphasized, "Pedestrians do not, they never, have the right of way."

Since Esim and I don't have a car, we are content to watch from the curb. As spectators; we watch cars jockey for position and wiz by.

Esim and I ride the bus. Buses in Turkey are really two buses hooked together, each seating thirty-two people. Every bus is jammed. In the beginning, the driver directs, "Please move back." As more jam on, the driver reasons, "Consider others that want to get on, move back please." Finally, jammed like sardines, "Move back or I'm stopping this bus."
Esim and I never experienced a bus to stop the entire year we were in Turkey. Passengers always move back on the third request.

The first time Esim and I rode a bus, I was offered a seat. I thought the offer was for Esim. I stepped aside. As Esim stepped forward, the considerate passenger jumped in front of Esim blocking her from being seated. Saying nothing, he smiled at me and motioned for me to sit. Startled, I looked at him. Then Esim said, "Go ahead." I sat while Esim stood for the entire ride. After getting off, Esim explained, "In Turkey older men are respected. Especially older men with beards." Then she warned, "Next time, I think you should decline." That was the last time I had a chance to sit down while riding a bus.

Prior to accepting the Fulbright, the United States Patent and Trademark Office granted me the official trademark, PeopleWise. PeopleWise replaced Differential Management. PeopleWise was billed as a wise way of dealing with self and others. It is the tick-tock of humankind. How we tick and tick better. How others tock and how to help them tock better.

PeopleWise was a big hit with the students and unquestionably it transcended the culture. The students understood and could relate to the theory but a couple of the concepts didn't fit.

The concept of time management was foreign. There is no hurry in Turkish culture unless you are in a car. Turks are relaxed. It isn't unusual to take two hours for a lunch break. The idea of maximizing time and getting more done in the same amount of time, they understood, but couldn't relate to. They thought time management to be funny and novel, but not useful.

Planning for the future was a lark. Depending on the family they were born into, that's the way they are going to be. Although far from a cast system, family ties are strong. Children grow up and stay with their parents or live next to their parents. Children are responsible for caring for their parents as they age.

A Turkish custom I learned to appreciate was drinking cay while watching the sun go down. In the United States, I was too busy, or in such a hurry, I never took the time to enjoy the sunset. I discovered sunsets are magnificent. In Turkey, every evening, adults gather to sip cay and absorb the beauty of the sunset. In the beginning, I felt it a waste of time. As I began to understand and value the culture, watching the sunset while sipping cay became natural and habitual.

The students enjoyed class as I did and they were learning as I was. I got a kick out of snacking and sipping cay in the courtyard in the saddle of the U. Their English was good and getting better. Idiomatic phrases fascinated them;

Deer in the headlights
The buck stops here
Fork in the road
Raining cats and dogs
Faster than greased lightning
Slow as molasses
Late bloomers

Every student picked up the southern 'you all.' One student was a juggler, on occasion he would entertain. Another wanted to be a comedian and tried routines out on us. A couple of the girls made up cute jingles. I, on occasion performed magic tricks.

I was contacted by my dean at The University of Mississippi to write a short blurb comparing Turkish students with Mississippi students. I wrote;

> Cell phones and belly buttons are big in Turkey. The University students here at Dokuz Eylul have a phone attached to their ear just like those at Ole Miss. They cell-phone-talk going to and from class, waiting for the bus, while eating in the Kantin (cafeteria)... everywhere, every when, and every place imaginable. Female belly buttons are displayed with pride. Some are so proud they accessorize them with a ring. I come from a generation where belly buttons are to be covered up, not seen in public, nor pierced in any manner whatsoever. Now, I'm not talking

about belly buttons on belly dancers. That's art, that's talent and in some cases erotic. But belly buttons in mass is sort of gross. I believe a law should be passed forbidding the open display of navels on anything except belly dancers and oranges.

The dean never shared my literary gem with anyone.

As a Fulbrighter, in addition to teaching, I was expected to guest lecture for groups throughout Turkey. I presented somewhere at least once a month. After completing the first semester, I received a call from Eliza-Al-Laham, Program Development Officer, U.S. Embassy, Cairo.

"Dr. Payne, we have heard much about your PeopleWise theory. We would like for you to present your research to the faculty of the American University in Cairo. We have cleared everything with Fulbright authorities and if agreeable, Dr. Farag will call and make all the necessary arrangements."

Dr. Mahmond Farag, Vice Provost of The American University in Cairo made arrangements. Esim and I flew to Cairo, stayed at the spectacular Semiramis Hotel. Our suite overlooked the Nile. Me, from Kansas, in Cairo, staying in a suite so close to the Nile, if I wanted, I could lean out the window and drop a pebble in it.

Pictures do not do justice to the Pyramids. Standing at the base, looking up, you feel small and insignificant. The stones so large, so massive, you can't understand how they could possibly be built when you realize they were built before the invention of the wheel.

Hot, painstaking, Esim and I climb, with our guide, up the Pyramid into its entrance. The entrance, a hole so small we crouch down and stagger forward. The tunnel is winding and so small we never stand up. It's not much to see but it is mind boggling to experience.

We are led to a camel. The camel kneels for us to mount. As the camel rises, I almost fall off. The camel lumbers around to where our pictures are taken, then the camel lumbers back to where we started. The camel kneels, we de-mount. Boring for the camel. An experience never to be forgotten for us.

The American University in Cairo is situated in the middle of downtown Cairo. There are barricades and police everywhere but Esim and I are far from afraid because we are captivated by the hustle and bustle, the markets, shops, vendors, bazaars, even the beggars.

We make our way to the building in which I am to present. It looks more like a Cathedral than a university building. Large white stone steps take us through two heavy, massive doors. The wooden floor is parquetted with walnut and pine that form geometric shapes that dazzle the eye. I enter the lecture hall filled with faculty.

There are over 100 faculty seated in chairs lined in rows on the main floor before a stage that contains a lectern and four high back chairs covered with crimson velvet. Surrounding the main floor another 100 faculty sit in tiered seating behind an ornate, 3-foot high, banister fence. Above the tiered seating is a surrounding balcony producing another 100.

The provost introduces me to the president, and then presents me to the faculty.

As I look over the 300 in this historic room, I am struck by the silence and respect. I wonder, will PeopleWise resonate with the faculty of The American University in Cairo.

I present and conclude to a standing ovation. Multiple individuals approach the stage to shake my hand and thank me. After some time, I'm led to a side room of reporters who question me about America and how PeopleWise was developed. The crowning achievement was when Provost Farag informed me, my paper would be the feature article in the published proceedings of the 17th Annual American University in Cairo Research Conference.

After a year I return to Mississippi knowing my theory transcends cultures and believing I am a scholar.

I taught in the American Studies
building at Dokuz Eylul University
in Izmir, Turkey.

The American Indian
Ten Commandments impressed me.

In the distance the pyramids look small.

I never realized the stones of the pyramids are so large. I can't imagine
how they were moved before the invention of the wheel.

Esim leading me.

I'm being escorted to The American
University in Cairo to present before
the faculty.

–Chapter 25–

All in the Family

2004

Granted, Fulbright Scholar, Turkey

(I learn I'm not so smart after all)

I am often asked if it bothered me, having to repeat third grade. The answer is "no;" in fact, I was relieved. Maybe I could catch up. Did it bother my parents? No, they respected teachers. They knew that school learning was important but irrelevant. A parent's job was to teach stuff like honesty, truthfulness, perseverance, purposefulness, caring, and respect. The school's job was to teach reading, writing, and arithmetic. Seemed simple enough to me at the time.

Did it bother me that I couldn't read? I have thought about this a lot, but truthfully, I was so involved in having fun and joking around I didn't have time to think about not being able to read.

Back in those days, elementary schools had reading groups: Cardinals, Bluebirds and the Crows. The Cardinals were all girls that read real books from the library. The Bluebirds, composed of both girls and boys, struggled with a basic text. They read stories about Dick and Jane, written for a specific grade level. Dick did everything while Jane watched Dick do everything. My group, the Crows, were all boys trying to learn the sounds letters make. Once we had figured that C and K made the same sound, teachers forced blends on us. Before I got to blends, I had trouble with b, d, p & q. I mastered the sounds but the letters kept jumping around. What good was it if I knew the sounds, but couldn't distinguish one letter from the other. I spent several years trying to figure this out. Today, when I get excited, I still can't see the difference.

While I continued to struggle with my reversal and inversion problems, along came vowels. Long and short, followed quickly by exceptions. Let's see "i before e," ok "except after c"-- are you kidding me -- "or when sounded like "a" as in "neighbor" or "weigh." Now for a kid that can't tell the difference among b, d, p, q, the 'i, e' thing is a real mind blower.

My youngest brother Randy couldn't read but he didn't fail any classes thanks to the concept of "social promotion." Supposedly, somebody -- probably a psychologist or social worker -- believed that if a person repeated a grade he got out of step with his peers, and this traumatic

288

experience produced feelings of inferiority. Thus, during this period of Developmental Education everyone was passed, no matter how unprepared.

I learned a lot from my brother. We lived down by the railroad tracks. My brother and his friends got a kick out of placing a penny on the tracks and watching a train roll over it and smash it flat. He had a whole Mason jar filled with compressed pennies that he proudly showed to anyone who wanted a look.

One day, he and his gang got the bright idea of placing a tire on the tracks, so as to watch the train cut it in half. My brother and his gang placed the tire and sat on the side of a nearby hill. The tire derailed the train. My brother, somewhat naïve, observed the commotion and excitement while the members of his gang got out of Dodge. According to my brother, it was a sight to behold. According to the judge, the act was worthy of reprimand.

Right after high school graduation my brother knocked up a thirteen year old. My mother was shocked and my dad was furious. My dad made Randy marry and before they divorced, they had three children.

While married, as an avocation, Randy raced cars every Friday at the Fairgrounds in Topeka. Each week he and his buddies would somehow get a car running well enough to enter it into the race. Randy had a devoted fan base of 35 to 40 people. They loved him and he loved them. He wore a white jumpsuit and a white helmet, resembling Evel Knievel but without the red and blue. When the cars lined up, his fans went crazy. His reputation as a fierce competitor was recognized throughout the Topeka race crowd. He would always start in last place, quickly move to the middle of the pack, and then to the front, sometimes leading. Before the race was over he usually blew an engine or a tire. The couple of times I watched, he received more applause when his car blew up than the winner got for winning. When his car blew up, he would coast off the track toward the inner circle of the field, jump out of the disabled vehicle, and proudly wave to the delighted crowd.

Randy hated the government and never paid any taxes. He worked for cash only. He never had any trouble getting a job because he was quite skilled as an unlicensed electrician and a non-certified plumber. He could also lay brick and build or repair anything.

After his divorce, he rented a house two doors down from my mother's. Every time I visited, the sink was filled with dirty dishes. The place smelled of garbage. He believed in washing the dishes only when there were no more clean ones available.

He loved to drink beer and collect empty beer cans and bottles. Entering his house, I was immediately greeted by a complete wall of empty beer cans and bottles, beautifully displayed on shelves, side by side, from floor to ceiling. I found the display artful. It was like a symmetrical, three dimensional collage of interesting colors and shapes. He was as proud of it as of his Mason jar filled with smashed pennies.

One day I was visiting and we were drinking beer, seated at the kitchen table -- red formica top with chrome legs. I heard a commotion in the back yard. I jumped up to look out the kitchen window to see a young kid chased by Randy's dog. The kid had crawled over the fence to take a short cut through the back yard. Randy's dog attacked. The kid began the chase fully clothed, but by the time he crossed the yard and jumped over the fence on the other side, he was stark naked. The dog had torn off all the kid's clothes. There was no tissue damage but it scared me and petrified the kid.

I was shook up. "Randy, you have to do something about your dog."

Randy looked up, surprised, but unconcerned for the terrorized kid. "What do you mean?"

I explained that someone could get hurt and he explained the kid shouldn't have climbed over the fence. I explained someone could get hurt bad and he explained it was his property and the kid was trespassing. We went back and forth for some time. Finally, I said "Your dog is dangerous."

"Dangerous? No, he's not."

"Look, Randy, your dog bites."

Randy put down his beer can, thought a second, then asked, "Jimmy, you are an educated person -- and we all admire that -- but explain this to me: why would anyone ever own a dog that doesn't bite?"

Randy's dog is named Savage; my dog is named Muffin. If somebody were to cut through my yard or come into my house, Muffin would go hide under the bed. Not only would Muffin not bite anybody, we had to cut his canned dog food into small pieces before he could chew it. Just what good was Muffin? I turned to my brother and said, "I think I'll have another Bud Light."

I'm at home watching television. My mother calls. Frantic. "Come quick, I need you. They have put Randy in jail. This time it is serious."

I said, "What happened?"

She said, "Come. Come now."

I drive all day and all night. My mother is beside herself. I try to calm her down. Finally, she explains, "Randy tried to rob a bank."

"WHAT?"

Sobbing, "Randy tried to rob a bank."

I go to the police station and they take me into the Chief's office. The Chief explains, "Jim, this time it is serious. Real serious."

My brother and his group of friends had been drinking, watching a Western on television. Apparently, the movie shows a bunch of cowboys robbing a bank. In his drunken stupor, my brother thought robbing the bank would be interesting. His friends thought he was joking. After they left the house, Randy got his shot gun, got his dog Savage, put a red bandana around the dog's nose and a second bandana around his own, got in the car and headed to the bank.

Randy gets out of the car while Savage looks on from the passenger's seat. Randy enters the bank. The tellers, members of his racetrack fan club, laugh at him. Even though he wears a bandana mask, his slim 140-pound body, his five foot eight inch frame, his shoulder length brown hair, clue them in. "Go home, you're drunk," they tell him.

"Hand over the money."

The tellers try to persuade him to go home. Randy gets mad, fires off the gun and shoots out the chandelier.

The next thing, I'm told, he is running out of the bank empty handed. He jumps in the front seat with Savage, and peels out of the driveway. A cop car with sirens blaring chases him.

From then on, according to the Chief, things go downhill. Randy floorboards the car. Savage sticks his bandanned nose out the side window. The cop car calls for help. The Chief explains, "We had every available police car in pursuit of your brother. We couldn't catch him. It's like he was on that damn track."

He zoomed up alleys, across residential yards -- like a scene from "The Dukes of Hazard." The local television station got wind of the event and their helicopter showed the chase on the news.

The Chief said, "Like O.J. Simpson's car chase, except much more exciting." "We would never have stopped him had it not been for that tree."

A policeman escorted me back to find my brother pouting in his cell with his broken arm in a sling. Before I could utter a sound, he said, "Jimmy, don't worry. Savage is O.K."

The judge wasn't impressed. Randy was sentenced to spend some time in prison. Not jail. Prison. First to Leavenworth, where all the hardcore convicts were sent. Just a couple of days. Then they sent him to Springfield, Missouri.

After about a month, my brother calls, tells me he likes it: free meals, a place to sleep, basketball with other inmates. He can watch television. But he misses Savage and is released on good behavior. Before you know it, he is back in prison. I check to find out why. I am told he refused to report to his parole officer. The police go to his house and tell him he has to report to his parole officer. Randy folds his arms. "You can't make me. What are you going to do, put me in prison?" They do exactly that: They put him in prison.

Randy being in and out of prison thing happened enough times that the judicial system decided -- since he was not a threat to himself or others -- it was cheaper to arrange for him to stay on parole at an apartment. They would pay for his room and give him a small stipend to eat and live on.

It looked like this arrangement would keep him out of prison, so my wife, Esim, and I decide to pay him a visit. We go to his house on 3rd street, a few blocks from Topeka Avenue. It's an old two-story house with four mailboxes on the front porch. One of the mailboxes is labeled with crooked lettering: R. Payne. I knock on the door. I knock again and again. No response. My wife waits on the porch while I walk across the street. A guy in the liquor store confirms it's the right house and that Randy is, in fact at home. "Go to the side of the house and yell. Randy should be sitting at the kitchen table next to the open window, smoking. Drinking beer."

I do that. "Randy."

Suddenly, Randy sticks his head out the window and yells, "Jimmy."

My wife and I are escorted up the steps to his small, rundown apartment. He fixes my wife a cup of coffee and gets me and him a couple of beers.

We sit at the kitchen table. This one has a yellow Formica top with chrome legs, and yellow plastic seats. We sit next to the sink full of dirty dishes. The walls of the kitchen are covered with posters of scantily clad women, race cars, and Pittsburg Steeler football players. The door to the bedroom is wide open to reveal a cluttered mess like on the TV show "Hoarders."

My wife sits on my right facing Randy. I am facing the open window. We laugh and reminisce about times long gone by. On the far side of the table, next to the wall, I notice a leather moccasin - new, obviously never used. Next to the moccasin is a six-inch stack of craft kits, a pair of moccasins in each envelope along with leather straps.

I ask, "Randy what's the deal with the moccasins?"

"They send them to me. In my spare time I put them together. It's therapy."

"Therapy?"

"Yeah. It's to keep me from getting depressed."

I've never seen my brother depressed in his entire life.

My wife asks, "Very nice. How much are they?"

"Oh, they aren't for sale. They're just my therapy."

Esim continues, "Well, what do you do with them?"

My brother's jaw drops. His eyes don't leave Esim.

Esim repeats, "What do you do with them?"

My brother's eyeballs roll to the right. His head jerks a little to the right.

293

Esim and I look on.

Randy repeats the eye roll and the head jerks, indicating for us to pay attention to his right. On his right is the open door leading to his bedroom. "I exchange them for sexual favors," he says.

Dead silence fills the room. Then Esim says, "I think I'll have another cup of coffee."

I repeated third grade, graduated from high school illiterate, and earned a BA degree in Psychology not being able to read a newspaper. My younger brother Randy also graduated from high school illiterate. Never paid any taxes in his entire life, but my tax dollars pay his room and board and pay for those therapeutic moccasins, which he exchanges for sexual favors. If I'm brilliant, my brother must be a freakin' genius. And he can't read any better than me.

Randy in his green jacket to match his race car but he actually raced in a white jumpsuit resembling Evel Knievel.

He never won but his fans didn't care. Unconditional devotion.

A freakin' genius.

After Thoughts

–After Thought 1–
Great Teaching
(I learn what a yacht is)

I am continuously asked how I learned to read. Truthfully, I don't know. Keep in mind as a Fulbright Scholar at 84 years of age, I still only read on about a sixth grade level. But that's pretty good for my age.

I believe what helped me achieve literacy (fourth grade reading level) was a combination of situations and opportunities. At the early elementary level they tried to teach me how to read using a traditional approach of learning letters, sounds, words accompanied by a basic text, the Dick and Jane type. After repeating third grade emphasis was placed on phonics. After sixth grade they tried whole language. None of these methods worked. I believe all my teachers were well intended and well trained to teach reading to the moderately average, average, and above average student. In other words, they were great at teaching the Cardinals, good with the Bluebirds and confused with the Crows.

What stands out in my mind as I reminisce, is learning the phonetic alphabet under the expert instruction of Mr. McCausland. Miss Southworth, who by the way later married Mr. McCausland, gave me confidence by making me think I had style. As a rehabilitation counselor requiring me to dictate narratives everyday and subsequently proofing the transcriptions, forced me to read and as a placement counselor having a personal secretary who was learning shorthand, helped the both of us advance and learn new skills. These unplanned situations and events inched me toward literacy.

I have taught thousands of teachers how to teach reading and I have taught hundreds of struggling readers, both child and adult, how to read. As a teacher or teachers and a remedial specialist, at this point in my life I believe, hypothetically, 50% of the population learn to read almost as easy as they learn to talk. Thirty percent learn through moderate instruction and good parenting. Ten percent learn through reasonable instruction, encouragement, reinforcement and love. The remaining 10% will struggle their entire life unless they receive professional help that is highly trained in assessment, diagnosis and remediation. Even then, I believe 1% will not get it. I represent the 1% and only became literate by luck and several quirks of fate.

For a period of time I served on the Governors Literacy Council in the state ranked number one on illiteracy. At the end of my tenure I concluded being unable to read is tragic but being able to read and choosing not to read bordered on being sinful. I cannot understand why a person that has the gift of mastering the skill of reading decides not to read. Now for those that struggle and fail to learn to read, they must keep in mind reading is important but there are an abundance of other things more important. You can live a good purposeful life illiterate.

One time I was asked, "As a nonreader, when you look at a page, what do you see?" That is a great question of which I have no answer, but I obviously see something you don't.

I have reversal and inversion problems. Even now, at 84, under stress I can't see the difference between d, b, p, q. Here is the crazy thing, I am a reasonable typist, know the key board, the home row real well: a, s, d, f, j, k, l, ;. But many times when I type my name, Payne, I hit the 'b' key instead of 'p'. The 'p' key is on the upper row, right hand, little finger and the 'b' key is lower row, left hand, first finger. Not only can I not distinguish the 'p' from the 'b' on sight, I can't even think it and hit the correct key from memory. Sometimes I have a lateral reversal, I want 'j' but hit 'g'. Both home row, both first finger but reversed hands.

I do my book writing with a pencil on a yellow pad. Even today I mix up the d, b, p, q. When ideas come faster than my pencil can move, I use a perpendicular slash through a circle representing each of the undistinguishable letters much like a person that can't remember if the apostrophe goes before or after the 's' and places the apostrophe directly above the 's'.

Being brought up in my culture the letters 'i' and 'e' sound the same. As explained in Chapter 3, as I mastered the phonetic alphabet I learned the difference but truthfully at 84 I can't hear the difference nor pronounce the sounds correctly unless I pay exceedingly close attention.

In the small town of DeSoto, the high school had no cafeteria so everyone brown bagged. During lunch we could eat anywhere. Several of us boys would walk a block to the only filling station, retrieve an RC from the drink machine, sit on an adjoining wall and consume lunch. Many times we would be joined by one of our teachers.

One day our science teacher joined us during his final days just before retirement. He was asked, "After you retire, if money were no problem, what would you do?"

His response, "I'd buy me a yatch (pronounced like catch with a 'y')."

"What's a yatch?"

"One of those fancy boats you see in magazines where the captain wears a blue blazer and a cap with a scrambled eggs emblem on the bill."

Sounded good to us. No further discussion.

After graduation, I go to Washburn University, first day, first course, first class session everyone is asked to stand, state name, where from, and what you want to do after graduation. Some wanted to be teachers, some lawyers, a couple doctors.

I stood up and said, "I'm Jim Payne, from DeSoto High and I'd like to make enough money to buy a yatch."

Everyone questionably looked while the teacher questioned, "What is a yatch?"

"One of those fancy boats you see in magazines where the captain wears a blue blazer and a cap with a scrambled eggs emblem on the bill."

"You are talking about a yacht."

"No. Yatch."

"It's not called a yatch, it's a yacht."

"No, it's a yatch."

"You mean yacht."

"No, Yatch."

"I'm telling you it's a yacht."

"It might be a yacht in Topeka, but it's a yatch in DeSoto."

I failed the class, not because I didn't know a yatch from yacht but because I couldn't read.

Hearing that unexaggerated true story, people think my high school science teacher must have been terrible. No, he was great. What made him great was he made us fall in love with science. He stimulated our curiosity and most importantly he made all of us think we were smart and of value.

He may not have known the difference between a yatch and a yacht but he was a great teacher. And I bet he knew the largest lake in the area was Shawnee lake, a man built lake, that wasn't big enough for a yacht. A yacht in the state of Kansas is an oxymoron.

I believe I conquered literacy by luck and happen stance. I was at the right place at the right time but I got to the right place at the right time by continuing to sharpen my pencil, refusing to quit and believing in myself.

DeSoto High School

Football 2-3-4, Football
All-Star 4, Track 2-3-4,
Baseball 2-3-4, Basket-Ball
2-3-4 , Junio Play 3, One Act
Play 3, Annual Staff 4,
Mixed Chorus 4, Minstrel 3,
Homecoming
Co-Captain 4, Forensics 3,
Class Officer 2-3, Student
Council President 4

Mr. Perkins, Sponsor;
Jim Payne, President

–After Thought 2–
Sharpen, Resharpen
(I learn second graders know more than me)

Thank you for listening and holding my hand as I sharpened and resharpened my pencil. Now I want to tell you what I hope, think, and believe that will help you sharpen your pencil and, more importantly, help you teach others how to sharpen their pencil.

Pencil sharpening involves two parallel interlocking chains, ACTION and REACTION that mysteriously and wonderfully feed each other, leading to a feeling of ecstasy and stellar performance.

On the ACTION chain, we do things we have complete control of doing, resulting in the development of grit. On the REACTION chain are physical and mental things that may or may not happen as a result of the ACTION taken. We may think we have control over the physical or mental things, but in reality, we only have influence. What I have learned in my lifetime is the difference between control and influence and how to increase the influence one has over the physical and mental things. In other words, I have learned how to sharpen and resharpen myself and help others by sheer mental toughness. I have learned how to get better, get real good, experience a personal best, and grind to becoming stellar.

Take a moment to look at the ACTION and REACTION chains. Notice the evolution of Play to Grit on the ACTION chain and Think to Mental Toughness on the REACTION chain.

EVOLUTION OF ACTION AND REACTION CHAINS

                                    Mental Toughness
                          Habit
REACTION: Think

                                    Grit
                          Work
                Persevere
ACTION: Play

As the pencil is sharpened over time, if the desire to become real sharp exists, the lead in the pencil becomes more pointed. If there is a push, outside or inside, to become point perfect, the pencil gets finely pointed and eventually begins to look like it writes itself. In reality it does not write itself but only the pencil knows that.

The ACTION chain starts with the link of Play. Play starts with the intent of having fun or a sense of curiosity. In time Play becomes more involved, more intense, The blocks get stacked higher, bridges arc made, block buildings are constructed, a city is formed. The mind is creating, solving problems, learning. In the sandbox, sand is pushed around, scooped in a bucket, piles made, underground tunnels formed and eventually a castle emerges.

As Play continues, blocks fall, sand collapses. The player tries different things. A few successes come here and there but a lot of mistakes are experienced. As the player tries different things and if refuses to quit, the second link, Persevere is realized. Through perseverance the city gets more complex and the castle more elaborate.

When a player is introduced to violin, basketball, chess, they first learn what the instrument does, what the sport is, how the game is played. Next, they learn the basics, the fundamentals; how to hold, finger and stroke the instruments, dribble and shoot, the various moves of the pieces.

As the players advance, music becomes more complex, layups and jump shots become more fluid, strategies for moving the pieces are more sophisticated. During this progression, perseverance becomes evident. The player returns to the activity because they want to or because they are forced to, it makes no difference. Regardless whether the player likes it or hates it, the player returns again and again and again. That is, they Persevere.

How is perseverance taught? Some parents, teachers, coaches continuously encourage, praise, reinforce, recognize and show approval while others force, yell, badger, scold and make the player practice. These are all methods and techniques for getting the player to stay with it.

Another way is to look at the curriculum or skill to be learned and make it easier and faster to learn. In other words, put it into smaller, easier to learn steps. When teaching the second graders in Batesville Intermediate School how to work a Rubik's Cube, it was important to get all the kids with different learning styles and rates to hang in there and stick with the task for the whole year. Yes, Sam Gilbert, the second grade teacher and I encouraged, praised, reinforced but some of the kids would invariably hit an impasse. They would hit a wall. No matter what, they just kept failing and making mistakes. They couldn't catch on. Gilbert and I needed to do something or they would quit but we didn't know what to do. We found the advanced kids knew more than we did about learning how to solve the cube.

To work the cube you have to be able to rotate the six sides; top, bottom, left, right, front, posterior. Over half the kids had trouble rotating the front. They would turn the cube sideways making the front the right side and then rotate it. So they weren't rotating the front, they were always rotating the right side. When you do this you will never solve the cube.

I thought they were having trouble because today's kids don't play with manipulatives like Legos, Tinker Toys, or Lincoln Logs. I spent a significant amount of time teaching good eye hand coordination. They got to where they could manipulate the cube as good as I, but they still would

305

turn the cube to the right when having to rotate the front. I believe some of the kids sensed my frustration. Then Phillip came to me and said, "Dr. Payne, make them sit the cube on their desk and tell them not to spin the cube." From that point on the kids were instructed to put the cube on top of their desk and not spin it while working the cube. Keep the front always in front. Immediately, all the kids were able to rotate the front. Every single one of the 24. They did not and would not spin the cube to the right while on the table. All the kids kept trudging forward while correctly rotating the front. Not a kid quit or gave up.

I spent time teaching right from left but half the kids just couldn't get it. JeLisa, an advanced kid, told me to forget about left because the left side is never rotated.

At first, I didn't believe it, then I looked at how to solve Step 1. No left. Step 2, no left. Step 3, no left. I'll be darned, you actually master the cube and never rotate the left. All that needed to be focused on was front, bottom, right. And that is what we did. Everyone got it and everyone moved on. Not a kid quit or gave up.

But next you had to know clockwise and counterclockwise. I bring a hugh clock to teach clockwise and counterclockwise. Over half the class can't get it. Carlos and Evelyn, two advanced students, tell me they have digital clocks at home, not analogs. Then Carlos said,

"Try using a jar."

"What jar?"

Evelyn answers, "Any jar. Screw the cap on, it is clockwise, unscrew – counterclockwise."

Carlos adds, "Hold the jar straight up and the cap is the top. Lay it down facing you the cap is the front, rotate the jar and lay it on its side facing right, the cap is right."

At that point, clockwise became screw on and counterclockwise became unscrew. Everyone got it and continued to work the cube. No kid quit or gave up.

Perseverance can be taught by encouragement, praising, reinforcement, recognition, approval or by force, yelling, badgering and scolding but we found breaking the task down into easy, understandable tiny steps kept the Gilbertoneons persevering for the entire year. And they liked doing it.

Another technique was once a step had been mastered, don't have them mix the cube up and do it again. We found during individual, one-on-one teaching sessions, after a step had been completed, move the cube with the completed step to the side and give the kid a scrambled second cube, when that was done give a third, then a fourth, fifth and sixth. As the cubes line up on the desk, we noticed the steps get completed faster. The cubist gets excited not just about mastering a step but how many can be mastered in a set amount of time. This technique increases learning, interest, satisfaction and perseverance.

How is perseverance measured? It is measured in length of time AND number of repetitions. The point is, perseverance can be taught and we are learning how to teach it. We know it when we see it, we can teach it and we can measure it. For some kids, when learning how to read gets hard, they give up and quit. Teaching perseverance has merit.

By returning again and again, by repeating a task over and over, through perseverance the third link is introduced, Work.

Work is an interesting link in the ACTION chain because Work doesn't automatically make the player better. Work takes effort but you can have work without perseverance. You can intensely work on a project like gardening or a hobby for a short time or do a difficult task off and on but when Persevere is attached to Work it sets up the fourth link, Grit. Grit makes you better.

Grit cannot be experienced without pain or discomfort. Grit is when you knuckle down, you will not be beaten or outdone. You have the will to not just survive but to thrive. You grind and are steadfast over time.

Play-Persevere-Work=Grit

The gritsy person realizes they are different from the masses. Grit is a part of their very being. They show stamina, steadfastness and a will to do anything and everything. Angela Duckworth (2016) in her best-selling book *Grit* studied United States Military Academy West Point graduates and Army Special Operations Forces better known as Green Berets and found the overwhelming majority of these elite professionals scored high in Grit. Duckworth, with a simple ten item Grit Scale, figured out how to test and measure Grit. Words she uses to describe gritsters are: dogged, ferocious determination, exceptional zeal, capacity for hard labor, never give up. But like poise in a beauty contest, style in a theater performer, or projection from the lectern by a gifted orator, we know it when we see it but we don't know how to teach it. She indicates she is not sure Grit can be taught but she believes, maybe, it can be cultivated.

We believe we have stumbled across a way to teach Grit with the second graders in Batesville. How do we know? First, we see an individual exhibiting Grit in multiple aspects of their life as they continue to struggle with the cube. Even at a second grade level, they stay at tasks longer, they are more focused and less distracted in their studies. They play longer. They tell their parents and siblings what they have learned and they begin to teach their parents and siblings what they have learned. Second, we measured Grit by the amount of time involved while mastering the cube, the number of steps and sub-steps completed that led to an abnormal increase in reading and math scores. Throughout the year, it appeared the kids approached their reading and math assignments with greater intensity.

In the context of second graders, a case can be made that all 24 demonstrated the characteristics of Grit; stamina, steadfastness, doggedness, determination and zeal. In the process, they got so engaged in their work, all work, it was difficult to get them to stop. As they talked with others, they indirectly showed they were different from the masses. They could do something their parents or older siblings couldn't do. They knew they were different from the masses.

All 24 stayed with the cube, all 24 increased their reading scores including two with special needs. The average reading score for the class was greater when compared to the other thirteen second grade classes in the same building. All fourteen classes used the same curriculum and the same methods. I believe we learned how to teach grit and the acquisition of grit transferred to superior performance and increased reading as well as math scores.

Along the ACTION chain the player has complete control of how they deal with each link. While evolving through each link, on the ACTION chain, the body and mind develop. Understanding how the body and mind develop can help the player and the player's teacher, coach, counselor or parent know how and when to advance from link to link or when to stop. In other words, the ACTION taken by the player effects or influences the development of the body and mind. Here is the trick, as the body and mind grow, advancement along the ACTION chain is accelerated and we know how to influence body and mind growth through the REACTION chain. By utilizing the REACTION chain we increase performance and proficiency.

Sam Gilbert, Second Grade Teacher and Master Cubist

–After Thought 3–
Influence
(I learn the importance of myelin)

Here is where we make the pencil dance. We know how to sharpen it and we have ways to make it point perfect, but now we have figured out how to make it dance. As the pencil dances, observers admire and appreciate the performance but when the dance becomes breathtaking, it is common to believe the skill was inherently born into the pencil: A prodigy pencil, so to speak. Only the pencil knows the secret was relentless practice that involved the development of mental toughness that influenced performance at the highest level.

Take a moment to look at the ACTION and REACTION chains. Notice as the links in both the ACTION and REACTION chains evolve, there is an automatic, instinctive interaction between the two. As the ying and yang between the two connect, skill development and performance increase.

INTERACTION OF ACTION AND REACTION CHAINS

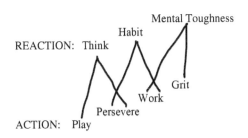

As an individual moves along the ACTION chain, things happen to the brain. Sometimes the links in the ACTION chain affect brain function on the REACTION chain and sometimes the brain function on the REACTION chain affects the links in the ACTION chain. We know as an individual moves along the ACTION chain the brain is very active. And, now we know ways to help and guide brain activity that, in turn, influences performance.

As one trains the body, it unquestionably affects the brain. But by reversing the process, as one train's the brain it unquestionably affects the body.

Instruments exist that somewhat accurately measure the activation impulses of the brain. Simply stated, electrodes that measure electrical currents (brain waves) are attached to the outside of the head. These instruments provide information that suggest in most, most of the time, the activation in the brain is scattered. However, when a person begins to concentrate or focus on something with some degree of intensity, the activation of the brain becomes more localized. When concentration or focus becomes more intense the activation becomes more pinpointed.

Amy Haufler and Bradley Hatfield, well known brain researchers, studied skilled and novice rifle shooters (Glover 1998), By placing electrodes on the skull, they measured brain waves simultaneously with the accuracy of the rifle shots. They found novice shooters' brain activation is scattered, skilled shooter's brain activation is localized and in Olympian shooters, five seconds before trigger pull, the firing of the brain is even more pinpointed, indicating superior focus and concentration. Just by simply showing the shooters how brain activation relates to the accuracy of the shots, improvement in shooting is realized.

The brain is complex and there is confusion and disagreement on how the brain works. But most neuroscientists and brain researchers agree on three points:

1. Emotion plays a major role on the impact of the brain.

2. The brain is physiologically affected by the environment.

3. The brain can't tell the difference from fact or fiction.

Emotion:

Joseph LeDoux (1996) and David Goleman (1995) have helped us understand the role of emotion in learning. Simply stated, the stronger the emotion connected with the experience, the stronger the memory of the experience. When emotion is added to the learning, the brain deems the information important and retention is increased.

Physiological Change:

Marian Diamond and Janet Hopson (1998) introduced the concept of 'neural plasticity.' Neural plasticity is the brain's ability to constantly change its structure and function in response to external experiences. The brain is similar to a muscle; you can change its shape by making it work.

Fact from Fiction:

One of the most unique findings of brain science is that the activation of the brain is the same whether it is imagined or real. This simple finding provides us with an abundance of opportunities and options for assisting brain development.

As one plays or starts to learn something, the brain goes through a trial and error process. It tries to figure things out. PLAY on the ACTION chain relates to THINK on the REACTION chain.

Through the thinking process, the learner dreams and envisions things. This fires up the brain which begins to shape or alter its structure and function. By providing things we have control over, like time to play and presenting opportunities to learn, we hope to influence brain growth. Ronald Kotulack (1996) uses a metaphor of a banquet to illustrate the interaction of the brain and the environment.

> The brain gobbles up the external environment through
> its sensory system and then reassembles the digested
> world in the form of trillions of connections which are
> constantly growing or dying, becoming stronger or
> weaker depending on the richness of the banquet. (p.4)

By feeding the brain nutritious, environmental food and supplying a steady stream of environmental vitamins, the brain grows.

Since the brain is essentially curious, we can help it make the connection between the known and the unknown. We did this with second graders by teaching them how to work a Rubik's Cube as mentioned in the previous chapter, by breaking the tasks down into tiny, understandable and relevant steps like, placing the cube on the table to keep it from turning, screwing a lid on a jar to teach clockwise and counterclockwise and realizing the left side of the cube is never used so focus on the sides used – front, right, bottom.

The relationship between the ACTION and REACTION chains is inevitable, but we don't have control over thinking. We can try to influence thinking by doing things we have control over. I don't have control over someone's thinking but I have 100% control of things I can do in hopes to influence thinking.

Play stimulates Thinking and Thinking stimulates Play. As Play continues, Perseverance sets in and when Perseverance continues, the Play activities become Work. Work can be enjoyable, unenjoyable or just plain Work but when Perseverance and Work connect, Habits are often formed.

Habits are learned functions and take over automatically; tying shoelaces, walking, speaking, memorizing, driving, riding a bicycle, adding, subtracting, multiplying, dividing, reading, working a computer, etc. The word "habit" originally meant garment or clothing. This gives us an insight into the true meaning of habit. Our habits are literally garments worn by us. They fit us and overtime become a part of us.

Habits can be helpful or not helpful. They can be good or bad. Through repetition, habits are formed. Habits are acquired behaviors and can be learned, unlearned, modified or changed. Most habits are formed by environmental influences like parents, teachers, coaches, counselors, ministers, and/or managers; teaching, telling or insisting, we do something over and over. We are told, reminded, praised when we do it and reprimanded when we don't.

When a bad habit develops and the individual wants to modify or change it they try to consciously force themselves to stop or change what they are doing.

It is possible to attack a bad habit or encourage the development of a good habit by focusing directly on the mental aspects of the habit. Since a habit is a part of us it forms a self-picture of who we are. Everyone has a mental picture of who they are and act in accordance with who they believe they are.

Let's say a person develops the habit of not remembering their keys. They have developed a mental picture that they can't remember where they place their keys. Dealing with the problem on the ACTION chain they can designate a place to put the keys, a special hook or bowl. Some people that have trouble remembering their keys attach to the key chain something big or something novel to make it easier to find.

To resolve the problem using the REACTION chain the person can change their picture of forgetfulness or not remembering to being smart, thoughtful and mentally tough. They form a different picture by repeating affirmations. "I am smart. My mind is like a memory vault. I see myself remembering my keys. I feel excited when I get my keys. Keys are a part of my very being."

The affirmations are repeated in the morning and in the evening when going to bed. Once the picture of remembering the keys replaces the picture of being forgetful, a new habit is formed not only for remembering keys but remembering names and other stuff.

The process of changing one's picture is explained in detail when covering the link, MENTAL TOUGHNESS on the REACTION chain. The technique is powerful and focuses directly on influencing the activation of neurons in the brain.

You start to learn a physical skill through trial and error. You usually learn a few basics, then you practice, practice, practice. As you get better, it becomes a habit. The habit is predominantly controlling the learned function of the subconscious. What separates the good player from the excellent player is mostly mental. The excellent player doesn't let failure bother them and they can't be influenced by outside negativity.

A habit is formed by transferring the thinking process from the conscious part of the brain to the subconscious part. Consider the interaction and role of the conscious and subconscious when catching a ball. Now elevate the complexity by catching the ball while running. Now distract the player by having people yell and scream. Finally, fill the subconscious with degrading comments to the point the player believes they are of little worth, are unsuccessful and can't do anything right. It is impossible to control the players thinking but there are things we have control over that might influence not only skill development in catching but develop a positive belief in self that will increase the skill of catching the ball.

Things we have control of on the ACTION chain are encouragement, praise, good instructions and multiple throwing to catch the ball. Control on the REACTION chain could be using affirmations in hopes to influence a positive picture.

Take a moment to examine the difference between Work and Grit. On the ACTION chain both grow out of Perseverance but you can have Work without Grit but you can't have Grit without Work. Both require Perseverance and both produce Habits.

The major difference is Grit requires hurt, discomfort, pain. Work may get uncomfortable but Grit gets downright nasty. My dad delivered milk for 30 years. He got up at 5:00am, reported to work, iced and loaded the wagon, hitched the horses and ran the route. I don't remember him missing a day and I don't remember him complaining. He did his job to put bread on the table for his family. He may have had grit but delivering milk for 30 years isn't what made him gritty. In addition to being a milkman, he was a body builder and every night he lifted weights. He had the burn. He would force himself to hurt and his body was solid as a rock. Lifting weights and working out is what made him a grit master.

A hard workout creates changes in the body. Certain muscles and the cardiovascular system are pushed to the point where homeostasis can no longer be maintained. Through hard exercise new capillaries grow and more oxygen is provided to the muscle cells so the body can return to the comfort zone.

This is how the body's desire for homeostasis can be harnessed to build the body. Pushing hard and long enough will reap a stronger, more coordinated body with greater endurance. So to have Grit, you have to push yourself to the limit for a long time. There are no easy shortcuts to Grit.

We have a pretty good handle on how the body responds to physical activity. We know much less about how the brain changes in response to mental challenges. A major difference between the body and the brain is that brain cells do not divide and form new brain cells. Instead the brain rewires networks, various connections between neurons are added and some are gotten rid of. Also, as concentration and focus increase the activation gets more localized.

Grit is formed through dissonance. Without dissonance there can be no Grit.

When an individual commits themselves to really working on something, the brain fires so often and with such velocity Mental Toughness automatically develops on the REACTION chain. Mental Toughness is developed from a combination of, Work and Grit.

As the gritsy person, gets Mentally Tough, myelin is formed around the neurons of the brain, which enhance performance.

Myelin is a neural insulator that surrounds nerve fibers similar to the way rubber insulation wraps around a copper wire, making the signal stronger and faster by preventing the electrical impulses from leaking out (Coyle, 2009). "The thicker the myelin gets, the better it insulates, and the faster and more accurate our movements and thoughts become." (p.5). Ericsson and Pool (2016) indicate:

> Myelination can increase the speed of nerve impulses by
> as much as ten times. Because these networks of neurons
> are responsible for thought, memories, controlling movement,
> interpreting sensory signals, and all other functions of the
> brain, rewiring and speeding up these networks can make
> it possible to do various things. (p.4).

Neuroscientists generally agree that myelin is built up through deliberate purposeful practice that is thoughtful and focused. It must be repetitious, challenging, and continuously move the individual out of the comfort zone but not so far out the individual quits.

The structure and function of the brain change in response to intense mental training, in much the same way your muscles and cardiovascular system respond to physical training. Using magnetic resonance imaging (MRI), neuroscientists have studied how the brains of people with particular skills differ from the brains of people without those skills. It is concluded skilled people have more myelin than unskilled people.

Myelin develops as an individual practices in deliberate, purposeful ways. But myelin can also be influenced through the technique of visual imagery and mental rehearsal.

The foundation for understanding visual imagery and mental rehearsal come from the seminal works of three great motivational experts: Maxwell Maltz (1967), author of *Psycho-Cyber netics,* Denis Waitley (1983), author *Seeds of Greatness,* and Louis Tice (1989), author of *A Better World, A Better You.* These bestselling masterpieces, written by these three scholars, have not only popularized the mental aspects of performance, they have operationalized it so it can be learned and taught.

The understanding of the mental aspects of visual imagery and mental rehearsal is simple but mastering it takes great discipline. Notice it takes discipline not practice.

Visual imagery and mental rehearsal are built on two concepts: mental picture of oneself commonly referred to as the Comfort Zone and the Creative Subconscious.

The Comfort Zone is so very powerful it locks us into acting and behaving as we see

318

ourselves and believe ourselves to be. We act and behave in accordance with our picture. Our picture is our life's target. Our comfort zone is nothing more than a target of life. What keeps us on target, what keeps us functioning within our comfort zone, is the creative subconscious.

Maxwell Maltz, a famous plastic surgeon and bestselling author, suggests the mind (creative subconscious) is like a homing system in a torpedo or an automatic pilot. Once the target is set, the self-adjusting mechanism guides the missile toward the target through a monitoring feedback system. This navigational guidance system constantly adjusts the flight of the missile by keeping it on target. Just as the propulsion of the missile drives it forward, the creative subconscious drives our behavior and actions. In other words, the creative subconscious is our motivator. The creative subconscious motivates us to perform within our comfort zone.

We cannot control the creative subconscious. The creative subconscious is always programmed to guide our behaviors and actions toward our picture, toward our comfort zone, toward our target. But the beauty is, we can move our picture, change our comfort zone, select a new target or refine an existing one. We can tell ourselves this over and over again, with such firm conviction, that we can actually see a new picture of ourselves, vividly, in high resolution. As we construct a new target of ourselves, the creative subconscious will drive us, monitor us, to become it.

You have the power to change or refine your target, but you cannot change or control the creative subconscious. The creative subconscious is nothing more than a homing device that drives your behaviors and actions toward the target.

Most of the kids that struggle with reading don't think they can do it and in many cases think they are not smart enough, so they stop trying and give up.

I have found I get the greatest results when I focus as much attention on their self-picture as I do on teaching them how to read.

I begin by getting a picture of building up myelin in their brain making them mentally tough. This is started by showing them they are smart while praising them for sticking with it. As I show them they are smart I continuously praise how smart they are, how tough minded their brain is, calling them a smarty pants. I don't just tell them they are smart. I show them they are smart as I tell them they are smart.

I show improvement in numbers and time: For example, increased number of correct sounds of letters and blends within a minute. Or showing the increased number of correct responses to comprehension questions. Using the cube I remind them what they have accomplished by listing the number of sub-steps mastered.

At the end of each learning session, I emphasize grityness, "I like the way you stayed with it and didn't even think of quitting." "You are like the Energizer Bunny that keeps on going."

Once a bond is formed I get the kid to affirm, with attitude, "I am smart." "I have value." After mastering a step related to the cube, I have the student stand before me and proclaim, "I am Master of Step 1," emphasizing 'Master.'

By the end of the year, of the 24, including two special needs, I felt all believed they were smart and each was a grit master.

Theoretically, the affirmations and praise imprinted a positive self-picture while the continuous work and never giving up, built myelin in their brain.

As we learn to use both the ACTION and REACTION chains the pencil is sharpened, the pencil gets more pointed, the lead gets point perfect, the pencil dances on its own.

Second Grade Cubists Teaching me how to teach the cube.

References

Coyle, D. (2009). *The talent code.* NY: Random House, Inc.

Diamond, M., & Hopson, J. (1998). *Magic trees of the mind: How to nurture your child's intelligence, creativity and healthy emotions from birth through adolescence.* New York: Penguin Putnam.

Duckworth, A. (2016). *Grit.* NY: Scribner.

Ericsson, A., & Pool, R. (2017). *Peak: Secrets from the new science of expertise.* NY: Houghton Mifflin Harcourt.

Glover, D. (1998). *Math like you've never seen it before* (videotape). Pittsburgh: WQED.

Goleman, D. (1998). *Emotional intelligence: Why it can matter more than IQ.* NY: Bantam.

Kotulak, R. (1996). *Inside the brain: Revolutionary discoveries of how the mind works.* Kansas City, MO: Andrews & McMeely.

LeDoux, J. (1996). *The emotional brain: The mysterious underpinnings of emotional life.* New York: Simon & Schuster.

Maltz, M. (1967). *Pyscho-cybernetics.* New York: Prentice Hall.

Payne, J. (2004). *PeopleWise brain to brain.* Pittsburgh, PA: Sterling House Publisher, Inc.

Tice, L. E. (1989). *A better world, a better you.* New Jersey: Prentice Hall.

Waitley, D. (1983). *Seeds of greatness.* New York: Pocket Books.

Cast of Characters

(Listed in order of appearance)

Nicole Erdim, ESL Teacher and my former daughter-in-law. The writing of my memoir started because of her comment, "you need to tell your story." I continued to write because of her encouragement.

Michelle Wallace, Typist and Copy Editor. We worked together for over 20 years. I could not have completed my memoir without her.

Myrtle Goodrum, my mother-in-law. Lived a full life of 99 years. I wish I would have taken the time to know her better and to thank her for what she did for me as I was maturing as an adult.

Mary Ann Bowen, Story Editor. She taught me how to do quotes and the importance of describing situations and places in detail.

Esim Erdim, my wife. The love of my life. She makes my life complete. I worship her and am thankful I found her across the hall.

Bob Simmons, my second son-in-law. He is smart, funny and he loves my oldest daughter, Kim. What more can I ask.

Kim Simmons, my oldest daughter. From her I learned how to be a father. She continues to call and visit. I am so very lucky and fortunate.

Dr. Walter Cegelka, Professor, The University of Kansas. He was my first graduate advisor. We later coauthored articles and books together. He was solely responsible for getting me on the right track to graduate.

Tom Kergel, former student that introduced me to Dr. Wright and continues to advise me spiritually. He critiqued the chapters on religion and helped clarify the main points.

Bill Herbert, former student in the Rehabilitation Techniques class I taught at The University of Virginia. Many years after graduating he contacted me about a book he was writing related to what he had learned from my class. We became friends and he clearly defined my purpose for the memoir.

J.C., fictitious name of real second grader that was taught how to make a cake he would never bake.

Frank, fictitious name of real second grader that liked the smell of Aramis.

Clyde, fictitious name of real second grader that wondered what elves were supposed to be doing.

Leigh, fictitious name of real second grader that was one smart cookie.

Helen Payne, my mom. She loved me and my brothers and taught us manners and to be civil.

JoAnn, fictitious name of real third grader that was in the Cardinal reading group.

Miss Campbell, Teacher, Third Grade, Gage Elementary School. Miss Campbell was a good person. I was a poor student that couldn't read. I have often wondered if the class were smaller and if she had been taught how to teach remedial reading, would I have learned how to read. The more I think about it the more I conclude, I wouldn't, because I still struggle with reading.

Cecil Payne, my dad. Modeled how to live the good life and what was right from wrong.

Hugh McCausland, Instructor, Speech 101, Washburn University. He captivated me by teaching me the phonetic alphabet. He made me think I was smarter than I was.

Margaret Southworth, Instructor, English 101, Washburn University. Her teaching techniques were unusual but every student learned enough English to graduate. She knew English but more important she knew how to inspire her students.

Robertson, fictitious name of real student in bonehead English. Miss Southworth would not let him quit. This inspired all of us to continue. He later became an internationally known artist.

Albertson, fictitious name of student in bonehead English.

Norris, fictitious name of student in bonehead English.

Owen, fictitious name of student in bonehead English.

Stevenson, fictitious name of student in bonehead English.

Hugh O'Brian, actor. Played Wyatt Earp on television. He could cuss like a drunkin sailor.

Monseigneur Robert Ballou, Instructor of French, Dodge City Jr. College. An excellent teacher that made me and every student in his class feel important as we fumbled with a strange language.

Emily, fictitious name of real student in my psychology class. Often times I think about her and I wonder what she did after getting her degree. She was a fascinating woman.

Allen, friend and employee, Allen's Drive-In. He was the first client I hired from Voc. Rehab. He taught me to be direct and compassionate in my teaching.

Kyle, fictitious name of real client from Voc. Rehab. He was my second hire from Voc. Rehab.

Sam, fictitious name of real client from Voc. Rehab. He was my third hire from Voc. Rehab.

Mr. Jones, President and CEO of Caterers Inc., the company that owned all the Allen's Drive- Ins. The first CEO I'd ever met in the first corporate boardroom I ever sat in. I was intimidated.

T.C. Llewellyn, Owner, Allen's Drive-Ins in Kansas. I learned more by watching him than I did by listening. He was so impressive. His clothes fit and he walked with purpose. Had I not met Dr. Haring I would have ended up in corporate emulating Mr. Llewellyn.

Dan Payne, my oldest brother. He cheered me on and helped in so many ways I can't count. He is full of life and so positive everyday and he can read.

Dr. Norris Haring, Professor of Special Education. He snatched me out of the restaurant business and gave me the opportunity to become a professional educator. He is nationally known for his work with special needs children.

Dr. Frederic Girardeau, Professor and Researcher, Children's Rehabilitation Unit, University of Kansas Medical Center. He was the first pure scientist I ever observed. I was taken by his methodology and precision in data collection.

Dr. Jim Lent, Professor and Researcher, Parsons State Hospital. I observed him masterfully dispense tokens in a sheltered workshop setting.

Jim Young, Placement Counselor, Vocational Rehabilitation Unit. He mentored me and took me under his wing.

Clifford, fictitious name of real client, Vocational Rehabilitation Unit. He would not lie but he had a clever way with words.

Rhonda, Secretary, The Kansas Vocational Rehabilitation and Special Education Cooperative Program. She could write in shorthand faster than I could speak. The process made me feel very important.

Henry, fictitious name of student used to illustrate how to properly dispense tokens for appropriate behavior.

Mike, High School student. I learned a great deal from him but his most important lesson was, relationships are important and more powerful than tokens.

Dr. Don Ball, Professor, The University of Virginia. He was a respected statistician and we wrote many articles together.

Dr. Jim Kauffman, Professor, Author and Scholar, The University of Virginia. We were students together at the University of Kansas and we both graduated together and went to the University of Virginia together. We coauthored articles and books together.

Dr. O.L. Plucker, Superintendent, Kansas City, Kansas United School District #500. He guided a big ship through turbulent times.

Dr. Bertrum Caruthers, Assistant Superintendent. My direct boss in Head Start. He counseled me and taught me how to work in a big system.

Walter Davies, Principal, Rosedale High School. He showed me the ropes of Kansas City.

Dr. Montrose Wolff, Co-director Juniper Gardens Project, Author and Researcher in early childhood. He and Dr. Risley helped me set up Head Start.

Dr. Todd Risley, Co-director Juniper Gardens Project, Author and Researcher in early childhood. He and Dr. Wolff helped me set up Head Start.

Sharon, Secretary to Walter Davies. She tried to keep him straight.

Carter Burns, Director of Purchasing, Kansas City, Kansas United School District #500. He handled money as if it were his own.

Peyton, Teacher, Head Start. His creativity and enthusiasm permeated Head Start faculty and staff.

Spencer, fictitious name of real gifted student in Head Start.

Ross, fictitious name for real Research Psychologist in Head Start.

Herbert, fictitious name for real Research Psychologist in Head Start.

Awilda Salard, Parent Coordinator, Head Start. She was a dynamo for Head Start. She later became the director.

Dr. Jerry Chaffin, Professor, The University of Kansas. He was my advisor, friend and boss as I worked as a Placement Counselor for the Vocational Rehabilitation and Special Education Cooperative Program.

Lucy Livingston, Director of Curriculum, Head Start. We shared offices together. She taught me how to write a curriculum for young children.

Joyce North, Social Worker and wife of Bill North. She was one smart cookie.

Bill North, Attorney who bailed me out of trouble with Head Start authorities.

Ruth Ann Payne, my first love. Married for 38 years. She unexpectedly passed away of cancer. A situation in my mind I can't get rid of.

Dean Ridgeway, Dean, School of Education, The University of Kansas. He set up an early defense of my dissertation and got me out of town.

Dr. Bill Carriker, Chairperson, Department of Special Education at The University of Virginia. He was so patient with me and never left my side.

John Zumwalt, Managing Director Economic Opportunity Foundation, Inc. His letter set me free.

Marc Columbus, graduate assistant that made me look good. We later became business partners.

Allen Miller, student that I learned so many things from. When I grow up I want to be like Allen Miller.

Ringo, Allen Miller's dog. The two of them were inseparable.

Mr. Sullivan, fictitious name of a farmer in Virginia who loved Allen Miller as if he were his own son.

Reverend Stuckhouse, fictitious name of Baptist minister. We traveled a lot together. He was such a kind and gentle person.

Mrs. Stuckhouse, fictitious name of wife of Reverend Stuckhouse.

Reverend Scott, fictitious name of real female Methodist minister.

Dr. Leon Wright, Minister, Author and Spiritual leader that taught me the Beware of Impending Forces prayer.

George Allen, Heach Coach and General Manager of the Washington Redskins, NFL football team. He taught me more than I taught him.

George Allen, Jr., student that introduced me to his dad. George, after receiving his law degree became Governor and later Senator of the State of Virginia.

Bill Hickman, First Assistant to George Allen. He helped me navigate through the professional world of football.

Lou Riecke, Weight Coach for the Washington Redskins.

Jim Curzi, Stretch Coach for the Washington Redskins.

Brian McCain, Assistant Director of National Association of Retarded Citizens. I served as chairperson of the Education committee for over 10 years and Brian was my confidant.

David Matthews, child that was the focal point in the 94-142 court case. As I observed him I gained strength. He made me believe in the spirit of the law.

Cecil Mercer, student that was so smart I couldn't keep up with him. We coauthored several books together.

Jim Patton, student that after graduation became a nationally recognized expert in special education. We coauthored several books together.

Dale C. Critz, Sr., President and General Manager of Critz, Inc. and Chairman of the Board of SunTrust Bank. He taught me the automobile business and the etiquette of smoking a cigar.

Dale C. Critz, Jr., student that introduced me to his dad. Upon graduation he took over the dealership and Dale was recognized by Time Magazine as Quality Dealer of the year.

No Neck, nick name of car salesman that became my dear friend and taught me tricks on selling cars not found in books or on tapes.

Harold, fictitious name of my mentor that taught me the art and science of selling encyclopedias.

Tenderfoot, the handle of a truck driver I sold two cars to for his two sons.

Darryl, fictitious name of a real person. Youngest son of Tenderfoot.

David, fictitious name of a real person. Oldest son of Tenderfoot.

Bruce, fictitious name of a real customer I sold an unusual looking truck to.

Dr. Ophonospour, fictitious name of real customer I sold a Buick to and later he returned for a Mercedes.

Janet Purdy, my youngest daughter. She keeps me on my toes. She is full of energy and smart.

John, fictitious name of real student. First student I dismissed because of mental issues.

Paul Hale, Director of Physical Plant, The University of Mississippi. With limited funds and decaying buildings he kept things a float.

Marjorie Douglass, Executive Secretary and Girl Friday. She actually ran the School of Education during my deanship.

Dr. Cooper, fictitious name for real professor in Counselor Education that raised the student evaluations to the very top in the course, Human Growth and Development.

David Horn, Area Supervisor, Division of Vocational Rehabilitation, Mississippi. Responsible for getting the first sheltered workshop in Northern Mississippi which was initially housed in the gym of the School of Education building.

John Cook, Director of the Division of Vocational Rehabilitation. Responsible for establishing Ability Works, a sheltered workshop in Oxford, Mississippi.

Dr. Malcolm Provost, Professor, University of Virginia. Creator of the Discrepancy Model that helped organizations plan for the future.

Dr. Don Deshler, Professor, University of Kansas. Designed a nationally recognized program to help university students take better notes, increase writing skills and improve study habits.

Dr. Nancy Swartz, fictitious name of real professor that taught the course Human Sexuality.

Dr. Main, fictitious name of real professor that co-taught with Dr. Horn. In the Burns and Allen duo he played Gracie.

Dr. June Horn, fictitious name of real professor that co-taught with Dr. Main. In the Burns and Allen duo she played George.

Dr. Brown, fictitious name for real professor that co-authored the nationally recognized Star Schools Project.

Jammie Whitten, U.S. Congressman. Secured the National Food Service Management Institute for The University of Mississippi.

Dr. Ray Hoops, Vice Chancellor of Academic Affairs. As a boss he protected me and kept me out of trouble.

Dr. Jeanette Phillips, Professor, Home Economics. Principal Investor for National Food Service Management Institute. A powerful yet sensitive professional woman.

Shirley Messer, Secretary, The University of Mississippi. World's fastest typist with an ashtray on each side of her computer while altering the smoking of two cigarettes. Also, award winning salesperson of Avon products.

Clyde Goodrum, my father-in-law. Served in both World War I and II. The gentlest man I've ever known.

Randy Brookshire, my ex-son-in-law. First husband of my oldest daughter. I continue to admire and respect him. We are life-long friends.

Ashley Brookshire, my granddaughter. A person that can do no wrong.

Dr. Jack Kevorkian, Physician. Nationally known for euthanasia of the sick and elderly.

Dr. Abby Fin, Professor in Counselor Education, The University of Mississippi. I owe everything to Abby for introducing me to Esim.

Major William E. Mayer, Psychologist that conducted an exhaustive study of prisoners of war captured in Korea by the Chinese.

Dr. Ron Cofman, Executive Director, Turkish-American Association of Ankara. I will never forget his presentation at the Fulbright Orientation, "Don't drink the water."

Eliza-Al-Laham, Program Development officer, U.S. Embassy, Cairo. Introduced me to Dr. Farag and made arrangements for me to present to the faculty of the American University in Cairo.

Dr. Mahmond Farag, Vice President, The American University in Cairo. He was instrumental in getting my paper featured in the proceedings of the 11th Annual American University in Cairo Research Conference.

Randy Payne, my youngest brother. A freakin' genius.

Savage, Randy's dog. I kept my distance from him.

Muffin, my dog. He couldn't bite or scare anyone.

Sam Gilbert, Master Cubist and second grade teacher. The two of us along with Kim Simmons and Grant Purdy developed the simplest, easiest, fastest way to work the cube, "5 Steps to Mastering the Cube."

About the Author

Dr. Payne is a Professor Emeritus and scholar who specializes in the methodology of teaching and program development. He is the author of over twenty-five books, three of which were best-selling texts in education. The three texts sold over 400,000 copies during the first 15 years. After 15 years of sales, Dr. Payne relinquished authorship of the books to his previous students so he could focus on his research related to his theory on management and motivation. Today the texts are published by Pearson Publishing as *Strategies for Teaching Learners with Special Needs 10th Edition, Mental Retardation 8th Edition, and Exceptional Individuals in Focus 7th Edition.*

Through the Mississippi Department of Education, Dr. Payne developed a four-day training program for public school administrators. Over 3,000 administrators benefited from the module entitled *Thinking Like a Leader.* Also, the Mississippi Department of Education sent Dr. Payne to Utah to study under Dr. Stephen Covey and become a certified facilitator for the *Seven Habits of Highly Effective People.* Dr. Payne modified the seven habits training to make it Mississippi specific. Over 2,000 public school teachers were certified through the five-day training program directly taught by Dr. Payne.

Over a 40 year period, Dr. Payne developed the PeopleWise® theory. PeopleWise®, a management and motivation theory dealing with self and others, is about the tick-tock of human-kind: How we tick and learn to tick better and how others tock and how to help them tock better. The United States Patent and Trademark Office granted Dr. Payne the official trademark, PeopleWise®, in 2001.

In 2004, Dr. Payne was awarded a Fulbright and as a scholar, he taught his PeopleWise® theory to university students in Turkey and presented to the faculty of The American University in

Cairo resulting in his paper being the feature article in the proceedings of the 17th Annual American University in Cairo Research Conference.

Dr. Payne developed *The PeopleWise® Series of Planners,* designed to help children, teens and adults stay focused and organized and *The PeopleWise® Profile System,* which is a self-scoring instrument that helps individuals understand themselves and others. His first book in the *PeopleWise® Series of Books, PeopleWise® Brain-to-Brain,* was featured at the Book Expo of America, June 2004; the second book, *PeopleWise® Putting: Get Your Brain in the Game,* was published in 2005 and featured at the PGA Expo, January 2006, and the third book *PeopleWise® Selling! The Art of Selling Brain to Brain* was released in 2006. In 2008, a training program including DVD, workbook, and instructor's guide was released by National Professional Resources. The training program is entitled *8 Steps to Captivating an Audience.* In 2010, Dr. Payne's first eBook was published, *Life Just Before Death,* and in 2011 the second book on putting was released, *So You Think You Can't Putt.* In 2012, Dr. Payne's first commercial film, *Leo Beuerman: A Legacy,* was produced. The film is about a pencil salesman that Dr. Payne bought pencils from as a child. Dr. Payne's first political book, *Obama is a Level 7,* was released in 2013. *Obama is a Level 7,* formed the foundation of his weekly television series that ran for one year and was aired on MUTV1 that serves the Memphis Metropolitan area. In 2015, Dr. Payne co-authored the first text to include both an intervention approach and a developmental approach to teaching, *Inspiring Kids to Learn: The Token Economy Playbook.*

Dr. Payne is the proud father of Kim and Janet. He was married for 38 years to Ruth Ann, who unfortunately passed away to cancer in 1999. In 2001, Dr. Payne married Esim, a university colleague. Esim originated from Turkey and has two sons, Burak and Firat. Jim and Esim currently reside in Chapel Hill, North Carolina.

Trailer

Noah enters with purpose. Smiling ear to ear, black horned rimmed glasses, two inches shorter than his classmates, blue t-shirt with red lettering that says…it is so faded. I can barely make it out. I move my head closer. Focus. S-H-A-Z-A-M.

While I am decoding he completes Steps 1, 2, and 3 and is examining the bottom four corners.

I am impressed, not surprised at his speed. "Man, you are cooking. So quick. Your brain is on fire."

Without looking up. Still focused on the cube. "I cheated."

"Cheated? How did you cheat?"

"This morning, I put sugar on my cereal. (hesitation) Don't tell my mom."

Noah continues to study the bottom four corners. "Dr. Payne, show me again how to match two corners. This is hard."

Using my pencil as a pointer I explain and show how to match two of the bottom four corners.

Focused on the bottom layer, laser sharp, continuing to study his cube, he simultaneously, with his left hand, reaches to my desk and grabs a second cube.

His attention turns to the new cube. He completes Steps 1, 2, and 3 with the new retrieved cube as fast as he did the first. Studies the bottom layer, carefully rotates the bottom layer until two corners match. Then out of nowhere, right minus, bottom minus, right plus, front plus, bottom plus, front minus, right minus, bottom plus, right plus and the 'coup de grace', two bottom clicks. Bingo. Bango. Bongo. The bottom four corners are perfectly placed All *four* corners perfectly placed.

Noah slams the cube on the table, gets up, takes two steps toward the door, turns around, comes back, slides his chair into its proper place in front of the desk and as he leaves. I hear him utter under his breath, "Damn. I good."

What happens in my room. Stays in my room.

Naomi enters. Thin as a rail, ill kept, average height and weight. Non-descript. Looks at the cube then, head turns toward me. "My parents are trying to get a divorce. This has been going on forever. I wish they would just do it. They don't like one another anymore. They yell, holler, fight all the time. It is getting to me."Head turns back toward the cube and without comment completes Steps 1 and 2.

Brycen, a special needs student, has had trouble learning Step 1, the white cross. The school is out for the winter vacation. Before vacation, I worked with him six times. He enters for the seventh session. Grabs a cube and completes Step 1 without error. Grabs a second cube and completes it. Then a third, fourth and fifth.

Stunned, I ask, "How do you remember how to do it?"

"I bought a cube."

"Where?"

"Walmart."

"How much?"

"Not sure."

"Where did you get the money?"

"My mom pays me to do the dishes."

"How much?"

"Twenty-five cents."

I calculate in my head. $10 for a cube at 25 cents a wash, equals 40 washes. Forty quarters. He must have wanted that cube awfully bad.

Ava after finishing Steps 1 and 2 several times, turns and says, "It gets frustrating, but if you keep going you will get better and better. A lot of things are frustrating like drawing an elephant. But you have to keep going."

For a second grader drawing an elephant must be a challenge.

334

Max catches his breath. "Kinda gives you exercise. Really makes your brain work."

Brandon finishes Step 1. "I'm proud of myself. It was awesome. I can make the white cross every time."

Daniyle gets up to leave the room. Turns and says, "I wanted to be a doctor, now I think I want to be a Rubik's Cube maker."

I'm not sure what we are doing is a good thing.

"Karegen, how can you remember all the moves?"

"I've got a Rubik's Cube in my head."

Kaitlyn slams down a completed Step 1, the white cross, and announces, "I am Queen of the Cross." Emphasizing Queen.

Ayla points to a corner die. "You see that? That is an Ole Miss corner."

I look and sure enough it is red and blue.

Clay is one of the smartest kids in the class or at least thinks he is one of the smartest. He confronts me. "Who was your favorite last year?"

"What do you mean?"

"Your favorite. The one you like the best."

"I had no favorites. I loved working with everyone."

"I want to be your favorite this year but you are not going to like me."

"Why?"

"I'm going to Mississippi State."

"I like Mississippi State. My son went to Mississippi State."

"Wow. What position did he play?"

"He didn't play football he is an architect."

Clay looks at me, confused, then says, "I still want to be your favorite."